Central America:
INTERNATIONAL DIMENSIONS
OF THE CRISIS

Edited by Richard E. Feinberg

Holmes & Meier Publishers, Inc.
New York • London

First published in the United States of America 1982 by
Holmes & Meier Publishers, Inc.
30 Irving Place
New York, N.Y. 10003

Great Britain:
Holmes & Meier Publishers, Ltd.
131 Trafalgar Road
Greenwich, London SE10 9TX

Library of Congress Cataloging in Publication Data
Main entry under title:

Central America, international dimensions of the crisis.

Includes bibliographical references and index.
Contents: The local setting. The background to the
current political crisis in Central America / Francisco
Villagran Kramer—United States interests and practices. The United States and Central America / James
Kurth. The recent rapid redefinitions of U.S. interests
and diplomacy in Central America / Richard E. Feinberg.
U.S. military interests in Central America in global
perspective / Margaret Daly Hayes. The interests and
perceptions of U.S. business in relation to the political crisis in Central America / John Purcell—[etc.]
   1. Central America—Foreign relations—Addresses,
essays, lectures.   2. Central America—Politics and
government—1951–   —Addresses, essays, lectures.
I. Feinberg, Richard E.
F1436.7.C46   1982   327.728   81-13232
ISBN 0-8419-0737-4   AACR2
ISBN 0-8419-0738-2 (pbk.)

Manufactured in the United States of America

Book design by Marsha Picker

Central America:
INTERNATIONAL DIMENSIONS
OF THE CRISIS

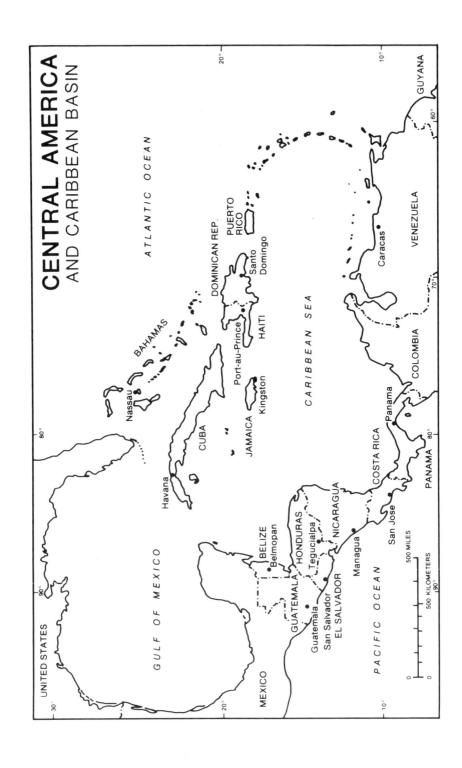

CENTRAL AMERICA
AND CARIBBEAN BASIN

UNITED STATES

ATLANTIC OCEAN

GULF OF MEXICO

BAHAMAS

Nassau

CUBA

Havana

MEXICO

BELIZE
Belmopan

GUATEMALA

Guatemala

San Salvador
EL SALVADOR

HONDURAS

Tegucigalpa

NICARAGUA

Managua

San Jose

COSTA RICA

PACIFIC OCEAN

JAMAICA

Kingston

Port-au-Prince

HAITI

DOMINICAN REP.

Santo
Domingo

PUERTO
RICO

CARIBBEAN SEA

Panama

PANAMA

COLOMBIA

VENEZUELA

Caracas

GUYANA

0   500 MILES

0   500 KILOMETERS

30°

20°

10°

90°

80°

70°

60°

20°

10°

Contents

About the Contributors

Robert D. Bond is program associate of the Latin American Program of the Woodrow Wilson International Center for Scholars, Smithsonian Institution. He has taught political science at New York University and Vanderbilt University, directed the Latin American program of the Council on Foreign Relations, and worked as an independent international political consultant. Dr. Bond's publications include: co-author, *Contemporary Venezuela and Its Role in International Affairs* (New York University Press, 1977), and articles in *Orbis, International Organization, Worldview,* and *Foro Internacional.* His most recent publication is "Political and Regional Stability in Latin America," a chapter in *The U.S. Role in a Changing World Economy,* a study prepared for the 96th Congress by the Joint Economic Committee.

Margaret E. Crahan is an associate professor of history at Herbert H. Lehman College of the City University of New York and a visiting professor at The John Hopkins University School of Advanced International Studies. Her books and articles include studies of Spanish colonial administration, church-state relations, religion and politics, twentieth century Cuba, and African cultural heritage in the Caribbean. Dr. Crahan has served on the Executive Council of the Latin American Studies Association, as vice-president of the Latin American Foundation, and on the board of directors of the Washington Office on Latin America. She is presently editing two books for publication: *Power and Piety: The Political Dimensions of Religion in Latin America* and *Social Transformations in Cuba, 1750–1950,* and has recently published *Human Rights and Basic Needs in the Americas* (Georgetown University Press, 1982).

Richard E. Feinberg served as the Latin American specialist on the Policy Planning Staff of the Department of State from 1977 to 1979. More recently he has held fellowships from the Council on Foreign Relations and the Woodrow Wilson International Center for Scholars, Smithsonian Institution. Dr. Feinberg is currently a visiting fellow at the Overseas Development Council and an adjunct professor at the Georgetown University School of Foreign Service. He has written numerous articles on United States foreign policy, Latin American politics, and international economics, and has just published *Subsidizing Success: The Export-Import Bank in the U.S. Economy* (Cambridge University Press, 1982).

Wolf Grabendorff is a senior staff member at the Stiftung Wissenschaft und Politik in Ebenhausen, West Germany. He has worked as the Latin American correspondent for a German national TV network (ARD), and has published numberous articles on the international relations of Latin American states. Mr. Grabendorff has studied at the Goethe University in Frankfurt, Grinnell College, Columbia University, and the Free University in Berlin. In 1980–81 he was a visiting fellow at the Center of Brazilian Studies, Johns Hopkins University School of Advance International Studies.

Margaret Daly Hayes is the senior Latin American specialist for the Senate Foreign Relations Committee. She has taught at The Johns Hopkins University School of Advanced International Studies and was associate director of the school's Center of Brazilian Studies. Dr. Hayes has worked as a consultant to the United States Information Agency, the Foreign Service Institute, and the Congressional Research Service and was a senior associate in the Policy Sciences Division of CACI, Inc., a private, Washington-based research firm. Her research, "Security to the South: U.S. Interests in Latin America," appeared in *International Security* (Summer, 1980). She is the author of *Latin America and the U.S. National Interest: Issues for the Future* (forthcoming).

René Herrera Zúñiga is a professor at the Center of International Studies, El Colegio de Mexico. Born in Nicaragua, he has taught at the Universidad Centroamericana in Managua, the Universidad Metropolitana and the Facultad Lationamericana de Ciencias Sociales (FLACSO) in Mexico City. He has published articles in numerous Mexican journals, is co-editor of *Centroamerica en Crisis* (El Colegio de Mexico, 1980), and author of a forthcoming book on Mexican relations with Central America.

James K. Kurth is professor of political science, Swarthmore College. His research interests and professional publications have dealt with United States foreign, defense, and industrial policies and with European politics. His publications include "Industrial Change and Political Change: A European Perspective," in David Collier, editor, *The New Authoritarianism in Latin America* (Princeton University Press, 1979); and *Testing Theories of Economic Imperialism,* edited with Steven J. Rosen (D.C. Heath, 1974). He has testified on three occasions before Congressional committees on United States foreign and defense policies.

Mario Ojeda is a professor and former director of the Center of International Studies, El Colegio de Mexico. He has also taught at the Massachusetts Institute of Technology. In addition to having published numerous articles on Mexico's foreign relations, he edited *Mexico y America Latina* (El Colegio de Mexico, 1974) and authored *Alcances y limites de la politica exterior de Mexico* (El Colegio de Mexico, 1976).

John F. H. Purcell is an assistant vice president in the Economics Division at Bankers Trust Company and is in charge of political assessment for Latin America and the Caribbean. His responsibilities include political assessment for Bankers Trust as well as consultation for the bank's corporate customers. He is also a consultant to the International Division of the Rockefeller Foundation. Until 1979 Dr. Purcell was an associate professor of political science at California State University, Fullerton.

James N. Rosenau is director of the Institute for Transnational Studies at the University of Southern California. His recent publications include *The Dramas of Political Life* (1980), *The Scientific Study of Foreign Policy* (rev. ed., 1980), *The Study of Global Interdependence* (1980), *The Study of Political Adaptation* (1981), and *World System Structure* (1981).

Jiri Valenta has in 1981–82 a joint appointment as an international fellow at the Council on Foreign Relations, senior research associate at the Institute on International Change, Columbia University and an international fellowship at the Rockefeller Foundation. He is on leave from the Naval Postgraduate School, Monterey, California, where he is an associate professor and coordinator of Soviet and East European studies. Dr. Valenta is the author of *Soviet Intervention in Czechoslovakia, 1968: Anatomy of a Decision* (Johns Hopkins University Press, 1979); co-editor of *Eurocommunism between East and West* (Indiana University Press, 1980); co-author of the monograph *The Soviet Invasion of Afghanistan: Three Perspectives* (University of California Press, 1980); and co-editor of the forthcoming book *Soviet Decisionmaking for National Security* (Allen and Unwin, Inc.).

Francisco Villagran Kramer was vice president of Guatemala from

1978 until his resignation in September, 1980. He holds a doctoral degree in international law from the University of Geneva, has taught at universities in El Salvador and Guatemala, and has written widely on Central American social, political and legal issues. His books include *Integración Ecónomica Centroamericana: Aspectos Sociales y Politicos* (1967).

Introduction and Overview

Internal factors have undoubtedly provided the central impetus for change in Central America, but a wide variety of external forces are taking an active interest in the region. As the old order crumbles in Central America, foreign governments and nongovernmental actors are attempting to mold a new Central America that is consistent with their own interests and values. The developments in Central America during the 1980s will not be comprehensible without an understanding of the role being played by these external powers.

Central America today is situated within an international environment characterized by intense competition between the United States and the Soviet Union in the developing world, the pursuit by Cuba of a foreign policy of activist internationalism, persistent divergencies between the United States and its Western European allies, and the emergence of regional Third World powers such as Mexico and Venezuela. Nongovernmental forces, including U.S. business firms, European political parties, and the Catholic church also have stakes in Central America. Central America has become a major battleground where these numerous forces are vying for influence and power.

The purpose of this volume is to describe and analyze the motivations, interests, and capabilities of official and nongovernmental external forces as they are likely to react to and affect the course of events in Central America. Taken individually, each chapter is an essay on the attitudes and behavior of its particular subject in today's world. Viewed as a whole, the volume seeks to explain the international environment as it interacts with Central America. The volume stands, in effect, as a case study of the dynamic relationship between a Third World subregion and a world in which East-West, North-North, North-South, and South-South forces interlock in an increasingly complex pattern. While not wishing to underplay the importance of internal elements, and at the risk of appearing to overemphasize the international dimension, this book seeks to fill a gap in the systematic study of the external forces now impinging upon Central America.

Earlier versions of the essays presented here were, with the exceptions, of chapters 9 and 10, delivered at a conference at the Woodrow Wilson International Center for Scholars, Smithsonian Institution, Washington, D.C., on April 2–3, 1981. The center's Latin American program, then under acting director Alexander Wilde, organized the symposium which drew upon the talents, not only of experts on Latin America, but on the knowledge of "globalists" and students of strategic studies, of specialists in international relations, as well as on individuals with experience in policymaking and journalism. The final, published versions of the papers were enriched by the criticisms of this diverse group of commentators.*

Each chapter examines one or two of the external forces or actors now interested in Central America, and addresses the following questions:

• What are the actor's perceptions of the causes of unrest in Central America, and the likely direction of future events?

• How does the external actor define its interests in Central America? What is the overall strategic framework determining the actor's outlook toward the region? How important is Central America, and what risks might be taken to preserve or advance objectives?

• Given the actor's perceptions of events in Central America and its defined interests, what strategy is likely to be pursued in the 1980s? How successful is the strategy likely to be? What levers are available for influencing events?

• Can the actor accommodate rapidly to changing events? Is it bureaucratically or ideologically rigid or skillful in responding to new circumstances? How do the domestic and international poltical environments in which it operates impinge upon its flexibility?

• What are the linkages, official and unofficial, with Central American actors?

---

*For a summary of the conference discussions, see Anne Florini, *A Rapporteur's Report: The International Aspects of the Crisis in Central America,* Working Paper No. 92, Latin American Program, Woodrow Wilson International Center for Scholars, Smithsonian Institution, Washington, D.C., 1981.

Background to the Crises

The eruptions that began to shake Central America in the late 1970s caught many external observers by surprise. For example, neither the United States government nor Cuba and the Soviet Union had been focusing sustained attention on what appeared to be a stable if backward region. The background chapter by Francisco Villagran Kramer, a Guatemalan writer and politician, describes for the reader the largely unnoticed economic and political processes that were at work in Central America in the 1960s and 1970s. The seeds of profound social conflict are located in both the failures and successes of the policies adopted by governments during those years. Spurred indus- trial growth and planned regional economic integration gave rise to new social classes and political movements that opposed the political and social status quo. Natural and man-made acts—earthquakes, the "soccer war" between Honduras and El Salvador—stimulated proc- esses already in motion that would prove disruptive of existing institutions. Ruling political elites in Guatemala, El Salvador, and Nicaragua were unwilling to accommodate to these new developments. Instead, they chose a "policy of polarization"—the erasing of demo- cratic processes and centrist political parties—to force a choice between the status quo and armed insurrection. Villagran Kramer argues that the apparent consensus of the early 1960s—built around the prospect of a modernizing and democratizing capitalism—thus broke down and was replaced by ideological confrontation and class struggle. Through the 1970s, at least, Honduras and Costa Rica escaped this symdrome by allowing for more open politics and more attention to social welfare.

The U.S. Response

The United States, traditionally dominant in the region, failed to notice that economic modernization was undermining the stability of the *ancien régimes*. Thus, in the late 1960s and early 1970s, rather than lend weight to the efforts at socioeconomic reforms or electoral processes, the United States often continued to support regimes that froze out newly emerging political groups through electoral frauds or other power plays. Thus, opportunities were lost that might have permitted a more peaceful evolution of Central American institu- tions.

James Kurth, professor of political science at Swarthmore College, argues in chapter 2 that great powers typically foster changes within their spheres of influence that produce new forces inherently antagonistic to the old order. In Central America in the 1970s new social forces emerged as a result of the region's deepening insertion into a dynamic world economy under the leadership of the United States. The impressive increase in Central America's foreign trade and in external capital inflows reinforced such processes as the commercialization of agriculture and the development of urban industry. These processes in turn produced peasant and urban working-class movements, a more modern entrepreneurial class, and middle-class professionals often discontented with the dominant political institutions.

Kurth draws parallels between the U.S. relationship to Central America, British power in the Middle East earlier in this century, and the hegemony of the Soviet Union over Eastern Europe. He uses this exercise in comparative history to shed light on the U.S.-Central American dynamic, and to argue that this hegemonic system, like others of its kind that are no longer stable, faces three alternative paths. The United States can simply withdraw, can stimulate other friendly powers to replace it (as the British did in the Middle East after World War II), or seek to reaffirm its control. Kurth contends that the choice will depend upon which coalition of interests within the United States succeeds in determining U.S. policy. Interests that might favor a reassertion of American power include declining U.S. industries, the military services, and traditional anti-Communist "patriots." An "anti-intervention" coalition might draw support from the churches, human rights groups, and some circles of international business and finance. A modified "anti-intervention" strategy could look to such friendly powers as Western Europe, Mexico and Venezuela to at least partially offset a decline in U.S. influence.

Richard E. Feinberg, who served on the Policy Planning Staff of Secretary of State Cyrus Vance, investigates in greater detail the policies that have actually been pursued by the U.S. government in Central America in recent years. His essay concentrates on the Carter period, contrasting it with the policies of Nixon and Ford and the initial days of the Reagan administration. U.S. perceptions and policies are found to change with surprising rapidity, including during the lifetime of a single administration. Moreover, the very definition of the U.S. national interest seems to shift significantly, travelling during a short period of time from defending human rights to containing Cuban influence. Changing circumstances in Central America, an evolving international environment, and shifts in U.S. domestic political moods account for these lurches in U.S. attitudes and policies.

Margaret Daly Hayes, a staff member of the Senate Foreign Relations Committee, discusses a definition of the U.S. national interest that was submerged during the Carter years but that has resurfaced in the Reagan administration—the traditional security perspective of the Department of Defense. Several former Defense Department officials have been influential in formulating Reagan administration policy toward Central America, including Secretary of State Alexander Haig, Robert McFarlane, a career Marine officer who, after serving as Haig's counsellor, was transferred to the National Security Council, Lieutenant General Vernon Walters, Haig's ambassador-at-large, General Gordon Sumner, special assistant to the Assistant Secretary for Latin American Affairs, and National Security Council staff member General Robert Schweitzer (dismissed in late 1981 for having given an unauthorized speech on Soviet military superiority and the danger of war). Concerned with securing the "southern flank" and with restraining Cuban influence, the Defense Department (DOD) views Central America as the Western littoral of a wider Caribbean basin. In accordance with its "economy of force" doctrine, DOD would like the basin to be free of potentially hostile forces. This accomplished, DOD would not need to allocate significant military forces to secure the basin should hostilities break out elsewhere with the Soviet Union.

Operating under a "worst case" planning mode, DOD considers that only strongly pro-American governments can be relied upon not to cooperate with hostile forces. Thus, the Defense Department has often advocated cooperation with friendly military regimes in Central America, viewing them as the best guarantor of U.S. security interests. This view differs sharply from the perspective dominant during the Carter administration, when some Central American military regimes were considered to be dangerously unstable. The Carter administration worried that the prolongation of conservative military regimes could lead to violence and polarization. Fearing such a revolutionary outcome, the Carter administration pressed for an evolution toward broader-based, civilian governments.

The importance that DOD attaches to Central America contrasts with the relatively minor stake that U.S. businesses have in the region. In earlier years, such firms as the United Fruit Company had major investments in Central America and were influential in both U.S. and Central American politics. Today, total U.S. direct investment in the region only approaches one billion dollars, less than 3 percent of the total invested in Latin America, and firms like United Fruit (now United Brands) have diversified into other markets and products. John Purcell, a political risk analyst with Bankers Trust, one of the most internationally active U.S. banks, infers from this relative insignificance of Central America to corporate strategists that U.S. firms will tend to react defensively, and to withdraw if instability in Central America is prolonged. Purcell's chapter includes a short- to medium-term political risk assessment of each Central American country based upon interviews conducted with U.S. businessmen and bankers.

Purcell finds U.S. firms willing to do business with regimes located along a broad spectrum of political ideologies, so long as they provide a predictable investment climate. These tendencies of U.S. business toward withdrawal and adaptation differ markedly from the more assertive Defense Department perspective, and from the fervently anti-Communist stance of the Reagan administration. Purcell's paper suggests that a simple materialist explanation for contemporary U.S. policy toward Central America would be in error.

The Soviet Union and Cuba

Jiri Valenta of the Naval Postgraduate School examines Soviet and Cuban policies toward Central America through the lens of an expert on Soviet policies toward Eastern Europe and the Third World. Valenta does not argue that Moscow has a preconceived grand design for seizing Central America. Nevertheless, the Soviets would like to take advantage of the discontent in Central America, and help establish there, as elsewhere, "progressive, anti-imperialist" (but not necessarily Marxist-Leninist) regimes. Valenta perceives the Soviets as inclined to view Third World politics as a zero-sum struggle for influence, in a mirror image of the U.S. security perspective as described in chapter 4 by Margaret Daly Hayes. The Soviets will want to increase their presence as American influence is diminished, and enlist the new regimes on their side in great-power competition.

Solid evidence on Soviet intentions in Central America is extremely sparse. Valenta notes that the Soviets have traditionally viewed Central America as a U.S. sphere of influence, and opines that Moscow, preoccupied with more pressing problems nearer its perimeter (Poland, Afghanistan, the Persian Gulf), may be willing to recede from Central America if Washington concedes the Soviets a freer hand elsewhere. Such an acquiescence to what Kurth refers to as U.S. "hegemonic reassertion" would require a parallel U.S. recognition of a Soviet sphere of influence in Eastern Europe or perhaps in other areas.

Valenta takes a centrist position in the hot debate on the nature of the Soviet-Cuban relationship. Seeing Cuba as neither a Soviet surrogate, nor as an essentially autonomous actor, Valenta argues that Cuba provides important informational inputs into Soviet decision-making on Central America. Cuban motives in Central America are portrayed as a mix of ideology, an interest in building diplomatic ties, and Soviet needs. Whether Cuba will seek to extend significant assistance to revolutionary movements will certainly reflect Soviet strategies. However, serious strains in the Cuban-Soviet relationship could arise should

Moscow prefer caution while Havana sees opportunities for a more aggressive approach.

Soviet policies are likely to be affected by the attitudes of the more important Latin American powers. Moscow, as well as Havana, will hesitate to cross a sustained policy of Mexico and Venezuela; except for the potential nuisance factor for the United States, Central America is of little inherent value to the Soviet Union compared to its relations with the richer Latin states or other regions such as Eastern Europe and South Asia.

The Regional Powers—Mexico and Venezuela

The Central American upheavals are occurring at a time when the wealthier and more dynamic of the developing countries are seeking to play a greater role in regional and even global politics. Oil-rich Mexico and Venezuela are both defining Central America as part of their own security zone, and are actively attempting to influence the flow of events there. Their interests are both defensive and offensive. Each nation wishes to avoid prolonged conflicts and superpower confrontation in the region, for fear that its own room for maneuvering might be diminished, and that its domestic political institutions could be destabilized. At the same time, both nations see opportunities to extend their influence in the area.

René Herrera and Mario Ojeda, of El Colegio de Mexico in Mexico City, emphasize the defensive motivations behind Mexican policies. Mexico's political elite are concerned that protracted violence in Central America will divert oil revenues toward the military and strengthen the hand of the security forces in domestic politics. Mexico might then move closer, in both domestic and regional politics, toward the security definitions of conservatives in the United States. To avert these developments, Mexican politicians are advocating relatively pragmatic approaches to Central American conflicts, stressing political compromises and accommodation rather than ideology and force.

Herrera and Ojeda are deeply concerned that perceived U.S. efforts to reassert American hegemony in Central America through military confrontations could both upset Mexican stability and disrupt U.S.-Mexican relations. Thus, Mexico is faced with reconciling its opposition to Reagan's Central American policies with its desire to maintain normal bilateral relations with its major economic partner. One solution to this dilemma lies in de-linking the Central America issue from the rest of the U.S.-Mexico relationship. Such a separation has been feasible in the past, when Mexico denounced as "interventionist" U.S. policies toward Cuba in the early 1960s and in the Dominican Republic in 1965. Today, however, Mexico's greater capacity for actually influencing events may take the Mexican-U.S. confrontation beyond the mere rhetoric of the past. For example, while Washington was depriving Nicaragua of financial aid in 1981, Mexico became the Sandinistas' benefactor and protector, providing the young revolutionaries with a wide range of economic and technical assistance. The Reagan administration was displeased with the Sandinistas' radical politics, while the Mexican government considered the Sandinistas to be Nicaragua's best hope for political stability.

As Herrera and Ojeda do for Mexico, Robert Bond of the Council on Foreign Relations and Woodrow Wilson Center, traces Venezuela's interest in Central America to decade-old security concerns and to petropolitics. Venezuela has been extending economic assistance to increase its influence in the Caribbean basin, to deflect charges that it has been benefiting from high petroleum prices at the expense of its poorer neighbors, and to foster democratic institutions and long-term political stability. But Venezuela's immediate diplomatic objectives have shifted as domestic power changed hands. The Acción Democrática (AD) government of Carlos Andrés Pérez (1974–1979) strongly supported the Sandinistas, and out of office the social democratic AD has inclined toward the opposition in El Salvador. For its part, the Christian Democratic government of Luis Herrera Campins (elected for the years 1979–1983) has been unhappy with the Sandinistas and has identified closely with their fellow Christian Democrats in the Salvadoran junta. It remains to be seen whether a new consensus will emerge and, if not, whether Venezuela will be able to continue to conduct an activist policy in Central America.

Will Venezuela and Mexico be able to pursue common goals in Central America? They generally agree that right-wing military governments are inherently unstable, and that the establishment in Central America of a Soviet client state would be undesirable. Both countries opposed General Anastasio Somoza, but the election of the Christian Democrats in Venezuela introduced differences in perspective regarding El Salvador, and placed Venezuela closer to the United States. Despite these contradictions, in 1980 Venezuela and Mexico agreed to provide oil jointly at highly subsidized prices to the countries of the Caribbean basin. Nevertheless, the inevitable competition for influence between the basin's two Latin non-Socialist powers, and differences in ideology, are hampering the formation of a true alliance.

Nongovernmental Influences

Governments are not the only external forces attempting to work their will in Central America. European political parties—notably the

Christian Democrats and Social Democrats—and the Catholic church have become deeply involved in promoting changes that accord with their own ideologies and institutional interests and those of their local allies.

Wolf Grabendorff, a West German specialist on Latin America, argues in chapter 9 that most Europeans view Central America through a "regionalist" lens, i.e., that they see the causes of unrest as inherent to the region, rather than the result of external forces such as Cuba or the Soviet Union. The Social Democrats and Christian Democrats, with established transnational links to their counterparts in Central America, share common perceptions regarding the profound decay of the old order, although the two parties would differ over the desirable instruments and directions of change.

Europeans are concerned, Grabendorff writes, that the security-oriented policies of the Reagan administration will carry high political costs in North-South, East-West, and Western alliance affairs. Because Western Europe is more dependent on Third World economies, and more interested in containing East-West tensions, it prefers to seek compromises to upheavals in Central America and elsewhere. Thus, Central America has become a divisive issue in relations between the United States and Western Europe, despite an underlying commonality of basic interests: guaranteeing economic cooperation between the West and Central America, and preventing Central American countries from aligning with the Socialist bloc.

Grabendorff also notes the potential for regional powers to play a constructive role in local crises. Indeed, the Mexican government and European Social Democrats share remarkably similar perceptions regarding the dynamics of change in Central America, and both believe that a policy of accommodation is the preferable strategy for containing Cuban and Soviet influence while avoiding an escalation of East-West tensions. Moreover, Mexico and Western Europe could play important roles in a U.S. policy that sought to escape from the traditional security mold without sacrificing essential interests.

The complex interplay among and within the Central American churches and the international Catholic church is described in chapter 10 by Margaret E. Crahan, prepared while the author was at the Woodstock Theological Center in Washington, D.C. Tensions between the Catholic church and local political authorities grew out of the church's commitment to the poor and oppressed during the second Vatican Council (1962–1965) and the increased social and political activism of clerics and lay missionaries in Central America. In turn, the Central American churches became themselves victims of violence, and the reflex of the Vatican, and of bishops in the United States, was to express solidarity with their brethren. Thus, both the local and international churches became embroiled politically in Central America, most notably in Nicaragua and El Salvador. The churches in Guatemala, Honduras, and Costa Rica have experienced less structural innovation and theological ferment; but even in these countries the churches have become increasingly involved with the urban and rural poor, and both clergy and laity are becoming more politicized. At the same time, Crahan cautions that the church remains apprehensive about Marxism. While polarization in some Central American societies has led the church to identify with the left, once leftist groups succeed to power, as has occurred in Nicaragua, political divisions within the church tend to reassert themselves. The church then is likely to adopt ambiguous positions to satisfy opposing factions.

Other international actors have been trying to secure the support of the local and international churches for their policies in Central America. For example, the governments of the United States and Venezuela, and both local and international Christian Democrats, sought to persuade the Salvadoran bishops and the Vatican to support the Christian Democratic-military junta led by Napoleón Duarte, but with limited success. Subject to numerous contradictory pressures, the Catholic church seems willing to lend its significant influence to particular causes at a given moment, but has so far refused to adhere definitively to anyone else's strategy.

The Central American Response

The volume's last chapter returns to a theme of the first chapter by Villagran Kramer: given a particular international environment, what options are available to Central America? James Rosenau, professor of political science at the University of Southern California, draws on his earlier theoretical work on the adaptation of small states in a world system to comment on the range of options now open to Central America. Rosenau notes that the entrance of a wide range of external actors has enlarged the number of options available both to Central American governments and to factions contending for power. The Sandinistas have turned to Mexico, Western Europe, the Socialist bloc, and some Arab states. Other governments continue to look primarily to the United States, although the Christian Democrats of El Salvador are pleased to have the support of Venezuela. The opposition in El Salvador has increased its legitimacy and diplomatic strength by gaining the sympathy of Mexico, France, and the Socialist International and has received some military assistance from Cuba. Throughout the region both Christian Democratic as well as more leftist parties have been seeking the moral and sometimes more concrete support of the Catholic church.

It remains to be seen which of these external forces are prepared to devote the resources and the sustained energies required to promote their friends and objectives in Central America over the long haul. Will their domestic politics permit consistent and well-funded strategies? Or will they become frustrated by the difficulties of attempting to shape events in turbulent Central America? Another matter is whether various external actors will be willing to compete with the United States. Central America will test the ability of Western Europe and the regional powers to influence events in the Third World in an era of renewed East-West tensions.

Central America's future will be decided by the complex interaction of international and local forces, as each strives to enlist others behind its own purposes. The expanded number of external and internal actors has made it increasingly difficult to predict the course of events in Central America. The essays in this volume, however, are meant to offer the reader a framework with which to comprehend better the forces at work in Central America—and the world—during the 1980s.

Richard E. Feinberg
November 1981

PART ONE

The Local Setting

---

1. The Background to the Current Political Crisis in Central America

Francisco Villagran Kramer

Basic and important changes have occurred in Central America during the past two decades, and these changes serve to explain the present and forthcoming fluid situation in the region. Some of the changes were the result of the Economic Integration Program, which has had greater scope than the Central American Common Market, which gained momentum in the 1960s and continued its impetus—despite institutional crises arising from the war between El Salvador and Honduras—until the downfall of General Anastasio Somoza in 1979. Some of the changes were brought about by population growth and by new forms of social organization and confrontation; others began taking shape as new ideologies entered the region. Mention should also be made of the impact that the war between El Salvador and Honduras had on those two countries, and of natural catastrophies, such as the severe earthquakes in Nicaragua and Guatemala in the 1970s, which brought to light many social problems that previously had been consciously ignored or simply swept under the rug for convenience' sake. Nature sometimes reveals what societies hide under the surface of folklorism, contributing to class awareness and releasing social energy that has long been repressed.

Perhaps the most significant overall change has been the abandonment of traditional agro-export economies of one or two basic products—coffee and/or bananas—which in the past largely determined the rigid social structure of each country.[1] The change in the traditional economic structure undermined political institutions—which had been easily controlled by the armed forces, the Catholic church, and the agricultural oligarchies working in close association with the U.S. Embassy in each Central

American capital—to the extent that the figure of a paternalistic and "omnipresent dictator"—*el señor Presidente*—has faded away. Greater interaction has, since the early 1960s, been a constant in the region, to the point where the economies of the Central American nations, once totally independent of each other, are now interrelated. This can be illustrated by the fact that, prior to 1960, intra-Central American commerce was less than U.S. $10 million and that, by the end of the 1970s, the Guatemalan and Salvadoran economies depended on exports to other countries of the region to maintain their levels of employment and their ratios of growth, because of the fact that one-third of their total exports are to the region itself. Nicaragua relies heavily on commercial relations with the other countries, and, by the same token, its balance-of-payments difficulties adversely affect the other countries. The spillover effect of a deteriorating situation in any one nation of the region—whether economic, financial, or political—has important implications for the others, as Costa Rica, for example, is now finding out.

From Precapitalism to Capitalism

Notwithstanding the fact that important political movements developed in each Central American country prior to the 1960s—for example, the Guatemalan Revolution from 1944 to 1954, and the 1948 Costa Rican Revolution,[2] which among other things nationalized the banking system and ensured a better distribution of national income—the mainstream of concern at the time centered on the ways and means of overcoming economic and social underdevelopment, and ensuring workable conditions for formal democracy while attempting to determine what the state's role should be in the process of change.

There were no major disagreements in Central America during the 1960s or most of the 1970s over whether to follow a capitalist path. To the principal political sectors, the basic issue was not socialism versus capitalism, but how to make capitalism viable. It was in regard to this basic premise that ideological and strategic conflicts arose, allowing other important issues to become more clearly focused. Among these issues were: (1) the need to change the pattern of development from agricultural export-oriented systems, independent of each other, to more balanced internal growth in each of the countries, and increased interdependency among them, in order to ensure the creation of an expanded internal market and the possibility of a broader range of autonomous decisions; (2) the need to modernize societies in order to adjust precapitalistic systems to the dynamics of capitalism; and (3) the need to establish new forms of popular participation in order to stimulate a process of democratization.[3]

The main concern was with *development*. Within this concept, participation and democratization, although stressed by liberal circles, were rejected by the traditional elites. Inasmuch as capitalism was not challenged but was advocated by all, liberal circles felt that some sort of political compromise would be worked out while the process was under way. In the long run, however, economic change did not expand the potential for political compromise in the same manner throughout the region. Only Costa Rica and Honduras were able to construct channels of active communication between economic and social sectors, while Guatemala, El Salvador, and Nicaragua greatly restricted the development of that potential. It is perhaps also important to mention that even the region's Communist parties, however small and holding fast to the orthodox thinking of the time, perceived that through a process of capitalistic modernization and a given amount of democratization they would eventually find space within which to surface, acquire legal status, and engage in organizational activity among the popular sectors. Despite their criticism of the new approach from a structuralist point of view, they nevertheless took advantage of the new stage of events.

Economic Integration as a Platform

Following efforts of the UN Economic Commission for Latin America (ECLA) to introduce basic changes in the pattern of development through import-substitution schemes, the governments of the Central American counties began to examine the potential for a joint effort, giving greater emphasis to a subregional forum within ECLA—the Committee of Cooperation of the Central American Isthmus, established in the 1950s. It was through this structure that liberal circles in each country foresaw the road to economic and social change and the possibility for broader political participation.

The fact that outstanding Central Americans had been in exile in Mexico, various countries of South America, and even some countries of Central America greatly contributed to understanding the potential of the economic-integration program as a political platform on which to work jointly. A major contribution was ensured by the gradual but steady incorporation of Central American scholars who had returned from abroad or would do so in the following years. All in all, this new political approach, covered with the cloak of "economic development and regional integration," allowed a broader range of action within each of the governments. A growing number of intellectuals and professionals incorporated themselves into advisory governmental bodies as "technocrats" and eventually rose to high political positions. This allowed the expansion of a network of political relationships at the national and regional levels, increasing the potential for acceptance of the new approach within different political circles, and reducing some of the apprehensions in more traditional circles by phasing out revolutionary terminology.

The emergence of revolutionary Cuba and its favorable attitude toward revolutionary change in Central America introduced another important element into the political process. The United States turned its attention to the region and to the preliminary efforts toward economic integration. The need to agree on a policy of containment of communism became evident. Along with military and counterinsurgency assistance, the United States expressed its willingness to support the regional-integration program, to help widen its scope by means of complementary action in the social and educational fields, and to enhance the role of political parties in the electoral process. While the U.S. government had reservations about some of the basic theories of regional development espoused by the new wave of technocrats—for example, state supervision over regional industries and eventual exclusion of foreign capital in certain areas—it nevertheless supported the overall concept, lending its weight to the process and to some of the resulting political implications.

While the new relationship was being established within the framework of the Alliance for Progress, changes were already under way in Central America. By liberalizing commerce between the countries, industrialization began, in different degrees, to affect the structure of power in each country in the sense that new or emerging commercial, industrial, and financial groups began to displace the traditional agricultural elites and their overwhelming influence in the affairs of government.[4] The expansion and diversification of economic activity brought about a correlative expansion of the labor force and trade unions.[5] Professionalization of the armies, a tendency favored by the United States, brought about a more flexible attitude toward development on the part of the military. There was increased demand for vocational training schools and for higher education to the extent that the national universities were no longer sufficient to satisfy existing needs. As a result, private universities broke the long-standing tradition of public education at that level. Among them, Catholic universities in El Salvador and Nicaragua played an important role.

As long as these changes did not immediately affect basic agricultural interests—in the sense that agrarian reform was not undertaken, the roles of the church and the army were not challenged, and economic trends remained within the realm of capitalism—there was no major opposition from these sectors to the changing pattern of development. However, the need to control an expanding labor movement, with its demands for more freedom to organize in the rural areas, soon began to be felt. Industrialization and agricultural diversification, while accepted and even promoted by labor, brought new demands from labor for higher wages, housing, and other social benefits that the system was unwilling to meet as long as those demands remained unnecessary to maintaining social tranquility. To offset rising expectations, the predominant economic sectors formulated what were called "social development programs," involving greater public expenditures in rural education and health, colonization programs, and construction of roads to penetrate the interior of each country.[6] The underlying theory was that urban social unrest could be controlled by expanding security forces, while existing relationships between landowners and the army could cope with unrest in the rural areas, where trade unions and *campesino* (peasant) organizations would not be allowed to gain strength. In any case, it was publicly stated by agricultural organizations that the masses were not prepared to understand and evaluate "exotic ideas" such as those espoused by trade unions and leftist political parties.

As economic growth emerged as a new phenomenon and the first changes became apparent, so did the need for adjustments among social and political organizations. Emerging industrial and commercial groups in each country perceived the need to take a more direct part in the decisionmaking process at the national and regional levels. Integration institutions such as the Central American Bank, the General Secretariat of the Common Market, and the Central American Monetary Council had been set up through a network of treaties and made responsible for formulating and carrying out economic and social policies, including the administration of external tariffs, fiscal incentives for import-substitution activities, transportation of goods, price controls for certain products, sanitary regulations, unfair trade practices, and dumping practices between states. Chambers of industry sprang up, and traditional importers soon saw themselves being displaced by a wave of commercial entrepreneurs. A modest "jet set" made its debut in the area, and something of a capitalistic "takeoff" seemed to be in the making. Agricultural producers followed suit and, by the end of the 1960s, regional chambers of commerce and industrial- and agricultural-production organizations (e.g., sugar, cotton, coffee, and so on) became active. The region's governments faced a new phenomenon—national and regional pressure groups, which were to play an increasing role in the years to come.

The traditional division between liberals and conservatives began to give way with the emergence of ideological parties of various tendencies. Social-Democratic tendencies began to take hold among the liberal sectors, and political elements once linked to the church began to form Christian-Democratic parties. The traditional conservative parties reacted to the trend by taking strong anti-Communist positions, and the military foresaw the need to establish closer working links with the conservatives in order to safeguard the political system.

Foreign political cooperation also appeared during the 1960s. European political parties gave assistance to their ideological brethren in Central America, introducing an important new element in the political spectrum by pointing out that—contrary to Communist parties, which represented a one-class party, the party of the proletariat—democratic parties should have a pluralistic composition and structure, with precise objectives that would allow them to move toward economic and social democracy, and that political parties needed to understand and work in close relationship with trade unions. To this end, three foundations in the Federal Republic of Germany began the practice of holding ideological seminars similar to trade–union-formation seminars throughout the region. European Christian Democratic parties also engaged in the same tactics. This brought about greater interrelation among the democratic parties of the region and broadened their relations with other Latin American political parties. Relations between national labor movements and labor organizations from abroad also increased. The AFL-CIO opened up active communication with Central American trade unions, sponsoring the training of labor leaders and encouraging the handling of disputes by collective-bargaining procedures. In addition, labor attachés in U.S. embassies arranged tours to the United States for Central American labor leaders.

Meanwhile, the armed forces perceived that they should establish closer working relations on a regional level. For this purpose, they created the Central American Defense Council (which Costa Rica agreed to join only as an observer). From then on, cooperation among the security forces and joint military exercises became common.

As the political spectrum broadened and the impact of new ideologies and the labor movement (which was mainly restricted to urban centers[7]) began to be felt, the far right introduced the strategy of polarization. It did this by drawing a line between communism and anticommunism on all important issues, primarily during election periods. The church joined in this strategy, and the suggestion that God endorsed a given ideology—anticommunism—created internal discrepancies that were later to affect the role of the clergy. The more traditional elements began to brand the emerging labor movements as Communist-inspired or subject to Communist directives, thus enriching the political terminology: filo-Communist, crypto-Communist, pseudo-Communist, shameful Communist, anti-Christian, and antipatriotic were some of the expressions coined, while their authors, on the other hand, portrayed themselves as the defenders of the free world.

As a result, civilian governments came under siege throughout the region, except in Costa Rica. The decade of the 1960s saw the last of civilian government. Social and economic developments could not be left uncontrolled, nor open to the social and political forces that were the products of the process itself. The "politics of antipolitics" from this point on became a reality.[8]

Insurgency versus Counterinsurgency

As a result of the fiasco of the Bay of Pigs invasion and the fact that the Guatemalan and Nicaraguan governments had provided training facilities for the Cuban exiles who participated in that operation, the government of Fidel Castro began to devote more attention to the different groups of Central American radical youths who visited Cuba to learn the art and science of revolutionary warfare. Revolutionary conditions were believed to exist in Central America, at least in Guatemala and Nicaragua. Training and small supplies of weapons were provided to insurgent groups in both countries, but an effective guerrilla movement did not materialize. Cuban-assisted insurgency did, however, create internal conflicts in Communist parties throughout the region, and posed a delicate situation for the democratic political parties, whose leaders had to exercise considerable restraint on the youth, which viewed the guerrillas through the eyes of Ernesto ("Che") Guevara and became a headache not only for the United States but for Central America's political leadership as well.

If guerrillas were not able to materialize in Nicaragua, despite the fact that not only the far left but also elements of the center (for example, Pedro Joaquín Chamorro) sponsored them, they nevertheless managed to take hold in Guatemala. Counterinsurgency was the logical corollary.

By 1967, after losing some of its leaders, the Guatemalan Communist party (PGT) chose the path of insurgency, coordinating its efforts with ultra-left guerrilla groups such as the Rebel Armed Forces (FAR). The reaction of the extreme right was immediate. It organized its own cadres of counterinsurgents and made them available to the army. For the first time Guatemalans were to become aware of paramilitary organizations, secret sects such as the Mano Blanca (White Hand), death lists published in the press, and repression as a rule. Small groups of urban and rural guerrillas, mainly in northeastern Guatemala, clashed with military units and security forces. Without spectacular news coverage or major criticism from abroad or from within Guatemala, the U.S. government came to the rescue, providing ample support to the government and its forces.[9] The assassinations of the U.S. and German ambassadors and members of the U.S. military mission and other advisors by the guerrillas led to the adoption of some of the counterinsurgency methods used in Vietnam, with the result that the death toll mounted to about three thousand during a period of five years.

Elections were held in the course of this period. The civilian government, elected in 1966 for a four-year term, gave way to a general as president, in difficult, violent, but to a certain extent honest elections. By 1972, counterinsurgency methods had become fully effective. As a result, the guerrilla movement declined dramatically, as the entire Communist party leadership and most of the leadership of the other guerrilla groups were killed.

All in all, the Guatemalan army and the radicalized right became familiar with guerrilla warfare and the somewhat unorthodox methods that it employed. In the course of the struggle, the democratic left, the trade unions, and the campesino organizations were weakened. The guerrilla movement, on its part, learned that the center-left, the trade-union movement, campesino organizations, and the Indian communities were unwilling to join it as long as the system allowed them to follow a reformist course and participate in the electoral process. But it also learned another important lesson: no process that seeks deep changes can ignore the Indian communities, their cultures, and their traditions.[10]

The So-called Soccer War

For many years, El Salvador's economic elite and army felt they could cope with a high rate of population growth and mounting social tensions by keeping the doors of emigration open, particularly to Honduras and, to a lesser extent, Guatemala.[11] As time went by, Honduras became aware that, whatever land distribution projects it implemented for its nationals, a substantial number of Salvadorans would be the beneficiaries and an active element in the Honduran labor market. The Salvadoran military, foreseeing that this problem would eventually erupt, desired a government in Honduras that would be inclined to maintain the flow of immigration. They in fact sponsored the ambitions of some of their colleagues in that country, going so far as to deliver substantial military equipment to a Honduran garrison commander at his post. The government of Honduras learned of this assistance and, while the delivery was being made, it captured the Salvadoran convoy. From then on, tension grew and nationalistic sentiments were aroused in Honduras. Finally, in 1969, a soccer match held in San Salvador between teams from the two countries ended violently, setting off short-lived but violent military confrontations. Honduras subsequently forced more than three hundred thousand Salvadorans to return to their homeland and established severe controls on further movements of Salvadorans into Honduras.

It has been argued, and largely proven, that the Salvadoran oligarchy feared that the impact of such a wave of returning emigrees, and their future numbers, would sooner or later bring about social upheaval in El Salvador. To prevent it, military action was needed, and financial assistance was offered and provided. The army, with mixed feelings at first, and later with strong geopolitical convictions, ventured into Honduran territory under the pretext that Honduras was occupying territories where the boundary between both countries had not been established by treaty.

Whatever the outcome of the conflict from a military point of view, the fact is that the ensuing war deeply affected both countries. Honduras during the early 1970s revised its participation in the Central American Common Market, looked deeper into the needs of its internal growth, and concluded that it had to make greater efforts to modernize its economy and stimulate social mobility. The military also concluded that they should withdraw from the strategy of polarization that they had shared with the militaries of neighboring countries, and that economic and social forces were a fact inclined to pressure governments, as political parties were important and instrumental for economic and political stability.

While Honduras remained basically a banana producer, incipient industrialization was taking place along the northern coast in precisely the area where two foreign companies ran their banana operations. The country therefore had two poles of development: the capital and San Pedro Sula on the northern coast. The labor movement, which originally developed on the Atlantic coast, extended to the capital and adjacent areas, maintaining a high degree of discipline and making use of collective-bargaining methods. As a result, it could no longer be ignored by the power structure.

Lacking a landed oligarchy or an extremely wealthy elite such as existed in neighboring Guatemala and El Salvador, Honduras's emerging entrepreneurial groups were more willing to concede labor a role in the decisionmaking process. Both capital and labor formed part of the two traditional political parties: the Liberal party and the Nationalist party. Within this social structure, the army soon observed that as an outcome of the war with El Salvador it would be displaced from its leading role if it did not promote social reforms alongside economic growth. To this effect, it recognized the role of social and economic forces in the affairs of government.

As a result, three major events took place during the decade of the

1970s. In the first place, a more extensive agrarian program was implemented, granting labor unions, cooperatives, and campesino organizations willing to set up production units the right to land and to farm credit. The second entailed a more or less balanced participation in the government by the two traditional parties. Third, there was established a new working system for the army in government, whereby the commander in chief and also president could be removed by a collective body composed of military commanders in whose midst the main political decisions were to be made.

Playing strongly on nationalism, the Honduran military also undertook responsibility for modernizing its equipment and for establishing closer working relations with intellectuals and the National University, thus avoiding major clashes with the student body throughout the decade. The fact that the army supported agrarian projects without necessarily confronting all of the business groups at the same time resulted in the general recognition that the army, although constituting an organized and disciplined political force, nevertheless downplayed that role and projected an image of a force seeking a wide margin of compromise between capital and labor, as between liberals and nationalists. This allowed the system to remove the president twice during the decade without provoking major confrontations and to set the course for the country to return to civilian government in the 1980s. Events in El Salvador hastened this process. Elections were scheduled for a constitutional assembly, and for presidential elections by the end of 1981.

The same war had a totally different impact in El Salvador. The mass return of Salvadoran nationals from Honduras, coupled with one of the highest rates of population growth in the hemisphere, increased social tensions and led to closer relations between the military and the business community. National security was the basic concern. It required constant communication between the army and its security forces on the one hand, and the business community on the other, with both participating in overall agreements. In this sense, the military was to head the government and carry out vast public-work projects in order to provide employment, and the state would channel resources to the private sector so that it would participate in social programs, such as urban housing, health services, and recreational facilities.[12]

The impact of the Peruvian Revolution on military circles soon became a concern to the Salvadoran business community, which thought that the Salvadoran military might implement similar programs. They thereby began sharing economic interests with the military elite, expediting financial contributions to paramilitary organizations (such as ORDEN, created in the 1960s). The trend, however, did not totally reverse the process. The young officers were becoming acquainted with the basic problems of development and the need to change their attitude toward popular sectors and populist movements, in order to achieve some degree of flexibility in the otherwise rigid social structure.

As the decade of the 1970s began, the first major conflicts within the Salvadoran left appeared. Cayetano Carpio separated himself and a segment of his youth movement from the Communist party to form a nucleus of what was later to become the Farabundo Martí front (named after the Salvadoran communist martyred in the 1932 massacre of 30,000 peasants), setting up the first revolutionary group that would follow the path of armed struggle. As elections approached in 1972, two emerging ideological sectors—Christian Democrats and Social Democrats—recognized that they both had populist commitments and were competing for membership and support among the middle and popular sectors. A joint effort was the best alternative open to them in order to face and defeat the strong government coalition at the polls. Together they persuaded the orthodox sectors of the Communist party not to oppose or discredit electoral participation, and established a set of links with liberal-minded army officers. Armed with a pragmatic and reformist platform, the opposition, headed by Napoleón Duarte as presidential candidate and Manuel Ungo as vice-presidential candidate, challenged the government. The support of labor was overwhelming, as was that of campesinos in rural areas. The outcome in fact was an electoral victory for the opposition—but a victory that was immediately annulled by the government. This set off a garrison rebellion that was effectively put down by the government with direct and immediate assistance from the governments of Nicaragua and Guatemala. The opposition political leaders and the rebellious military then went into exile, and the new government of Colonel Arturo Armando Molina was free to pursue its course.

Brief mention should be made of the efforts by the new military government to implement a very modest and reformist agrarian program, as well as a policy of sponsoring collective bargaining by the trade unions. The latter soon led to the accusation that the government was endangering national security and was paving the way for a Communist takeover. Colonel Molina's government soon backed away from the agrarian program and consented to support General Carlos Romero as his successor.

Again in 1977, the same political formations—although with less support from labor leaders and from the Communist party, which by now saw armed struggle as the only valid path—tried the electoral course, choosing as presidential candidate a distinguished military officer, Colonel Ernesto Claramont. Manipulation of the elections combined with severe repression against the opposition in rural areas did not prevent the opposition from gaining a slim victory, which was immediately denied by the government. The presidential candidate soon led protest demonstrations that ended in his exile to Costa Rica, together with political leaders of the Christian Democratic and Social Democratic parties, including Antonio Morales Erlich and Manuel Ungo.

The turning point for those political sectors that had favored electoral participation all along and were open to compromise occurred when they realized that this approach had reached its end. Even the Communist party, which had remained aloof from the Farabundo Martí front, saw that armed struggle was the only revolutionary way of defeating the oligarchy and its military associates. The platforms of the early 1960s—of making capitalism viable—gradually faded out as ideological confrontation and class struggle became the predominant factors among the left and the ranks of the trade unions.

Amidst the deteriorating situation, center-left and center-right groups, mainly from the industrial and commercial sectors, still perceived that a compromise could be worked out, and that the new situation called for a political space in which the left could move. The situation also called for recognition of the role that the trade-union movement was entitled to play within the power structure if armed confrontation was to be avoided. Structural reforms could no longer be deferred, among them the need to reduce the overriding influence of the landed oligarchy in decisionmaking processes. Younger military officers understood the potentials of change and the need to avoid civil war, an effort to which the Catholic church gave its warm support. General Carlos Romero was then deposed as president in late 1979, in order to open the way to a centrist coalition, but the officers were unable to displace the more traditional elements in the army's upper echelons, who, while accepting the new reform platform, were unwilling to dismantle the repressive apparatus erected during the preceding years, or to submit to trying individuals responsible for gross violations of human rights. As the 1970s ended, so did expectations for peaceful change in El Salvador, given the contradictions that existed in the new situation.

The End of a Cycle of Integration

Costa Rica managed its social policies along with Common Market developments with keen awareness of the impact that events were having elsewhere in Central America on countries with rigid social structures and manipulated elections. Honduras managed to offset social and political tensions by allowing more or less fluid communication between different sectors and its armed forces. El Salvador—as has been seen—was setting the stage throughout the 1970s for profound confrontations, as were Guatemala and Nicaragua.

Costa Rica   Costa Rican political parties, long dominated by either center-left or center-right coalitions, have increasingly placed more emphasis on education and vocational training than on security forces, allowing the left ample political space within which to move and thereby reducing its potentials. They also agreed to adopt an open diplomatic and commercial framework of relations with the Soviet Union and some Eastern European countries, while maintaining a close association with the United States. As a result, Costa Ricans have not engaged in ideological controversies over capitalism versus socialism, but rather have moved toward a welfare state, where free enterprise and private property have not been issues of concern. Instead, the principal issues have been: (1) how to maintain high levels of economic development and expansion or reduction of welfare policies; and (2) centralization versus decentralization of the state and how to cope financially with the increasing tendency of the population toward consumption. The Communist party and other radical leftist groups, while able to engage in open political activity, have not managed over the years to gain more than three seats in a Congress composed of fifty to sixty members.

While its internal problems have been more in the financial than in the political arena, Costa Rica nevertheless experienced frequent difficulties with neighboring Nicaragua, and especially with the government of General Anastasio Somoza, who was constantly attacked in the Costa Rican press and Congress for his despotism and nepotism. According to a majority of Costa Ricans, the main threat to their democratic system came not from within Costa Rica but from Somoza. This serves to explain the favorable reception that anti-Somocista elements always found in Costa Rica and the freedom accorded them to organize against Somoza. This brings us to Nicaragua.

Nicaragua   Perhaps the most significant factor in the case of Nicaragua was the continual effort of the Conservative party and emerging Social and Christian Democratic groups to evict Somoza from power by electoral means, and Somoza's manipulations to prolong his stay in power through legal machinations and repressive means. In the early 1970s, the opposition found itself facing a new phenomenon that was to have a profound effect on the struggle against Somoza and the "guardians of the dynasty."[13] This was the formation and gradual strengthening of the Sandinista movement, which firmly opposed further electoral participation and favored armed struggle.

While the Sandinista guerrilla movement did not conceal its adherence to Marxism, it nevertheless did not make an issue of it. The issue was Somoza and his family's economic control of the country, and the repressive methods used by his system against all opposition—whether center-left, center-right, or even far-right conservatives. Gradually, Nicaraguan society found itself facing, not class confrontation, but a vertical split extending through upper-, middle-, and lower-income groups. The business community came to realize that its capability to influence government decisions in the economic, financial, and fiscal fields was limited not only in scope but also in effect, because of the fact that all decisions were made by Somoza himself, and the only way out was to join him or oust him. Pluralism was thus a significant element within the opposition, and the need to find an area of compromise in the opposition's ranks soon began to be felt.

Apart from the earthquake that destroyed Managua in the early 1970s and that deeply affected the country's economy because of the heavy concentration of economic activities in the capital, mounting unemployment began to produce political effects. The mishandling of aid relief and a visible slowness in reconstruction programs had an adverse effect on Somoza. The Sandinista movement soon took advantage of this and proclaimed the need for structural and political reforms. As these two factors became interrelated, so did different sectors within the opposition . An area of compromise began to clearly appear in the ranks of the anti-Somoza forces. The Sandinista movement was ready to make a distinction between the armed-struggle front, which had gradually developed, and the political front; the former was open to all Nicaraguans willing to join under the nationalist, anti-Somoza banner of Sandinismo (Sandino being the guerilla who fought the U.S. marines in the 1920s), while the Sandinistas still expressed a willingness to participate in the political front on an equal footing with other political sectors and factions.

The Nicaraguan government and Somoza in particular were unable to perceive the dangers in the Sandinista strategy. They resorted to the only method they knew well: generalized repression. While his adversaries were able to discuss and progressively agree on future courses of action, thereby reducing the normal contradictions and conflicts between the far-left, center-left, and center-right, Somoza closed the door to the economic and political sectors with which he had an ideological affinity and which believed that civil war could be averted by holding truly democratic national elections.

By adopting a two-front strategy—the armed front and the open political front—the Sandinista leadership exposed itself to the risks of political compromise earnestly being sought by the center-left and center-right. Nevertheless, the Sandinistas were willing to explore and even accept such a compromise, provided they were not forced to hand in their weapons. The leadership of the political front prepared itself for a possible compromise and, in order to stimulate and receive support from abroad, it set up a directing body composed of twelve representatives (*el grupo de los doce*) from the main ideological sectors, the Sandinistas included. This was a major step in that the opposition was able to perceive the potential of a political solution and agree on unified political participation in elections in the event that a compromise with Somoza could be worked out. It also weighed the risks of armed struggle and, in preparation for such a contingency, refined the elements of a common platform with the Sandinista movement.

The fact that Somoza rejected all formulas for a political compromise that involved his removal from power (as the opposition demanded), and that he was able to undercut inter-American support by securing military aid from the governments of Guatemala and El Salvador, increased the opposition's support from abroad, and forced the opposition to accept the leadership role that the armed front would play from then on. This meant that the Sandinista movement would play a leading role. Difficult discussions took place among the forces opposing Somoza, but the common objective of deposing him gave way to a compromise in which substantial modifications in the structure of the state were accepted by all. No longer was the viability of capitalism seen as a common objective, nor was the establishment of a socialist model agreed upon. A mixed economic system with political pluralism was to be the main ingredient of the common platform. Market forces were no longer to determine economic growth, but were to act within a planned economic system. The social base of the country would have to be expanded so as to include rural workers. The new government would not be run by technocrats and a political elite, but by the forces that had participated in the struggle.

As the decade of the 1970s came to a close, Nicaragua was undergoing its most profound transformation in the present century, with spillover effects in other countries. The collapse of Somoza and the *Guardia Nacional* not only led to the establishment of a new system but offered a profound lesson to the armies and oligarchies of El Salvador and Guatemala. Central America faced new challenges, and each country again began to look for its own way out of mounting difficulties. Fears of an uncertain future deeply affected the business communities, and talk of digging trenches began to increase.

Guatemala   It has often been said that underdeveloped countries do not examine or reflect on the mistakes committed by deposed governments or displaced economic sectors. Instead, external factors and the weakness of the security forces are brought to light and blamed for the outcome. While these latter factors are to a certain extent relevant, the fact remains that rigidly structured societies tend to refuse to look inward and determine how vulnerable they are when confronting mounting dissatisfaction within the prevailing system. Less rigidly structured societies that have learned to exercise the art of compromise, or are in the process of learning it, tend to take actions that will steer them away from possible confrontations. The question whether privileges and the weakening of social controls might give way to "uncontrolled changes" seems to blur perceptions of events and useful lessons. Such was the case in Guatemala.

In order to place events in Guatemala in proper perspective, it must be remembered that with a good record of economic growth, mounting foreign reserves, and increasing benefits from participation in the Central American Common Market, the country appeared during the 1970s to be capable of "taking off" as far as development was concerned. Guerrilla movements sponsored by the far left had, for all practical purposes, been defeated with the assistance of the U.S. government, and the political right and the army felt that the situation was under control. Capitalism had in fact taken hold, to the point where the center-left—Christian Democrats and Social-Democratic groups— insisted not on profound structural changes but rather on pursuing modernization, greater popular participation, and more profound democratization, and carried out strong campaigns in favor of free elections. The conformation of center-right groups became evident, so that it was possible to draw a somewhat clearer distinction between the progressive-right and the traditional-right. Similar distinctions were apparent within the center-left, between populist and reformist elements unwilling to sponsor class struggle but willing to back social integration between Indians and non-Indians, and the far-left, composed of the Communist party and other ultra-left groups who, according to the Communists, were engaged in adventurism.

As in the economic sector, a line could be drawn between progressive elements and traditional agricultural groups, each having leverage of its own. The working class still remained divided between Indians and non-Indians. The Indians held fast to their traditional cultures and remained subject to social and racial discrimination. They constitute the main work force for seasonal agricultural crops: coffee, sugar, cotton, cardamom. The non-Indians are more inclined to form and join trade unions. It has been in the trade-union movement that basic ideological and strategic conflicts have arisen—conflicts over whether to take a reformist course of action and make use of collective-bargaining procedures to ensure better working conditions and social benefits, or to pursue the revolutionary course in which the labor movement would engage in confrontation, so that it could prepare itself to assume power. Insofar as the center-left had space in which to move and act, and inasmuch as national elections provided a way to achieve political power, a majority of the labor movement chose the reformist path. The Indian communities also supported this path by voting for opposition parties in national elections.

Since the center-left and center-right concurred on the need to reduce social tensions and make necessary adjustments in the structure of power, they worked on opening channels of communication. This also afforded trade unions an opportunity to become aware of the thinking among progressive capitalists and the traditional sectors. As labor strikes spread from industry and banking institutions to agricultural enterprises, however, and as government employees began to organize to press for wage increases, the far-right openly voiced its concern and fears, declaring that there would soon be a Communist takeover, calling for a hard line, and pressing the army not to fall into a trap.

As the political spectrum broadened, the possibility of an understanding between the center-left and center-right groups increased. By 1977, these groups were exploring the formation of a broad front that would make room for the election of a centrist government. The trade-union movement, which favored reforms, expressed its willingness to support the effort insomuch as the freedom to organize would be extended to the rural areas, and an effort would be made to return to civilian rule in the near future, an objective shared by centrist forces. The need for compromise was accentuated by the fact that newly formed guerrilla groups had appeared in the highlands—for example, the Guerrilla Army of the Poor *(Ejército Guerrillero de los Pobres, EGP)* —proclaiming the strategy of prolonged warfare.[14]

Agreements between center-left and center-right forces did in fact materialize, and an elected government displaced the far-right from political power in early 1978. The experiment was short-lived, however, as events in Nicaragua and El Salvador increased the fears of the right, which now returned to its previous hard-line tactics and impressed its fears on the army.

Confirmation of their apprehensions came from General Somoza personally, who during the course of 1979 convinced the Guatemalan military high command of the need to take a hard line, and to ignore the pursuit of democratization and popular participation, which would only lead eventually to an armed struggle similar to the one he was then facing. While the governments of Costa Rica, Venezuela, and the

United States did their best to persuade the Guatemalan government not to diverge from its original course, the far-right pressed for action against the center-left, the trade unions, the university, and religious institutions—"in order to clear the way of potential subversives, and be able to fight the guerrillas," as its main spokesmen expressed to the army's high command.

Throughout this period, and drawing from past experiences, two of the guerrilla movements—the Guerrilla Army of the Poor (EGP) and the People's Organization in Arms (ORPA)[15]—turned their attention to the Indian sector of the population, seeking support by showing deep understanding of their plight and aspirations. They thereby confirmed their statement that each "guerrillero" must known how to handle his weapons: the rifle and political science.

As trade-union leaders, center-left political leaders, highland community leaders, and priests began to be assassinated, the ranks of the guerrillas began to grow. The assassinations of businessmen and military officers led the right to close ranks and further identify with the army. What was to have been a broad front began to contract, and the government moved to the far-right, giving way to polarization. Economic and military sectors interlocked, thereby displacing the center of gravity of national security and opening up further ground to insurgency. According to the far-left, this entailed drawing the line between the "rich and its army" on one hand and the "poor and its army" on the other.

What was once a healthy economy began to suffer serious deterioration as foreign reserves dropped because of transfers of capital abroad, investment declined, and unemployment increased. By the end of the 1970s, radical anti-Communist sectors again looked north for support and relief, no longer having confidence in their own ability to meet the challenges of subversion and of exploring new ideas and solutions. Events in neighboring El Salvador further narrowed the perspective of analysis and increased the conviction that trenches had to be dug.[16] The decade began with violence and ended in violence, with breathing spells of tranquility and major earthquakes that shook the foundations of a traditional society.

The end of the decade also showed Central America as a whole that economic integration would no longer be the common platform in the region unless new realities were recognized, among them: Panama; the emergence of an independent Belize forming part of the Central American isthmus; political and economic pluralism in the region; and the expanding interests of Mexico and Venezuela.

NOTES

1. In 1950, a single export product typically provided 60–70 percent of all foreign-exchange earnings; in the case of El Salvador, it reached 90 percent. By the end of the 1970s, no single product provided more than 50 percent of exports, except in the case of El Salvador, where coffee still accounted for 65 percent. Subsistence farming also decreased. Thus while in the 1950s 20 to 25 percent of agricultural Gross Domestic Product (GDP) typically originated in the subsistence sector, this percentage had fallen to roughly 14 percent by 1980. The vital link between export-oriented agriculture and subsistence farming has been seasonal labor, which larger and more modern plantations need and without which the subsistence farmer could not survive. I express my gratitude to Dr. Gert Rosenthal and Dr. Isaac Cohen Orantes of ECLA for valuable statistical information provided for this study.

2. For more detailed reading, see: Ralph Lee Woodward, Jr., *Central America: A Nation Divided* (New York: Oxford Univ. Press, 1976); Jose M. De Aybar de Soto, *Dependency and Intervention: The Case of Guatemala in 1954* (Denver: Westview Press, 1978); Richard H. Immerman, "Guatemala as Cold War History," *Political Quarterly* 95; no. 4 (Winter 1980); J. P. Bell, *Crisis in Costa Rica* (Austin: Univ. of Texas Press, 1971).

3. Until the decade of the 1950s, there was little or no popular participation in national affairs other than in electoral periods. The trade-union movement was reduced to the capitals of the countries and very restricted in banana operations and related activities such as railroads and ports. Cooperatives were limited in number and the Catholic church did not encourage community activity, other than that related to religious festivities and church repairs.

4. The contribution of primary activities to GDP for the region as a whole dropped from 38 percent in the 1950s to 27 percent in 1978, while relative participation of secondary activities grew from 15 percent to 24 percent during the same period. As the economies began to be more "open" than ever, the ratio of exports to GDP grew from 18.6 percent in the 1950s to over 30 percent in the 1970s, while the ratio of imports grew from 16.3 percent to 34 percent during the same period.

5. The composition of the work force changed significantly. For the region as a whole, about 65 percent of the economically active population lived off agriculture in the 1950s; that percentage had dropped to 50 percent by 1980 (28 percent in the case of Costa Rica), while the percentage of the work force employed in industry increased from about 10 percent in the 1950s to almost 20 percent by 1980. The most important growth of employment of the work force has been in the service sector, which absorbed less than 20 percent of the work force in the 1950s and over 30 percent in 1980, often in urban activities of very low productivity.

In the case of Guatemala, the contribution of primary activities to GDP dropped significantly during this same period, but the percentage of the economically active population that lives off agriculture has remained the highest in the region. The work force is predominantly Indian and the "family" unity is in itself a work unit, mainly in seasonal crops and subsistence farming.

6. For the region as a whole, the literacy rate increased from 38.7 percent in 1950 to a still appalling 57.1 percent in 1975. Life expectancy at birth increased from 49 years to 59 years between 1960 and 1975; the percentage of the population with access to drinking water increased from 22 percent in 1960 to roughly 46 percent in 1975. For all of these indicators, Costa Rica is well above the average and Guatemala below.

The public sector emerged as a relatively more important and autonomous actor with a greater commitment to developmental goals than in previous years. Total expenditures of central governments grew from 11.2 percent of GDP in 1960 to 16.3 percent of GDP in 1978. The tax systems also experienced considerable change. Total fiscal receipts to GDP increased from 10.7 percent to 12.1 percent in the same period. The relative participation of direct taxation increased from 14 percent to 23 percent and that of sales taxes from 30 percent to 38 percent during the same period.

Weekend and Sunday entertainment facilities for workers began to be constructed by governments and turned over to employers' organizations, thereby keeping within the paternalistic tradition.

7. The urbanization index increased from 16 percent in the 1950s to 43 percent at present. The population of the capital cities, which are virtually the only important truly metropolitan centers in the region, increased from 11 percent to 19 percent of the total population during the period under examination.

8. The phenomena and policies examined by Brian Loveman and Thomas N. Davies, eds., *The Politics of Anti-Politics* (Lincoln: Univ. Nebraska Press, 1978) also appeared in Central America. The marked disdain by the military toward civilian political leadership did not affect the relationship with the technocratic sector. The Peruvian model temporarily had more influence in El Salvador and Guatemala than other South American military models, although the Brazilian theory of national security received wider acceptance.

9. For a more detailed analysis, see: Caesar D. Sereseres and Brian Jenkins, "US Military Assistance and the Guatemalan Armed Forces," *Armed Forces and Society* 3, no. 4 (Summer 1977): 575–594.

10. EGP., *Compañero,* revista internacional del Ejército Guerrillero de los Pobres de Guatemala, ca. 1980. Tom Fenton, in "Special Report from Guatemala," Associated Press, May 14, 1981, examines this trend.

11. While the whole of Central America experienced rapid population growth—from eight million in 1950 to over twenty million by the end of the 1970s—the growth rate in El Salvador had a greater impact due to the small size of the country and the limited available land for farming, most of which has been owned by a social and economic elite known as the "Fourteen Families," who throughout the period under examination, not only expanded in number, but whose set of values was shared by emerging entrepreneurial groups who ventured into agriculture. Cotton and sugar plantations in Guatemala relied heavily on Salvadoran migrant labor.

12. For a more detailed analysis, see the excellent study by William Leogrande and Carla Anne Robbins, "Oligarchs and Officers: The Crisis in El Salvador," *Foreign Affairs* 58, no. 5 (Summer 1980): 1084–1103.

13. For a more profound analysis and understanding of the role of the Guardia Nacional of Nicaragua, see Richard Millet, *Guardians of the Dynasty* (Maryknoll, N.Y.: Orbis Books, 1977), pp. 251–274.

14. As a result of the formation of a broad-front coalition and agreement on a minimum program of action between center-left, center-right, and members of the Guatemalan army's high command, I agreed to be a candidate for the vice-presidency and was elected to that post in March 1978 for a four-year term. The EGP defined its strategy of prolonged warfare in January 1978 in manifestos published in the press as a condition to the release of Roberto Herrera Ibarguen, who was held hostage.

15. ORPA (*Organisación del Pueblo en Armas,* The People's Organization in Arms) formed in late 1979 as a revolutionary guerrilla movement, including in its ranks young Indians of both sexes. Although proclaiming itself Marxist, it did not align itself with any specific current or tendency. The other two guerrilla movements—FAR *(Fuerzas Armadas Rebeldes)* and PGT *(Partido Guatemalteco del Trabajo)*—became public in 1980, both Communist-oriented.

16. On September 1, 1980, I submitted my resignation as vice-president before the Guatemalan Congress, stating, among other points:

> The resulting crisis is profound. The younger generations show signs of dissatisfaction and their protest banners are already visible on the horizon. The nation demands wide national agreements which take into consideration these young people and their hopes, as well as ideological freedom and respect for the basic human rights of the individual. This cannot be achieved by erecting barricades and trenches. History has amply demonstrated this to be the wrong alternative. Due to my differences with the President of the Republic and in the absence of institutional forums to debate the serious problems affecting the nation, my retirement from the Vice-Presidency has become imperative. Therefore, I respectfully submit to the Congress my irrevocable resignation as Vice-President.

PART TWO

United States
Interests and Policies

2. The United States and Central America: Hegemony in Historical and Comparative Perspective

James R. Kurth

Hegemonic Powers in International Politics

Much may be learned about the future of the United States in Central America by a look at other historical analogies, by comparisons with other cases of relations between a great power and several small states. For the relations between the United States and the countries of Central America and the Caribbean have been, since the Spanish-American War of 1898, an example of a special kind of international system. Traditional historians and political analysts have often described such systems as areas of "hegemony" or "spheres of influence," and they have often called the small states within them "client states" or "protectorates."

In addition to the United States in Central America and the Caribbean, other major examples of hegemonic systems since World War II have been the Soviets in Eastern Europe, the British in the Middle East until the 1950s and in the Persian Gulf sheikdoms until the early 1970s, and the French in Subsaharan Africa. The United States in Central America and the Caribbean has had a good deal in common with these other systems of relations between states of unequal power and societies of unequal development. And, as we shall see, there were also several comparable hegemonic systems in the past.

More formally, a hegemonic system can be said to be characterized by each of the following four features:

Military Alliance There is a formal military alliance between the great power and the several small states (e.g., the Rio treaty, the Warsaw treaty, the French agreements with several African states). Often military assistance or protection extends beyond mere alliance to include military aid, military advisors, or military bases.

In Central America and the Caribbean, the United States has organized and supported both the Rio treaty (1947), covering Latin America in general, and the Central American Defense Council (CONDECA, 1964), covering Guatemala, El Salvador, Honduras, and Nicaragua in particular; it has provided military aid and military advisors to most Central American and Caribbean states since the beginning of the twentieth century; and it has maintained military bases on its own territories in the area—the Canal Zone and Puerto Rico (and also at that anomaly, Guantanamo in Cuba).

Economic Dependency   The economic relations—trade, investments, economic aid, or economic advisors—of most small states in the alliance system with the great power are much more intensive than their economic relations with any other great power. Often certain important economic ratios reach the level of 20–25 percent or more (e.g., the small state's exports to the great power as a percentage of the small state's total exports; the great power's investment in the small state as a percentage of the total foreign investment in the small state; the great power's grants and loans to the small state as a percentage of the small state's total government budget). In the case of small states in Central America and the Caribbean, these trade and investment ratios with the United States have often exceeded 50 percent.

Foreign Intervention   The great power has undertaken foreign intervention—military, advisory, or proxy—in several small states in the alliance system. Often there is a general expectation, among elites and counterelites in the states of the system, that there are certain diplomatic and political limits to a small state's behavior, the transgressing of which will provoke the great power to undertake intervention within the offending state.

One such transgression is the imminent defection of the small state to a competing great power. This is what the United States claimed was occurring when it undertook CIA interventions in Guatemala in 1954 and in Cuba in 1961. Another such transgression, relatedly, is the imminent displacement of a friendly regime within the small state by an unfriendly one, together with signs that the new regime will move internally toward ideological and institutional forms that are similar to those of a competing great power, increasing the probability of defection of the small state to that power. This is what the United States claimed was occurring when it undertook its military intervention in the Dominican Republic in 1965 and when it recently sent military advisors to El Salvador.

In some cases of intervention, the great power uses an international organization to help provide collective legitimization for its operation (e.g., the Organization of American States in Guatemala in 1954 and in the Dominican Republic in 1965, the Warsaw Treaty Organization in Czechoslovakia in 1968).

System Stability The system has shown a capacity for stability, in the sense that the system has endured for at least a generation.

Since the Peace of Westphalia of 1648, which ended the Thirty Years' War and established the legal grounds for a multitude of small but formally independent states within *Mitteleuropa,* there have been a number of hegemonic systems or close approximations to them. In addition to the modern systems already mentioned, there were also earlier cases such as (1) France in the Rhineland (1648–1713), (2) Austria in the German states (1815–1866), (3) Austria in the Italian states (1815–1859), (4) Germany in southeastern Europe (1934–1945), and (5) Britain in the Indian princely states (1858–1947). (This last system was a limiting case between a hegemonic system and a colonial one, an extreme form of the indirect rule that Britain often employed elsewhere in its empire.) There have also been abortive hegemonic systems, such as Japan in East Asia (1931–1945) and Italy in southeastern Europe (1924–1943).

Thus almost every great power has undertaken at some time some sort of hegemonic system, be it actual, approximate, or abortive. This might suggest that hegemonic systems are merely a predictable result of great power status. Such a view might stress the many similarities among them and especially the similarities with the hegemonic system of the United States in Central America and the Caribbean: there were, for example, the Austrians in Germany, with their use of international organization (the German Confederation) for collective legitimation of political intervention; the Austrians in Italy, with their use of military intervention against revolutionary movements and in support of client regimes; and the Germans in Southeastern Europe with their use of their large market for foreign goods as a powerful bargaining tool with underdeveloped countries.[1] The United States in Central America and the Caribbean has had some similarities in its methods with these three hegemonic systems in the Mitteleuropa of an earlier day.

But for most observers, the most relevant comparisons will be with more contemporary hegemonic systems—the Soviets in Eastern Europe and the British in the Middle East.

Soviet Hegemony in Eastern Europe

At the end of World War II and as a consequence of it, the Soviet Union occupied or at least overshadowed each of the nations on its western frontiers. The way in which it organized its relations with these nations of Eastern Europe tells us something about the dynamics of a hegemonic system and about three interrelated hegemonic logics—strategic, political, and economic.[2]

Stalin himself observed at the time, "This war is not as in the past. Whoever occupies a territory also imposes on it his own social system [as far] as his army can reach."[3] Here, as in so much else, Stalin understood the logic of a great power in international politics in the contemporary era.

Like all great powers, the Soviet Union sought to achieve a ring of buffer states, a protective *glacis,* as soon as it had the military strength to do so. The compulsion, and indeed the justification, seemed especially strong in the case of the Soviet Union. After all, historically the greatest powers of the West had periodically invaded Russia through Eastern Europe and especially through Poland, as in 1812, in 1914, in 1919, and in 1941. The true "Polish Corridor" lay between Germany and Russia and was Poland itself. But the smaller nations to the north and to the south of Poland had also on occasion been springboards for invasions of Russia, as all of them had been once again in 1941. It was thus wholly natural, indeed inevitable, that Stalin would insist that these East European nations become buffer states with, in the words of the Yalta agreements, "governments friendly to the Soviet Union."

This logic of international politics soon led to a logic of internal politics, however, and the Soviet Union's strategic imperative became the East European nations' political imperative. The social structure and the national traditions in most of the East European nations made it most unlikely that a government friendly to the Soviet Union would issue from a wholly indigenous or independent political process, be it a democratic or an authoritarian one. Most of these countries were still in the early stages of industrialization; their working class was small, their middle class was weak and divided, and their landlord class was powerful. This was the case in Poland, Hungary, Romania, and Bulgaria. In these countries, it was likely that, in a few years after World War II, the old conservative elites would regain their political power, just as they had a few years after World War I. Being anti-Communist by class interest and anti-Russian by national tradition (except in Bulgaria), these elites would then readily ally themselves with the newest great power to the West, the United States of America, and would once again become a threat to the Soviet Union.[4]

This meant that the Soviets had to replace the natural social structure with an artificial one, that the Soviets would have to manufacture their friendly governments by a revolution from above and from without, and they would have to impose Communist party rule and maintain it by authoritarian, even totalitarian, means. And this was the pattern and the process in Poland, Hungary, Romania, Bulgaria, and also the Soviet zone of Germany in the years immediately after World War II.[5]

Missing from this list were Czechoslovakia and Finland, the exceptions that prove the rule. For these nations were considerably more industrialized in 1945, had maintained democratic rather than authoritarian systems in the interwar years, and had large mass-based Communist parties. These differences in social structure preserved Czechoslovakian democracy from Soviet-imposed revolution for three years, until 1948, when the division of Europe and the polarization of the cold war caused the Soviets to end this particular state of exception. But the similar differences in social structure have preserved Finnish democracy to the present day.

The internal political logic in Eastern Europe soon turned into an internal economic one. The Communist parties of the Soviet Union and the new satellites were committed to a particular economic program, that of rapid, forced-draft industrialization.[6] This in turn resulted in rapid urbanization and in rapid growth in the number of industrial workers, bureaucratic employees, and intellectuals. These social changes had something in common with those that occurred in Central America in the 1970s, with the rapid economic growth encouraged by the United States and by American multinational corporations.[7]

It is difficult, however, to govern an industrialized and urbanized society with a small authoritarian party, even a highly organized Communist one. The Soviet army and the Communist party had brought into being in East European countries a new society that then pressed upon the bounds of the party and on occasion broke into open rebellion, as in rebellions of workers in East Berlin in 1953, of workers and intellectuals in Hungary in 1956, of intellectuals in Czechoslovakia in 1968, and of workers or intellectuals in Poland in 1956, 1970, 1976, and 1980–1981.

Had the East European nations been allowed to follow their natural tendency, to line up their political systems with their new social structures, they probably would have become social democracies. When allowed to vote their preferences, industrial workers tend over the long run to vote for Socialist parties and bureaucratic employees tend to vote for Liberal or Progressive ones. In a situation where there is a large industrial working class and a large bureaucratic employee class, where there is no longer a powerful landlord class, and where there is a large state sector in the economy, as in both Northern Europe and Eastern Europe, there is a natural, solid base for a governing coalition of Socialist, Progressive, and Liberal parties and for Social Democratic policies. The political *telos* of Eastern Europe is probably Finlandization, so to speak. But the Soviets have not dared to permit this.

First, in the historical crucible of Eastern Europe with its traditions of opposition to Russian domination, the Soviets have assumed that there is too great a risk that a newly democratic and newly neutral nation might go all the way and become an ally of the West. Second, the liberalization of an East European Communist state carries implications for the liberalization of the Soviet Union itself. Thus, for the Soviets the monopoly of the Communist party (i.e., the Soviet system) in its East European satellites had to be maintained; and in East Germany, Hungary, and Czechoslovakia this could only be done by Soviet military intervention and then by continuing military occupation.[8]

The particular timing of the Soviet military interventions seems also to reflect conditions in the West. In each case, the Soviet problem with its ally had been growing for some time, yet the moment that the Soviets invaded was one when the West was diverted and engaged elsewhere (concluding the armistice negotiations in the Korean War in 1953; the Suez crisis in 1956; the turmoil surrounding the antiwar protests and the Democratic National Convention in 1968). Similarly, the Soviets invaded Afghanistan in December 1979 when the relationships between the United States and Iran and Pakistan, the two countries most immediately threatened by the Afghan intervention, had never been worse (the occupation of the U.S. Embassy in Tehran and the burning of the U.S. Embassy in Islamabad both having occurred in November, the previous month).

The dynamics of the Soviet hegemonic system in its client states, then, seem to have condemned the Soviets to continuing military occupation, to being a "brooding omnipresence," in East Germany, Poland, Czechoslovakia, Hungary, and now Afghanistan.

There have, however, also been cases where an East European nation was able to gain a very large degree of independence from the Soviet Union without provoking Soviet military intervention, i.e., Yugoslavia in 1948, Albania in 1961, and Romania in 1964. These exceptions illuminate the rules of the Soviet hegemonic system. In each case, at the time of its move toward independence, the local Communist regime was at least as authoritarian, as insistent upon its political monopoly, as the Communist regime in the Soviet Union itself. (Later, Tito in Yugoslavia would allow very substantial liberalization.) The move toward independence did not immediately challenge the domestic political formula within the Soviet Union. For the nations of Eastern Europe, it seems, there is a rather sharp contradiction between political liberalization and national independence, between internal freedom and external freedom.

British Hegemony in the Middle East

When the British created their great empire in the nineteenth century, they organized most of it into a vast system of colonies or direct rule. Other parts were governed as protectorates or with what was sometimes referred to as indirect rule. And still other countries, most notably in the Middle East, retained various degrees of formal independence while experiencing pervasive British influence. The way in which the British conducted their relations with the countries of the Middle East from the end of the nineteenth century until the middle of the twentieth also tells us something about the dynamics of a hegemonic system.[9]

Like the Soviets in Eastern Europe, the British in the Middle East were originally propelled by a strategic logic. The British sought to achieve a string of secure territories and bases along their "lifeline" to India. But India itself was primarily of enormous economic value to the British.[10]

The British accordingly sought friendly governments, "most loyal allies" in the phrase of the day, in the countries of the Middle East, first in Egypt and in the Persian Gulf, then in Persia, and then in particular successor states of the Ottoman Empire, such as Iraq. At first, this was not very difficult to achieve. These were traditional societies, and the kind of government most natural to them was traditional monarchy. This comported well with the form although not the reality, with the "decorative," although not the "efficient," elements of the British political system itself. The form of the British monarchy and the life-style of the British aristocracy provided a natural model for emulation by Arab kings, Persian shahs, and Gulf sheiks.[11]

Here too, however, the strategic logic and the political logic led to an economic one. British hegemony and local monarchies, Pax Britannica and Trucial States, provided stability, both international and internal. This stable environment, in turn, became an attractive area for British investors. And so the wealth of Britain flowed out from the home country to foreign countries, "from industry to empire," including the countries of the Middle East. And the discovery and the development of oil in Iran, Iraq, and the Persian Gulf sheikdoms greatly accelerated and accentuated the process of investment and the consequent process of economic growth and social modernization. There was created a large middle class grounded in commercial activities and in local bureaucracies. But this class was a natural source for nationalism and anti-imperialism. Thus, as in the case of Soviet hegemony in Eastern Europe and, as we shall see, in the case of American hegemony in Central America, by a comparable dynamic a gap opened up between the political system supported by the hegemon and the social system energized by the hegemon, between the "official country" and the "real country."[12]

The strength of nationalist, anti-British (and pro-German) movements was great enough in Iran and Egypt by World War II that the British feared that they might successfully convert their monarchs from most loyal allies into German agents. The British intervened militarily in Iran in 1941, when they deposed the shah and placed on the throne his young son who would become the shah that we would come to know all too well in later years. They intervened militarily also in Egypt in 1942, when they occupied the grounds of King Farouk's palace.

After the war, the British no longer had the resources and then no longer had the will to sustain a vigorous hegemony in the Middle East. In some countries, those without economic value, they chose to turn their hegemonic enterprises and responsibilities almost immediately over to the Americans, who seemed to have interests similar enough to the British so that one could be confident that they would do the job. The years 1947–1948 were the time of the first phase of the Great Recessional of British hegemony in the Middle East and adjacent areas, as they turned over the responsibility for Greece to the Americans (e.g., the Truman Doctrine) and for Palestine to the American-supported State of Israel.[13] And by 1954, the Americans had assumed dominant responsibility for even oil-rich Iran, after the CIA helped the young shah overturn the populist and nationalist government that had come to power.

By the early 1950s, it would have been reasonable to calculate that the authoritarian monarchies of the Middle East were unstable equilibria. The recent history (1910s–1940s) of monarchy in the modernizing societies of Eastern and Southern Europe suggested that the institution was really only a transitional phenomenon, doomed to disappear in a political upheaval after a few generations of economic growth and social modernization had brought into being new groups, classes, and conflicts. Given their position on the near periphery of industrial Europe and given the income from their growing oil production, the Middle Eastern states would undergo economic growth and social modernization and, therefore, political stress and strain comparable to that which had occurred on that earlier periphery on the eastern and southern fringes of Europe, including countries such as Greece and Turkey, which obviously had much in common with the states of the Middle East. Indeed, the oil wealth and the new means of mass communications would accelerate and accentuate the process in the Middle East compared to Europe. A warning had been given by the populist and nationalist Mossadegh government in Iran. But the real prototype of the new political formula was the military-nationalist revolution that overthrew the Egyptian monarchy in 1952.

If the Middle East countries were allowed to follow their natural tendency, to line up their political systems with their new social structures, the result seemed to be a nationalist and often populist military regime. The political telos of the Middle East seemed to be Nasserism. The Middle Eastern countries lacked the heavy industry and the large industrial working class of Communist Eastern Europe. They were rather at an economic level similar to the "import-substituting industrialization" of the major Latin-American countries at that time.[14] And it is not surprising that something like "national populism," like Juan Domingo Perón and Getulio Dornelles Vargas, would be the political result. The military-nationalist revolution in Egypt was followed by similar ones in later years in other most loyal allies of British power in the Middle East—in Iraq in 1958 and in Libya in 1969.

Finally, in the early 1970s, the British cooperated with the Americans in turning over the last remnants of their hegemonic system, in the sheikdoms of the Persian Gulf, to what was hoped to be a sufficiently powerful and responsible local hegemon, the shah of Iran, but this hegemon soon turned out to be incapable of protecting his own rule, much less that of the assorted sheiks of the Gulf. It was in the ancient mosques and bazaars of Tehran amid the revival of Islam that the sun finally set upon the British hegemony.

American Hegemony in Central America and the Caribbean

Like the Soviets in Eastern Europe and the British in the Middle East, the Americans in Central America and the Caribbean have been propelled by a strategic logic, although like them not by that logic alone. The threat of the Germans in the 1910s and the 1930s and the threat of the Soviets since the 1950s have periodically energized and justified American hegemony in the region.

The proximity of Central America and the Caribbean to the United States and the smallness of the countries there would have made the region a natural sphere of influence, no matter what the particular political, economic, or ideological character of the "colossus of the North." If somehow either the British, the French, the Germans, or the Russians had established a unified nation on the southern portion of the North American continent by the end of the nineteenth century, they too would have composed a hegemonic system over the states of Central America and the Caribbean. Indeed, given the style of imperial rule of the time and given the actual practice of the British and the French in the region, the system would probably have been a colonial rather than a hegemonic one.

Here, too, the strategic logic of hegemony soon worked its way into a political and then an economic logic. In the first half of the twentieth century, the social structures of Central America and the Caribbean had much in common with those of Eastern Europe and the Middle East. The countries of Central America and the Caribbean were of course exporters of primary commodities with only the beginnings of industrialization; on the basis of this economic pattern alone, their natural political system would probably have been traditional monarchy, as in Eastern Europe and the Middle East. But, of course, this political form had been made wholly impossible by the revolutions of the nineteenth century, first the Latin-American Wars of Independence, then the revolution against the Brazilian monarchy in 1889, and finally the Cuban War of Independence culminating in 1898. Given the role model of the United States in the region, the political form for those countries after their revolutions normally had to be a presidential republic rather than a traditional monarchy. But, given the social structure of the region, a presidential republic could only be a political form that covered a different political reality, that of personalistic dictatorship.

Personalistic dictatorship lacked, however, an important feature of traditional monarchies, that of dynastic legitimacy. And thus the dictators in Central America and the Caribbean often compensated for the absence of this element of political power by resorting to enhanced brutality. Thus it was that the most liberal and democratic of the hegemonic powers, the United States, ended up supporting some of the most brutal and repressive of client regimes.

Still, personalistic dictatorship had a certain congruence with the social structure of Central America and the Caribbean in the early decades of the twentieth century; and when that congruence on occasion broke down, American intervention reestablished it. Once again, as with the British hegemony in the Middle East, conditions of international and internal stability largely prevailed. And American investors also found an attractive area for their capital. And once again, economic development, new social classes, and new political strains ensued.

The United States was thus confronted with the overthrow of several of its client dictatorships in Central America and the Caribbean, at roughly the same time and the same rate as the British in the Middle East and the Soviets in Eastern Europe (General Jorge Ubico in Guatemala in 1944 culminating in the crisis of 1954, Fulgencio Batista in Cuba in 1959, Rafael Trujillo Molina in the Dominican Republic culminating in the crisis of 1965, and Somoza in Nicaragua in 1979).

For some of these countries, their most natural political formula, given their particular level of economic development and social structure, would have been some form of national-populist military regime, like that which had earlier appeared in Argentina and Brazil, which currently appeared in the Middle East, and indeed had appeared with Jacobo Arbenz in Guatemala. These countries were entering their stage of import-substituting industrialization; they contained a rapidly growing local business class, industrial working class, and class of white-collar employees and intellectuals, with the workers, white-collar employees, and intellectuals adding up to a substantial urban popular sector.[15] The political telos of Central America and the Caribbean perhaps was something like Perónism. But the politics of national-populism in an economy dominated by direct American foreign investments meant that national-populist movements would attack and call for the nationalization of these investments. And this meant a direct political conflict between the national-populist movements and the government of the United States.

Unlike the British when they confronted nationalism and populism in the Middle East, the United States was at times powerful enough, proximate enough, and determined enough to do something about it, as in the CIA intervention in Guatemala in 1954 and the military intervention in the Dominican Republic in 1965.

More interesting, perhaps, than the successful interventions are the unsuccessful interventions, the Bay of Pigs invasion of Cuba in 1961 and the more or less nonintervention in Nicaragua in 1979. The cases of Cuba and Nicaragua may give a glimpse into possible paths out of the apparently deterministic logic of a hegemonic system.

In both Cuba by 1958 and Nicaragua by 1978, the major portion of the local business class had withdrawn its support from the dictator. This made it reasonable for American businessmen and American officials to withdraw their support too. And, relatedly, in both Cuba and Nicaragua, the revolutionary leadership seemed at the time more populist than Communist. In each case, this conjunction of populist movement with business support temporarily gave rise to hopes among U.S. policymakers for a viable third way between a personalistic dictatorship that no longer fit a new social structure and a revolutionary Communist regime that might fit it so well that it could do without American investments and U.S. influence. But in Cuba, in the end, the political conflict over American direct investment followed its logic and destroyed the option of the regime's being merely a populist one.

The very fate of the Cuban Revolution, moreover, tended to innoculate the business class in other Latin-American countries against such populist adventures in later years. Cuba became not so much the first domino in Latin America, as was feared by U.S. policymakers in the early 1960s, but rather became a barrier to other populist-business alliances in the region for almost a generation. And the fate of the recent Nicaraguan Revolution may yet perform a similar innoculation. It seems to have helped to do so in El Salvador and Guatemala. If so, the particular path that leads away from hegemonic intervention through a populist-business alliance will not be taken by the United States in the 1980s.

American Hegemony in the 1980s

What will be the course of American hegemony in Central America and the Caribbean in the 1980s? Our comparative review of hegemonies in other times and other places suggests a number of different possible paths rather than a simple and inevitable recapitulation of the past history of American hegemony in the region. These different paths might be termed devolution, dissolution, and reassertion.

Hegemonic Devolution   One path could be a devolution of American hegemony to other countries in the region capable of their own miniature hegemonies. In particular, this would mean Mexico and Venezuela, now grown into substantial economic powers. This path would be comparable to the devolution of British hegemony (and of American influence) in the Persian Gulf to Iran and Saudi Arabia in the early 1970s. The fate of these particular "twin pillars" (as they were called by Henry Kissinger) or "regional influentials" (as they were called by Zbigniew Brzezinski) does not in itself inspire confidence in the solution of devolution. Yet the idea may be more viable outside the area of its origin.

Hegemonic Dissolution   A second path could be a dissolution of American hegemony, a disengagement of American power from local political conflicts undertaken by a Republican administration whose credentials and reputation would otherwise be impeccably conservative. This path would be comparable to De Gaulle's withdrawal from Algeria in 1962. It also would have some similarities with Eisenhower's withdrawal of support from the French in Tonkin in 1954 and from Batista in Cuba in 1958, and with Nixon's withdrawal from Indochina in 1973. Here too, unfortunately, the actual events that followed these earlier American disengagements do not inspire confidence in the solution of dissolution.

Another path might be something of a combination of the first two and might be more promising, that is, hegemonic devolution to Mexico and Venezuela undertaken by a Republican administration.

Hegemonic Reassertion   A final path, of course, could be the reassertion of American hegemony, that is, a systematic and sustained effort with U.S. military advisors and probably combat troops to contain and suppress revolutionary movements in El Salvador, Guatemala, and perhaps elsewhere. And here our closest comparison would be with the Soviet Union in Eastern Europe. The likely costs and consequences of this path for both North Americans and Central Americans are well known and would be severe.

Which path is the United States likely to take in the 1980s? As we shall see, the answers given by the three logics of hegemony—strategic, political, and economic—are ambiguous.

The strategic logic has now split into two somewhat contradictory logics, a logic of defense and a logic of deterrence. From the viewpoint of territorial defense of the United States and its concrete material assets, such as foreign military bases or foreign direct investments, Central America is probably less important now than it has been at any time since the opening of the Panama Canal in 1914.

From the viewpoint of nuclear deterrence, however, the "credibility" of the United States *vis-à-vis* the Soviet Union is probably lower now than it has been anytime since the beginning of the nuclear age in 1945. To theorists of deterrence, credibility is central; and for restored credibility, a successful military repression of Communist revolutionary movements in Central America would be useful.[16]

As for the political logic, it now falls between two stools. The economic development and consequent social structure of Central America seem to have reached the point that a stable personalistic dictatorship (e.g., Somoza) is no longer possible; the number, the size, and the degree of mobilization of different social groups probably require some degree of "institutionalization" of political and governmental actors.[17] On the other hand, the economic development and social structure of Central America do not yet seem to have reached the point where a stable bureaucratic-authoritarian regime (e.g., Brazil, Argentina, Chile) becomes possible; such regimes probably require the economic resources and social allies found only at a later stage of industrialization than import-substitution, i.e., that which is sometimes termed the capital-goods or "deepening" stage of industrialization.[18]

If this is the case, the local political ally of American hegemony may have to be either an unstable obsolete personalistic dictatorship (e.g., Honduras) or an unstable premature bureaucratic-authoritarian regime (e.g., Guatemala), and any stability will have to be imposed from without, i.e., by American military advisors or combat troops. But this natural political instability or this imported political stability will likely create its own economic logic. Such political conditions are likely to result in a flight of local capital, a reduction in private American investments and loans, and a declining economy less and less able to meet increasing political demands.

The actual path that the United States takes in Central America in the 1980s will primarily be a function of the political and economic logics within the hegemonic power itself. It will be the product of conflicts and coalitions between major economic interests, bureaucratic organizations, and social groups in American society. We will examine two major coalitions, one now in favor of a reassertion of American hegemony and another one potentially in favor of a diminishment of American hegemony.

The Hegemonic Coalition   The cluster or coalition of interests and organizations in support of a reassertion of American hegemony and in particular of intervention in Central America is composed of four major elements. These are (1) industries that have direct investments in Central America and the Caribbean and that have traditionally been targeted for nationalization by national-populist regimes, a rather small group; (2) industries that are no longer competitive in the wider world market, a very large group indeed; (3) the military services and the covert intelligence services; (4) and a mass base that holds traditional definitions of patriotism and anticommunism.

Industries that have direct investments in Central America and that fear nationalization have an obvious interest in preventing revolutionary regimes in the region. By themselves, these firms would not be a significant political force. But they can be joined by the more numerous and more substantial firms with large direct investments in South America and Mexico that may come to fear a domino effect from revolutions in Central America.

The more interesting group is composed of industries that are no longer competitive in the world market. These have an interest in somehow creating *de facto* preferences for their goods in Latin-American markets over the goods of European, Japanese, or even Brazilian and Mexican competitors, a sort of "imperial preference" system. In the British colonial system, colonial administrators gave de facto preference to British goods by utilizing a network of government purchases and regulations, even though until 1932 the empire *de jure* was supposed to be governed by free trade, with an absence of trade barriers. Similarly, in the American hegemonic system in Central America as in Latin America more generally, an authoritarian military regime with long-established ties with U.S. government agencies and with the local American Chamber of Commerce is far more likely to give preference to American goods than would a populist or revolutionary government. The interest of American industries in a system of de facto preferences will almost certainly grow in the next few years, as these industries face more intense competition in a stagnant or depressed world market.

The military services have their own reasons for intervention in Central America. Military bureaucracies traditionally value a stable, controllable environment. Revolutionary regimes in Central America would introduce elements of risk and unpredictability into their strategic calculations.[19] In addition, the U.S. military services in general and the army in particular want to rewrite the history of the Vietnam War, and to undo the current conventional wisdom about it, by winning a counterinsurgency war in Central America.[20]

The Foreign Policy of the Sunbelt.   The southern states of the United States assume a special place in the hegemonic coalition. The South is obviously that region most proximate to Central America and for that reason alone would be most sensitive to events within it. In addition, some of the industries mentioned, most notably the textile industry, are located in the southeastern states. The military services also have a long-established presence in the South, with their military bases, their defense contracts, and their large numbers of personnel drawn from the region. The South, too, was long the region that was most labor intensive in both its agricultural and its industrial production, that has been most hostile to labor organizations, and that has been most hostile to anything that sounds like Marxism (or for that matter Catholicism).

It is natural, then, that in Congress the prime opponents of the Panama Canal Treaty in 1978, the prime backers of Somoza to the end in 1979, and the prime backers of increased U.S. military intervention in El Salvador in 1980–1981 have been southern senators and congressmen.

When President Carter undertook his 1980 campaign for reelection, he had to take this massive political reality into account. He had to win the South to win the nomination and to win the election. This largely explains his shift toward more anti-Marxist policies in 1980 and his inability to allow El Salvador to go the way of Nicaragua.

Any presidential candidate in the 1980s, Democratic or Republican, will also face this same reality. The "new South" is a two-party South, and it is now the largest swing-bloc in the nation. As such, presidential candidates in the 1980s will be under heavy and continuous pressure to be anti-Communist in general and anti-Communist in Central America and the Caribbean in particular.

The Potential for a Nonintervention Coalition   At present, there is no cluster or coalition of interests and organizations in opposition to intervention that is comparable in strength and persistence to the hegemonic coalition. However, it is possible to perceive some potential members whose wider interests may lead them into opposition to intervention.

As chapter 5 by John Purcell in this book suggests, many American business firms with interests in Central America do not favor U.S. intervention in the region. Political and economic instability damaging to profitable operations can issue from U.S. intervention in support of a violent and ineffective authoritarian government as well as from a revolutionary national-populist regime. Some firms, by the nature of their operations, could continue to engage in profitable business dealings in a postrevolutionary situation. There have, after all, been previous cases of revolutionary national-populist regimes in Latin America that eventually stabilized, that underwent a sort of "routinization of charisma," and that became good arenas for renewed business operations by American firms. Mexico is the most substantial case, but Venezuela and Peru also provide useful examples. A recent and relevant example outside of Latin America has been Portugal.[21]

One American business group worth special consideration is the major international banks. Banks, of course, do not look forward to populist or revolutionary regimes in Central America. The recent public statements of David Rockefeller, chairman of Chase Manhattan Bank, in which he praised military regimes in Latin America, make this clear enough.[22] However, the nature of the banks' interests in the region (e.g., loans more than direct investments) make them far less exposed than the firms in the hegemonic coalition. Further, international banks are sensitive to sharp increases in the inflation rate of the dollar, and they thus prefer not to have sharp increases in U.S. defense spending. Finally, and most importantly, international banks are sensitive to the positions and reactions of the governments of the West European nations and of the most impressive of the newly industrializing nations, such as Mexico and Brazil. Systematic and sustained opposition to U.S. intervention in Central America by nations such as West Germany, France, and Mexico could well be translated into a degree of opposition by the international banks.

The reaction of Mexico could also be an especially important consideration to the great American multinational corporations with direct investments in that country, which they will not want to see become the targets of repeated anti-American demonstrations protesting Yankee intervention "in their own backyard" so to speak.

The potential bureaucratic members of a nonintervention coalition are difficult to discern. There are no obvious counterparts to the military services. The State Department and its Foreign Service might be expected to be especially sensitive to the local realities and subtleties in Central America and to be especially sensitive to the opinions of the West European allies and Mexico. However, the Reagan administration's replacement of Ambassador Robert White, the U.S. envoy to El Salvador, doubtless had a chilling effect on Foreign Service officers. In any event, they know what happened thirty years ago to those Foreign Service officers who had advised U.S. policymakers not to undertake intervention in the Chinese Revolution in the 1940s.

The Catholic church could provide a mass base for a nonintervention coalition. The recent statements and activities by the U.S. Conference of Catholic Bishops on El Salvador are a prefiguration of what could be. Yet here, too, the pressure and energy that would be systematic and sustained enough to counterbalance the hegemonic coalition would probably have to come, not from the American Catholic hierarchy itself, but from outside the United States, in this case, from Pope John Paul II and the Vatican. Nevertheless, for at least the next year or two, the hopes of American noninterventionists will probably have to reside, not in economic or bureaucratic elites, but in committed Catholics or in believing Christians more generally.

The Foreign Policy of the Democratic House   Within the institutions of the U.S. government, the hopes of American noninterventionists will probably have to reside not in the Executive but in Congress, most particularly in the Democratic House of Representatives and its Committees and Subcommittees on Foreign Affairs, Armed Services, and Appropriations, i.e., those committees that must authorize and appropriate the new monies for the renewed assertion of American hegemony.

The Reagan administration seeks a broad array of controversial measures from these committees of Congress, such as domestic budget cuts, MX missiles, F-15 and AWACS sales to Saudi Arabia, new manned bombers, new naval shipbuilding, and even the taking out of mothballs and recommissioning of two old aircraft carriers and two old battleships, as well as military aid to authoritarian regimes in Central America. Each of these measures has formidable enemies within the committees. The administration may be able to get any one program through or even several. But it would be an ineffective Congress indeed that allowed the administration to get every measure through.

One way in which the American noninterventionists might get their way and might deny military aid and military advisors to Central America would be by using the classical bargaining and log-rolling process in these congressional committees, by helping to compose compromises and compensations by which Congress would grant the administration some of its programs while denying it the military program for Central America. The most obvious trade-offs would probably involve Democratic congressmen accepting domestic budget cuts or new weapons programs. But the legislative process, like "the cunning of history," sometimes follows twisting and surprising paths. And so it might happen that the condition for the end of U.S. military involvement in Central American politics, the scuttling of "gunboat diplomacy," could well be the refloating of aircraft carriers and battleships first launched almost forty years ago. And the devolution or dissolution of American hegemony will have come about because of a re-creation and reassertion of something like "the Great White Fleet."

NOTES

1. On Austrian counterrevolutionary interventions, see Henry A. Kissinger, *A World Restored* (New York: Grosset & Dunlap, 1964). This book was originally Kissinger's Harvard Ph.D. dissertation. On German foreign economic policy in Southeastern Europe, see Albert O. Hirschman, *National Power and the Structure of Foreign Trade,* revised edition (Berkeley: Univ. of California Press, 1980). I have discussed the concept of hegemonic systems in more detail in my "United States Foreign Policy and Latin American Military Rule," in Philippe C. Schmitter, ed., *Military Rule in Latin America: Functions, Consequences, and Perspectives* (Beverly Hills: Sage Publications, 1973), pp. 244–322.

2. A useful comparative analysis is Edy Kaufman, *The Superpowers and Their Spheres of Influence: The United States and the Soviet Union in Eastern Europe and Latin America* (New York: St. Martin's Press, 1976).

3. Quoted in Milovan Djilas, *Conversations with Stalin* (New York: Harcourt, Brace & World, 1962), p. 114.

4. Hugh Seton-Watson, *Eastern Europe Between the Wars, 1918–1941,* 3rd ed. rev. (New York: Harper & Row, 1967); Joseph Rothschild, *East Central Europe Between the Two World Wars* (Seattle: Univ. of Washington Press, 1974); Robert Wolff, *The Balkans in Our Time* (Cambridge, Mass.: Harvard Univ. Press, 1957).

5. Hugh Seton-Watson, *The East-European Revolution* (New York: Praeger, 1964).

6. The politics of East European industrialization are discussed by Zbigniew Brzezinski, *The Soviet Bloc: Unity and Conflict,* rev. ed. (Cambridge, Mass.: Harvard Univ. Press, 1967).

7. Central American economic growth and social change are discussed by Francisco Villagran Kramer in chapter 1 of this book.

8. The political implications of East-European liberalization for Soviet domestic politics are discussed by Adam Ulam, *The New Face of Soviet Totalitarianism* (New York: Praeger, 1965); also see his *Expansion and Coexistence,* rev. ed. (New York: Praeger, 1974).

9. On the variety and complexity of the British Empire, see D. K. Field-house, *The Colonial Empires* (New York: Grosset & Dunlap, 1967).

10. E. J. Hobsbawm, *Industry and Empire* (New York: Pantheon, 1968).

11. On the British in the Persian Gulf, see J. B. Kelly, *Arabia, the Gulf and the West* (New York: Basic Books, 1980); on their role in the Middle East generally, see Elizabeth Monroe, *Britain's Moment in the Middle East, 1914–1956* (Baltimore: Johns Hopkins Univ. Press, 1963).

12. On the political consequences of social modernization, see Samuel P. Huntington, *Political Order in Changing Societies* (New Haven: Yale Univ. Press, 1968).

13. William R. Polk, *The United States and the Arab World,* 3rd ed. (Cambridge: Harvard Univ. Press, 1975), chapter 21.

14. On the politics of import-substituting industrialization, see Guillermo A. O'Donnell, *Modernization and Bureaucratic-Authoritarianism: Studies in South American Politics* (Berkeley: Institute of International Studies, Univ. of California, 1973); and David Collier, ed., *The New Authoritarianism in Latin America* (Princeton: Princeton Univ. Press, 1979). I have discussed comparisons between Latin American and European development in my essay, "Industrial Change and Political Change: A European Perspective," in Collier, *The New Authoritarianism in Latin America,* pp. 319–362.

15. The development of import-substituting industrialization in Guatemala, Nicaragua, and El Salvador since the 1950s and its impact on politics have been analyzed in detail by Federico G. Gil, Enrique A. Baloyra, and Lars G. Schoultz in the chapters on these countries in their study, "Democracy in Latin America," done for the U.S. Department of State, December 1980.

16. The concern of U.S. policymakers in the 1960s to maintain credibility was one powerful factor propelling them to undertake military intervention in Vietnam; see Jonathan Schell, *The Time of Illusion* (New York: Vintage Books, 1976).

17. On the general issue of the relationships between social mobilization and political institutionalization, see Huntington, *Political Order in Changing Societies,* chapter 1.

18. On the general issue of the relationships between capital-goods industrialization and bureaucratic-authoritarian regimes, see the essays in Collier, *The New Authoritarianism in Latin America.*

19. See chapter 4 by Margaret Daly Hayes in this book.

20. For a review of recent efforts to reinterpret the U.S. military failure in Vietnam, see Walter LaFeber, "The Last War, The Next War, and The New Revisionists," *Democracy* 1 (January 1981): 93–103.

21. Tom J. Farer makes a persuasive analysis that the United States has a natural, comparative advantage (e.g., its large economic resources and its large market for foreign goods) in working out a long-term, mutually beneficial relationship with revolutionary regimes, an advantage that permits it to have even better relations with such regimes than does the Soviet Union. See his "Searching for Defeat," *Foreign Policy* 40 (Fall 1980): pp. 155–174.

22. *New York Times,* Nov. 19, 1980, IV, p. 1; Nov. 24, 1980; p. 27; Dec. 5, 1980, p. 20.

3. The Recent Rapid Redefinitions of U.S. Interests and Diplomacy in Central America

Richard E. Feinberg

During the last decade, Central America has passed from being a quiet backwater of little interest to American policymakers to an area of priority concern. Between 1975–81, U.S. policy passed through five phases. Initially, the United States was satisfied with the surface stability provided by conservative, military-dominated governments. In phase two, the Carter administration's human rights policies disrupted traditional ties. In the third period (roughly 1978 to mid-1979), the United states sought to stage-manage a controlled evolution of disintegrating political systems. When this failed, first in Nicaragua and then in El Salvador, an administration confronted with discontinuity applied distinctive policies to cope with different situations. Finally, in 1981 the Reagan administration redefined Central America as a major theater of U.S.-Soviet competition. What follows is the story of this rapid evolution in U.S. perceptions of and policies toward Central America.

A Difficult Inheritance

Important shifts occurred in the economies and societies of Central America during the 1960s and early 1970s.[1] A dynamic and modern export agriculture transformed the rural sector. Urban industry, stimulated by the Central American Common Market, expanded impressively. The growth of urban professional and entrepreneurial associations attested to the dynamism, however uneven, of the local economies. Nevertheless, the growth in the labor force exceeded the

58

demand for full-time rural and industrial workers, and underemployment rose.

The impressive economic modernization of the region stimulated pressures for political change. The urban white-collar and blue-collar workers sought a transfer of political power to more reformist political leaders and parties. Discontent mushroomed among the underemployed in the urban service sectors, and among seasonal workers and other underemployed peasants in the rural areas. Thus, in 1972, a broad centrist coalition of Christian Democrats, Social Democrats, and Communists apparently won the presidential elections in El Salvador. Similarly, in Guatemala in 1974 a broad centrist coalition led by General Efrain Rios Montt and Social Democrat Alberto Fuentes Mohr also appeared to have won a pluralty of votes. In both cases, however, the armed forces intervened to maintain their hold on power. In Nicaragua, President Anastasio Somoza's first term ended in 1972, and the constitution prohibited his reelection. Instead, Somoza altered the constitution to permit his effective continuity in office.

In these and other instances, historic opportunities that might have permitted a peaceful adaptation of political systems to the newly emerging social forces were lost. As the 1970s wore on, the governments became increasingly rigid, and their power depended less and less on consent or passivity, and increasingly on coercion.

Just as the political processes were hardening, the central motor of economic growth—the regional Common Market—began to lose its dynamism. The process whereby local production was substituted for imported light manufactures was rapidly exhausted. The uneven spread of benefits among the member states, foreign exchange pressures on national balance of payments, and the 1969 "soccer war" between Salvador and Honduras increased the tensions within the Common Market. Global inflation and rising oil prices added to the region's economic problems.

American foreign policy failed to respond to these new trends. In the late 1960s and early 1970s the United States did not question the essential stability of the military-dominated regimes, not understanding that the viability of the existing political models was being undermined by economic modernization. The United States failed to react to the electoral frauds and other power grabs that impeded the accession to power of the newly emerging social forces.[2] Indeed, in some cases, notably in Nicaragua,[3] the United States gave its benediction to these acts, believing the beneficiaries were conserving an acceptable political status quo.

In addition to supporting the conservative military-civilian governments and regional economic integration, the United States had fostered the creation, in 1965, of the regional defense council, CONDECA. But partly as a result of the "soccer war" between Honduras and El Salvador, the pact lost much of its vitality.

By 1976, an astute observer might have noticed that the main elements of U.S. policy toward the region, in the political, economic, and security areas, were all in need of revision.[4] Yet Washington was paying little attention to a region that, on the surface, appeared secure. Not only was high-level attention focused elsewhere, but the size of the U.S. diplomatic, military, and intelligence presence in the area had substantially declined.

Globalism

The Carter administration's first policy thrusts in the Central American region were the negotiation and ratification of the new Panama Canal treaties and the initiation of a process of normalizing relations with Cuba. Neither was seen as a Central American issue per se, although the principles behind each initiative might have been applicable to the region. The new Panama Canal treaties were advertised as exemplifying new U.S. respect for the national autonomy of small states. The normalization of relations with Cuba was to have symbolized a new willingness to tolerate a wider political diversity.

During its first year, the Carter administration paid less attention to Central America than to any other subregion in the hemisphere. Thus, U.S. policies there tended to reflect hemispheric or even global postures (as well as the personalities of particular ambassadors and middle-level policymakers). When denouncing state terrorism before the Organization of American States (OAS) in June 1977, Secretary Vance was stating a universalist principle, and to the extent that he was thinking of particular countries, the Southern Cone states (Argentina, Chile, Uruguay) were undoubtedly uppermost in his mind. Yet, when Vance warned that governments that abandon respect for the rule of law "descend into the nether world of the terrorist and lose their strongest weapon, their moral authority,"[5] the Central American governments were deeply resentful. They feared that the international legitimacy of their regimes was being challenged, and they worried that this could have consequences for internal stability. The Carter administration's clear preference for such Caribbean-basin, democratic nations as Jamaica, Costa Rica, and Venezuela, and for the "transition" states (Honduras, Peru, Ecuador, and, for a time, Bolivia) deepened the sense of rejection felt in Managua, San Salvador, and Guatemala City.

It was in response to the human rights policy in general, more than in opposition to any bilateral slight, that the governments of Guatemala and El Salvador rejected U.S. security assistance in 1977.[6] In the absence of high-level attention, the Latin American Bureau (ARA) in the State Department took few bilateral initiatives in Central America; if anything there was a tendency to try to protect formerly friendly "clients" from those political appointees pressing for a more activist human rights approach. During this first phase, the human rights policy as applied to Central America was not based on a clearcut strategy that, for example, detailed the political actors and institutions in each country and included a game plan for their desired evolution. Indeed, the strong currents of "noninterventionism" present in portions of the administration inhibited such an approach.

The human rights policy was, of course, based on a liberal conception of freedom that inherently opposed rightist authoritarian as well as collectivist, or Leninist, models; but the policy was not actively and explicitly targeted toward the prevention of a collectivist outcome. The initial thrust of the Carter human rights policy in Central America,[7] as well as throughout most of the hemisphere, gave greater weight to the more positive benefits that resulted from improved human rights conditions than to the barriers that democracy erected against radical change. The Carter administration did, however, adhere to a general theory regarding the nature of social change. Stated simply, the administration believed that social explosions leading to radical outcomes were less likely if tensions could be directed through open government channels.[8] Exclusivist regimes might retain power through coercion for a while, but a more open system was more likely to be relatively stable in the long run.

In Guatemala, El Salvador, and Nicaragua, the immediate results of globalist expressions on human rights and democracy were not satisfying. (In Honduras, the more tolerant political atmosphere remained essentially unchanged.) By the end of 1977, all three nations were still under authoritarian rule. In Nicaragua, however, U.S. policy did provoke a dramatic and tangible response. Somoza sought to make some concessions to appease Washington and, more importantly, an already agitated opposition decided that the United States would tolerate, and might even support, a change of regime. Oppositionists among the business sector and middle classes especially were encouraged. Thus, U.S. policy reinforced an internal dynamic already under way, and the result was explosive. When a leading opposition figure, Pedro Joaquin Chamorro, was assassinated in January 1978, widespread demonstrations, strikes, and rioting ensued. A second, more impressive insurrection occurred nine months later. Washington began to focus more carefully on Central America.

Controlled Evolutionism

During 1978 and 1979, the Carter administration attempted to formulate a more detailed and considered policy toward the region that would preserve many of the original intentions of the globalist human rights policy but would reduce the perceived risks inherent in sudden or rapid regime transformations. In this new policy approach, here called "controlled evolutionism," the United States would play a much more active role in trying to control the political process within the Central American states.

The administration concluded that, indeed, the region's existing political institutions had failed to evolve in response to changing economic realities and that new social groupings were being excluded from political participation.[9] The exclusivist regimes were necessarily becoming more repressive. Otherwise moderately reformist or centrist political movements, deprived of an opportunity to enter a meaningful political process, were being driven toward considering more extreme measures or else joining other groups that were already so inclined. In an increasingly polarized environment, an undesirable radical outcome became more likely.[10] The inherited policy of supporting the military-dominated governments no longer guaranteed stability. But an unconsidered globalist human rights policy was also dangerous.

The advocates of controlled evolutionism (my name for a policy tendency, not a self-identified group) worried that Central American political institutions, always fragile, had become even less secure during the 1970s. A growing proportion of the population no longer had faith in existing political institutions. Thus, a process of political evolution, no matter how gradual, would be a delicate and dangerous affair. The greatest fear was that the existing structures might quickly disintegrate should a leftist political movement capture the popular imagination.[11] The threat of a defensive coup by the most intransigent conservative forces—which in turn could lead to rapid polarization and revolution—was another reason for caution.

The advocates of controlled evolutionism believed, or hoped, that the rulers of Guatemala, Salvador, and Nicaragua could be prevailed upon to begin a process of political transition. The proponents of evolutionism recognized that Presidents Romeo Lucas Garcia and Carlos Humberto Romero were unimaginative and mediocre men, and that Somoza was devious and accustomed to arbitrary rule. Yet, U.S. policymakers hoped that a gradual opening could be sufficiently attractive to each of these three men. The integrity of the institution of first loyalty, the military, would be preserved, any associated political parties would continue to play an important and perhaps dominant role, and the presidents' personal wealth, or most of it, would be safe-guarded. Moreover, having presided over a praiseworthy process of political transition, each president would gain an honorable place in his nation's history.

The proponents of evolutionism believed that a guiding U.S. hand could compensate for the personal limitations of the Central American rulers. U.S. shrewdness and leverage could also help overcome destructive personal or group clashes that threatened to undo the delicate transition process. U.S. loans and grants could provide economies with the resources needed to compensate those whose financial interests might be sacrificed in the reform process.

The character of the controlled-evolution model can be clarified by comparing it to two contrasting approaches: supporting the status quo, or disassociating the United States from the regime in power. Supporting the status quo was rejected as being unrealistic, illegal, and immoral: propping up visibly decaying regimes would have been costly, perhaps futile, and would have contradicted legal prohibitions against providing economic and security assistance to governments guilty of systematically violating human rights and been contrary to the Carter administration's own global human rights posture. The alternative of sharply reducing or eliminating U.S. aid programs and maintaining a cool, distant diplomatic posture was considered too risky. Accomplished in the absence of a transition plan agreed upon by the incumbent government, a policy of disassociation might weaken the regime without preparing for its replacement. The United States could be left without leverage with either the government or its opposition and be unable to shape the outcome of an ensuing power struggle. The United States would become irrelevant, and project an image of impotence, both in the region and beyond. Moreover, the disassociation policy was also risky for domestic political reasons. If the situation went sour, conservative critics in the United States would charge that the administration had abandoned its responsibilities, and failed to protect United States interests energetically. Yet, the proponents of controlled evolutionism had concluded that the globalist human rights approach, especially as advanced by some liberal members of Congress, was leading U.S. policy in this direction.

How did Central American regimes respond to the evolutionist approach? In Honduras, the military kept its promise, and the civilian parties elected a constituent assembly in April 1980. In Salvador, Guatemala, and Nicaragua, however, the presidents resisted U.S. advice and pressures. Somoza preferred to fight from his bunker rather than accept a peaceful transfer of authority. In El Salvador, President Romero became increasingly isolated until he was overthrown in a coup in October 1979. President Lucas Garcia of Guatemala decided that repression was a better guarantor of stability than even moderate reform. A closer look at each country's case will suggest where some of the obstacles to U.S. policy were hidden.

Honduras

The U.S. human rights policy reinforced a process already under way in Honduras, where the military had previously announced its intention to hold elections for a constituent assembly and for the presidency. The U.S. Embassy in Tegucigalpa, in numerous private meetings and public pronouncements, reinforced Washington's broadly stated preference for elected governments. In addition, when President-General Melgar Castro visited the White House at the time of the signing of the Panama Canal treaties, President Carter personally urged him to proceed with the promised elections. In the year preceding the April 20, 1980, elections for the constituent assembly, the United States doubled its economic aid levels and allocated $3.4 million for military assistance.[12] And according to some reports, the United States also helped prevent a coup by dissident officers in February 1980.[13]

In Honduras, the task was relatively easy: the United States simply encouraged the Honduran military to remain true to its own promises. The Honduran military recognized that its de facto government lacked legitimacy, and that popular discontent was increasing; thus, the United States was reinforcing an internal process that was obeying its own dynamic.[14]

Guatemala

Among the Central American countries, only Costa Rica received less attention than Guatemala from the Carter administration. With the traditional alliance of military, business, and most of the Catholic church hierarchy intact, Guatemala appeared relatively stable, at least in the short run. Moreover, General Lucas scornfully rebuffed the liberal U.S. critique of his methods of rule. Many in the Guatemalan government and military believed that the United States was a declining world power, unable or unwilling to meet its commitments to old allies, and dangerously naive with regard to Central American realities. Many blamed the turmoil in Nicaragua and Salvador on "destabilizing" U.S. human rights policies. With a firm hold on the reins of government, a strong balance of payments, and access to alternative sources of weaponry, the Guatemalan government felt no need to sacrifice its perceived security interests to appease the United States.

The United States recognized that it had very limited room for maneuver in Guatemala. Nevertheless, concerned that the political situation was gradually deteriorating, the United States sought to convince the Guatemalans to undertake social reforms and improve the respectability of the political process. Specifically, the United States proposed that the Lucas government try to restrain its security forces and end political assassinations as a necessary precondition for holding legitimate presidential elections in 1982.[15]

The United States basically followed a low profile approach inside Guatemala, moving neither to complete disassociation nor granting immediate concessions in hope of inducing the desired behavior. Instead, "quiet" private diplomacy was employed to advance basic objectives. The embassy avoided public criticism and did not become a focal point for local human rights activists or political centrists, as occurred in Nicaragua and some South American countries. On the other hand, the administration rejected internal recommendations made throughout 1979 and 1980 that the United States offer "carrots" to the Guatemalan government and military to increase U.S. influence and the Guatemalans' own sense of security, as preparatory steps toward persuading them to liberalize. Moreover, a $250,000 administration request for the renewal of military training (IMET) for Guatemala was deleted from the FY 1980 budget by the House Foreign Affairs Committee, in reaction to the worsening human rights situation in Guatemala.[16]

Had the Lucas government demonstrated any inclination to work with the United States, the administration would surely have responded favorably, and been supportive of a modest political reform process. Ironically, in the absence of a serious internal challenge, the Lucas government felt it did not require U.S. advice and support.

Nicaragua

The human rights policy introduced a new, critical tone into the U.S. relationship with Somoza. By alternatively applying pressures and offering positive inducements, the administration sought to improve President Somoza's respect for civil liberties. The administration did not, however, appear to question the legitimacy of the regime itself, and to the extent that a long-term strategy existed, the administration seemed to be hoping to create a climate propitious for genuine presidential elections in late 1980. The U.S. Embassy in Managua encouraged the opposition politicians to "dialogue" with Somoza, in order to arrive at mutually acceptable rules of the game.

The popular insurrection of September 1978 convinced the United

States that a more urgent and deeper U.S. engagement was required. The administration had concluded that Somoza's removal was a *sine qua non* for avoiding a deepening spiral of radicalization and violence that would consume moderate and centrist elements and present the Sandinista Liberation Front (FSLN) with the opportunity to seize power. With the backing of the Organization of American States, the United States led a three-nation mediation team to Managua in early October.[17] The opposition parties, including the Group of Twelve who spoke for the FSLN, soon presented the mediation team with their proposal: that President Somoza and other Somoza family members in the National Guard immediately resign, and that, in effect, the United Opposition Front (FAO) form a new government. But the mediation team rejected this proposal, as being clearly unacceptable to Somoza and as failing to provide for sufficient continuity. In response, the FAO submitted an amended proposal that would have allowed the existing Congress, controlled by Somoza's Liberal party, to remain in office, and the National Guard would have been reorganized under the purview of a team of incumbent National Guard officers. These concessions to gradual evolution (the "control" was provided by the umbrella of the U.S.-led mediation exercise) contributed to the bolting of the Group of Twelve and several other opposition groups, but were not sufficient for Somoza.

When the administration first entered into the mediation, it understood that Somoza's tenure was the issue, and that U.S. pressures would probably be necessary to bring about his resignation. Nevertheless, when the moment came to support decisively the amended FAO plan for an orderly transition, the Carter administration balked. Instead, it allowed the mediation team to drop the FAO proposal and pick up on a proposal by Somoza's Liberal party to hold a plebiscite, despite the warning of the State Department's Latin American experts that the plebiscite proposal was a diversionary ploy. Following drawn-out negotiations on details, Somoza rejected the electoral reforms and international presence that the mediation team deemed necessary for a fair balloting. The last chance for an orderly transfer of power was lost.

Somoza had used the mediation to splinter the opposition, buy time, and rearm his National Guard. The United States chose not to attempt to apply pressures against Somoza until after the FAO had agreed upon a carefully structured transition plan. The U.S. failure to halt the Israeli arms flow to the Guard[18]—while the United States was pressing other governments to dry up weapons flow to the FSLN—deepened Somoza's confidence that the United States was not firmly resolved to force his departure. When the mediation team finally left in frustration, Somoza felt strong enough to resist at least mild U.S. slaps.

Why did the United States not act in accordance with the irresistible logic of its own mediation plan and its earlier analysis that Somoza's permanence in power was feeding radicalism? The administration vacillated for several reasons. Some officials had both political and moral qualms about forcing out a friendly head of state; the fear of hostile congressional hearings was pervasive, and the memory of the McCarthyite period remained vivid in the State Department. It was especially difficult to appear to be opposing Somoza's call for elections. Members of Congress favorable to Somoza were threatening the White House that they would delay or defeat legislation important to the administration. Some U.S. officials were not thoroughly convinced that Somoza was really vulnerable, or believed that he could at least withstand one more round of fighting, after which another mediation effort might be mounted. Others, notably in the Department of Defense (DOD), simply believed that Somoza was, in fact, the best guarantor of U.S. interests. Some argued that Somoza was unlikely to bow to the relatively mild pressures being considered (e.g., withdrawal of the U.S. military mission, severence of the Agency for International Development [AID] pipeline). The administration would have confronted powerful domestic opposition had it attempted more biting pressures (for example, working alone or in the OAS to curtail official and commercial credits and arms supplies, and/or to sever diplomatic relations). Whether Somoza would have bowed to concerted U.S. pressures will forever remain a hypothetical question.

Ironically, it was the pressure of conservatives, both within and outside, which inhibited the administration from acting to preempt a Sandinista military victory. The original FAO proposal (supported by the FSLN) would have elevated a truly centrist triumvirate into power, consisting of the businessman Alfonso Robelo, the traditional politician Rafael Cordova Rivas, and the center-left intellectual Sergio Ramirez. The mediation team tried to forge a center-right transition government by including the Liberal party and the National Guard, but the United States was not even prepared to press this solution with vigor. In the end, Robelo, Cordova Rivas, and Ramirez would all play important roles in the post-Somoza juntas, but in the shadow of Sandinista commanders.

El Salvador

The United States first tried a "carrot and stick" approach with President Romero, a conservative general who took office in July 1977 following a disputed election capped by a harshly repressed protest demonstration. The United States delayed a $90 million loan in the

Inter-American Development Bank (IDB) until Romero responded with what were interpreted by Washington as significant reforms, including a lifting of the state of siege and the inviting of the Inter-American Human Rights Commission to make a visit. However, only a month after the IDB approved the loan, the Romero government decreed the "Law of the Defense and Guarantee of Public Order," giving the government broad powers of arrest.

The United States then decided that political conflict, and the resulting coercive actions of the security forces, would only deepen unless the electoral process was rekindled. Widespread fraud by previous military governments had discredited elections, and the opposition had refused to participate in the March 1978 legislative contest. In December of 1978, the U.S. Embassy in San Salvador was instructed to attempt to persuade Romero, the Catholic church, the National Association of Private Businessmen (ANEP), and the moderate opposition (mainly the Christian Democrats and the Social Democratic National Revolutionary Movement [MNR]), to "dialogue." The intention was to produce an understanding on the necessary steps Romero would need to take for the opposition to participate, first in the upcoming March 1980 municipal and legislative elections, and then in the 1982 presidential contest. Such an agreement, it was felt, would draw people away from confrontational and insurrectionary strategies and back into electoral politics, and provide for an orderly and constitutional transition of power.

Senior Romero government officials responded by forming a "high-level commission" to engage in lengthy discussions with the U.S. ambassador, Frank Devine, and the government announced the creation of a "national forum" in which it offered to negotiate with the opposition in an open, public meeting. However, contrary to U.S. urgings, even the moderate opposition, while willing to talk privately with the government, interpreted the government maneuver as a ploy to improve its image and divide the opposition: since the more leftist elements clearly would not participate in highly publicized negotiations with government officials. The opposition also argued that, because of the repressiveness of the security forces, the climate was not propitious for a political campaign and fair elections.

The United States persisted. In June 1979 Ambassador Devine presented the Romero government with a detailed list of reforms intended to improve the electoral climate and election machinery. Despite lack of progress, in early August the Policy Review Committee (PRC) of the National Security Council reaffirmed the dialogue strategy: in the wake of the July Sandinista victory, the PRC gave greater emphasis to the instrumental value of an electoral process intended to strengthen Salvadoran moderates and isolating the growing left. On August 16, Romero publicly acceded to several of the U.S. reform proposals, including an invitation for the OAS to attend the 1980 elections. The State Department immediately issued a public statement: "We consider these [reforms] positive and statesmanlike moves which should reduce tensions and establish credible democratic processes." Devine urged the moderate political opposition to react positively to Romero's statement and to engage the government in private conversations.

Once again, raised U.S. expectations were frustrated. In early September, Romero abruptly canceled a private meeting scheduled with the moderate opposition to consider electoral reforms. The government's "national forum" issued conclusions that failed to include significant steps to improve the electoral climate or procedures. Some observers close to the Salvadoran government commented that the very favorable U.S. response to his August 16 speech had led Romero to believe that the United States had already been satisfied.

Despite the widening rift and distrust between the government and even the moderate opposition, the United States still hoped to work through Romero,[19] and lobbied hard into early October, urging all groups to converse with the government. However, on October 15, Romero was ousted in a palace coup engineered by reform-minded military officers who had concluded that Romero was either unwilling or unable to undertake the reforms needed to halt the spiralling radicalization and violence.

Explaining the Outcomes

Why did the controlled-evolution approach fail in three out of four cases? Two broad explanations are possible: one emphasizes problems in policymaking and implementation, while the other locates the basic cause in the local actors and dynamics.

The carrot-and-stick tactics, which are so important to the controlled-evolution approach, can be extremely difficult to orchestrate. Judging the seriousness and importance of a positive step by the government requires a profound understanding of the nation's history and political structures, as well as good intelligence gathering and analysis. A premature positive response might lead the foreign ruler to believe the United States to be either naive or cynical. Responding too slowly can convince the ruler that he can do nothing to placate the United States—a conclusion that hard-liners in and around his regime will encourage him to reach. The United States generally possesses only a limited number of instruments, and they must be used sparingly and well.

U.S. diplomacy is further complicated by intrabureaucratic rivalries at home. Some bureaucrats may have ideological or sentimental attachments to either the regime in power or to the opposition that cloud their perception of reality. Each agency will object to the use of its particular program for more general diplomatic purposes. The occasional orders issued by the president or other high officials not following a situation on a day-to-day basis can be disruptive. Finally, interference from Congress, private economic interests, and other lobbyists complicate the implementation of a consistent policy.

The alternative explanation argues that the controlled-evolution approach often misjudges the nature of the local actors and the dynamics of their interaction. It overestimates the willingness or the ability of the local governments to compromise. It fails to recognize the fear of opposition leaders that striking deals with the government will cost them credibility with their followers. Moreover, a compromise sufficient to satisfy the government may be acceptable to only the more moderate opposition. Yet if the more radical parties break from their more moderate allies, the government may decide that it no longer needs to yield to a splintered and weakened opposition.

U.S. policymakers are likely to have the interests and leverage needed to pressure a regime toward even a gradual evolution only when the opposition has reached an impressive strength. Yet in this polarized environment, compromise can be very difficult. Conservatives fear that moderate reforms, far from pacifying the opposition, will only encourage it, while radicals are aiming for a thorough regime transformation.

Either policymaking or local dynamics offers sufficient explanation for the failures of the controlled-evolution model in Nicaragua, Salvador, and Guatemala. The model seemed to demand a sophisticated orchestration of policies beyond the apparent capabilities of the U.S. political system. Yet, even if the U.S. bureaucracy had been more unified and intelligent, the controlled-evolution model would have seemed to demand too much from the local incumbents while being too cautious for much of the opposition. Both bureaucratic inefficiencies and U.S. caution contributed to the frequently noted impression that the United States was continually seeking solutions that were running behind local events.

Political systems can, of course, undergo a controlled transformation, even from authoritarian to democratic rule, as Spain and perhaps Brazil are demonstrating. But Central America was to witness more abrupt processes of social change.

Dealing with Discontinuity

The Nicaraguan mediation collapsed by the end of January 1979. By May, the Sandinistas had launched their final offensive. The mainstays of the Somoza regime, the National Guard and the Liberal party, dissolved and, along with the Somoza family, fled into exile. Discontinuity, not gradual evolution, marked the end of the Somoza era.

The year 1979 also witnessed the fall of the shah of Iran, an event that accelerated but did not initiate important transformations in American foreign policy. The Soviet intervention in Afghanistan capped a year in which the United States had become increasingly concerned with Soviet activities in the Third World. The Carter administration was bracing for a presidential campaign in which it would be attacked for having "lost" Nicaragua and Iran, and having failed to respond with sufficient vigor to Soviet probes and advances elsewhere. The Carter White House did not want any new countries added to these lists before the 1980 elections.

With these concerns forming the prism through which the administration was perceiving events overseas, the main lesson drawn from the Nicaraguan experience was the urgency of deeper U.S. involvement in Central America. The very day after the Sandinistas entered Managua, the administration decided to augment its economic and diplomatic commitment to the region. To better coordinate the use of these resources, the administration selected three of its most creative and activist hemispheric ambassadors then serving in more prestigious South American posts.[20] The appointment of Lawrence Pezzullo (Nicaragua), Robert White (El Salvador), and later, George Landau (never granted agreement by the Guatemalans) illustrated the administration's determination to shape events in Central America to conform with U.S. interests.

In El Salvador, the United States continued to try to convince Romero and his more moderate opposition to enter into negotiations not unlike those unsuccessfully pursued in Nicaragua. But only three months after Somoza fled Managua, a bloodless coup ousted Romero. Once again, the United States was confronted with discontinuity. The new Salvadoran junta, consisting of reformist colonels and civilians, did not represent as total a break with the past as the Sandinista-dominated government in Nicaragua, but its composition and stated intentions were markedly different from those of the Romero regime.

The October 15 Junta

In retrospect, the junta formed on October 15, 1979, was the golden, last opportunity to avoid civil war in El Salvador. Here was a genuinely broad-based government containing all the centrist elements in Salvadoran society. Once the junta was established, the United States publicly and privately offered its support: A reformist, democratic junta could advance U.S. interests in human rights and, at the same time, be capable of containing the more radical left. Yet, when the junta collapsed at the end of December 1979, the U.S. did not mourn its passing. What had happened?

Most of the civilians in the cabinet and the junta resigned in protest at the military's slowness in implementing the proposed social and economic reforms, especially the agrarian reform, and, more importantly, in opposition to the aggressiveness of the security forces in responding to mass demonstrations, strikes and sit-ins. The civilians believed that the stability and durability of their progressive experiment would require the participation, or at least the support, of some of the leftist unions and political movements.[21] The aggressiveness of the security forces undermined whatever opportunities existed for the junta to reach out toward these groups.

The United States was not, of course, in control of the Salvadoran security forces. But the United States may have, perhaps inadvertently, encouraged their aggressive behavior. In December, the U.S. Embassy, while continuing to underline its support for the promised social and economic reforms, began to place greater emphasis, especially in private conversations with military officers, on the need to restore authority.[22] This attitude was reinforced by the chilling report of a U.S. Department of Defense survey team. The report, presented in mid-December to the Salvadoran Ministry of Defense, warned that the Salvadoran security forces were ill prepared to cope with the advancing insurgency, and suggested the immediate purchase of counterinsurgency equipment.[23]

The embassy appeared generally unaware that efforts by the security forces to restore "authority" would rend the junta. Indeed, poor communications with the civilians in the government resulted in the embassy being taken by surprise by the announcement on December 27 that the civilians were threatening to resign.

The United States failed to react with vigor to try to prevent the junta from collapsing. Because of inadequate embassy reporting, Washington had been unprepared for the civilian withdrawal, and was in the midst of the Christmas holidays. The United States did not try to mediate the differences between the military and civilian tendencies in the junta. Nor did it suggest to the military that U.S. security assistance was conditional upon a compromise. Instead, the United States quickly seized upon the offer of the Christian Democrats to enter the government, and indicated to both the military and the Christian Democrats that the United States would support such a junta.

While the United States was not unfavorable toward the civilians in the October 15 junta, it found the Christian Democrats to be more moderate, flexible, and cohesive—in short, easier to work with. Indeed, a Christian Democrat-military understanding had been the basic objective of U.S. efforts during the Romero period.

Whether the October 15 junta could have survived with greater U.S. support and sensitivity is another hypothetical question whose answer cannot be known. Some U.S. government analysts believed that important leftist elements might have come to accept the junta and even participate in elections had reforms proceeded and the security forces been restrained. One of the three civilian junta members subsequently argued that, had the civilians and the more reform-minded officers moved immediately to purge some fifty conservative officers, the junta might have steadied itself.[24] Instead, the United States had counseled the younger officers to compromise with their superiors in the name of institutional cohesion. Perhaps if the United States had placed its weight behind the reform-minded officers and civilians, they might have had the necessary strength and determination. But the risk that such a purge could have split the armed forces—and opened the gates to a leftist insurrection—was sufficient cause for the United States to demur.

The Christian Democrat-Military Juntas

The United States recognized that the Christian Democratic-military government was extremely weak and vulnerable to either a rightist coup or, in the medium term, to a leftist insurrection.[25] The junta did not enjoy the firm support of either business, the church, most unions, or of the other civilian political parties and movements. The security forces themselves were politically divided, and the Christian Democratic party was a shell of what it had been during its apogee in the early 1970s. The junta's political base was narrow—considerably narrower than the October 15 junta—and its military capabilities shaky. Nevertheless, the administration's overriding concerns with regional security and domestic politics—the fear of "losing" yet another country—dictated that the United States commit its resources and efforts to the new junta.

The United States undertook to shoulder a series of major tasks intended to strengthen the junta. The United States helped design the agrarian reform,[26] and gain military acceptance of it, while giving the officers the backing they needed to break their traditional financial and psychological dependence on the large landowners. The United States lobbied hard with the business community, especially the urban industrialists and merchants, to convince them that limited reform was preferable to revolution.[27] American economic aid helped fund the agrarian reform, and thereby indirectly financed the transfer of property from the traditional large landowners to the peasantry. The United States lobbied, with less success, to persuade the center-left political parties and the church to back the regime. When disputes arose within the government, the United States served as mediator, while threatening aid cutoffs to avert rightist coups. U.S. diplomacy was supported by increasing levels of material resources. Economic assistance reached $56 million in FY 1980 and surpassed $60 million in FY 1981. Though military aid remained modest, it increased steadily throughout 1980, and U.S. military advisors were stationed in the headquarters of the army high command.

The United States also lobbied hard throughout the hemisphere and in Western Europe to gain international support for the junta, and pressed the multilateral development banks to assist the deteriorating Salvadoran economy. Policy was closely coordinated with Venezuela's ruling Christian Democratic government, which was especially friendly to the junta's leading Christian Democrat, Napoleón Duarte.[28]

In sum, the United States acted as the junta's foreign ministry, close domestic political counselor and propagandist, arbiter of internal disputes, liason with business interests, consultant on agrarian reform and labor organization, and, increasingly, military advisor. The United States had not become so deeply involved in assisting a government in the hemisphere since the Dominican crisis of the early and mid-1960s.

It is still too early to judge definitively the results of Carter administration efforts. A number of successes and disappointments could be listed. The formation and perseverance of the Christian Democratic-military junta and the implementation of the agrarian reform, however flawed, did seize the political initiative from the left, and the guerrilla offensive of January 1981 failed to defeat the armed forces or even splinter the junta. Relations improved between the government and most of the business sector. The Carter administration also succeeded in winning some international as well as Congressional support for the junta.

On the other hand, U.S. officials recognized that the junta had failed to gain significant popular support, or the adhesion of other centrist parties, in part because of the widespread terror generated by the right-wing "death squads" and the security forces.[29] U.S. efforts to make the counterinsurgency efforts more refined and selective were unsuccessful, and the security forces seemed unwilling to move against privately funded assassination teams. If the left was unable to gain the intensity of popular support needed to stimulate a mass insurrection, the guerrilla forces themselves grew in numbers, tactical skill, and armament during the course of 1980. In this climate of widespread violence and uncertainty, the economy declined by 8–10 percent, and international commercial credit dried up. Finally, as the intensity of the fighting increased, so did the danger of a regionalization of the conflict.

Accommodation with Nicaragua

The United States had worked hard to prevent the Sandinistas from acceding to power. When the FSLN columns entered Managua on July 19, 1979, the United States faced circumstances not of its own choosing, and a new set of options. The United States could either adopt a policy of hostility toward the new Sandinista-dominated government, could simply grant it unqualified acceptance, or else seek to accommodate and moderate the new government. The Carter administration chose accommodation.

The administration had several motives for adopting an accommodationist strategy. Given the strength of the FSLN and its control over the armed forces, a policy of hostility would only serve to radicalize the internal political dynamic and drive the FSLN to look to Cuba for security assistance; a "second" Cuba might be avoided by not repeating the mistakes made with the first Cuba. Moreover, a policy of hostility would create the impression in U.S. domestic opinion that the administration had, indeed, "lost" Nicaragua. But if a policy of hostility seemed counterproductive, a policy of laissez-faire was not even considered. The United States was prepared to accommodate itself to a liberalized definition of what could be tolerated in Central America, but outer boundaries would still be drawn.

The United States made clear that Nicaragua ought not to allow foreign troops or bases, nor attempt to "export revolution." Otherwise, the United States was prepared to tolerate radical rhetoric on international issues distant to the Central American reality. The administration decided to focus less on these immediate foreign-policy postures of the FSLN, and more on assuring the continuity of Nicaragua's material interaction with the rest of the world, and on the maintenance of a domestic private business sector. A Nicaragua enmeshed in trade and financial links with other Central American, Latin, and industrial nations was bound to moderate its foreign policy over time. A strong private sector within Nicaragua would be an important advocate of a pragmatic accommodation to international economic realities. Nicaragua seemed especially fertile ground for applying this strategy of "neorealism"[30] which was fundamental to the approach of some Carter administration officials to radical change in the Third World. Nicaragua was a small, open economy, with tight trading and financial links to the United States and Western Europe; the Sandinista leadership were materialists in need of the West's economic resources;[31] and the Nicaraguan business class, having participated in the anti-Somoza struggle, enjoyed some post-revolutionary legitimacy.

The Carter administration did not clearly define, either publicly or in its own mind, exactly what its vision of an acceptable "pluralistic" Nicaragua entailed.[32] Many recognized that the FSLN was determined to retain control of the executive branch of government, with Nicaragua perhaps evolving toward a Mexicanlike model with a dominant official party within a mixed economy, while other U.S. officials seemed to hope that Nicaragua would become a truly competitive, multiparty system similar to Costa Rica.

The $75 million aid package announced in late 1979 was intended to signal to the international financial institutions, other bilateral donors, and commercial lenders and traders that they ought to do business with Nicaragua. Some 60 percent of the $75 million was to be channeled to the Nicaraguan private sector. The large AID program would, of course, provide the United States with potential avenues of influence in Nicaraguan society, and allow for a direct U.S. presence to compete with the large influx of Cuban personnel. To reduce distrust, President Carter invited Nicaraguan government leaders to the White House in September 1979. To alleviate regional tensions that threatened to upset the delicate political balance in Managua, the United States urged other Caribbean-basin states to befriend the Nicaraguan regime. The United States especially urged Honduras to prevent former National Guardsmen from using Honduran territory as sanctuaries from which to harrass the FSLN.

At first the United States was reasonably pleased with the FSLN response.[33] The government's economic team was composed largely of businessmen and technocrats. Nicaragua acknowledged foreign debts accrued during the Somoza era and renegotiated its debts with the international banking community.[34] Internally, the government sought to moderate wage demands and repressed the ultraleft. Opposition political activity and media were tolerated.

By the second half of 1980, however, U.S. officials were increasingly disturbed with Nicaraguan developments. The reasons were numerous. Those U.S. officials who hoped Nicaragua would become a second Costa Rica became disillusioned.[35] Nearly all officials reacted negatively to the FSLN's approach to mass mobilization, which was seen in Washington not as legitimate popular participation but as a form of political control. Since the United States looked to the fortunes of the private sector as the key to pluralism and the continued integration of Nicaragua into the international economy, Washington was very sensitive to the heightened, if not yet inflamed, tensions between the FSLN and Nicaraguan businessmen. The presence of large numbers of Cuban propagandists and security advisors was viewed ominously, especially in light of Washington's growing agitation over Cuban and Soviet activities in the Third World. Nevertheless, given the Nicaraguan government's pragmatic economic policies, these developments might have been seen as irritating and worrisome, but not cause for abandoning the accommodationist policy—were it not for the civil war in El Salvador.

The Nicaraguan government had indicated its willingness to support the October 15 junta, in part because it recognized that deepening conflict in Salvador could threaten U.S.-Nicaraguan relations. But the conflict in El Salvador did polarize, and the United States and the FSLN were inevitably drawn in on opposite sides. One of the Carter administration's last acts was to suspend economic aid disbursements to Nicaragua, on the grounds that the Nicaraguan government was funneling arms to the Salvadoran guerrillas.

The Reagan Administration

Paralleling the early days of the Carter administration, the Reagan team approached Central America through globalist lens. But whereas the early Carter administration had emphasized human rights principles, Reagan saw the need to rescue the isthmus from what were perceived as Soviet bloc incursions. In its campaign to reverse the decline in American power, the Reagan administration made Central America, and El Salvador in particular, its initial foreign-policy priority. This extraordinary show of interest proceeded from two convergent concerns within the administration. First, having argued that the Carter administration had been overly tolerant of leftist political forces in the Third World, especially when supported by the Cubans or Soviets, the Reagan administration chose El Salvador to demonstrate its counter-revolutionary anti-Sovietism.[36] Second, responding to perceptions in the Defense Department[37] and in branches of the intelligence community, the administration sought to reassert U.S. control of the Caribbean basin, and to eliminate any actual or potential threats to U.S. security interests.

Central America offered favorable geopolitical terrain for a demonstration of U.S. resolve to respond forcefully to Cuban or Soviet "risk-taking" (a term used repeatedly by Secretary of State Alexander Haig). If the United States failed to act decisively so near to home, the Soviets would not be convinced of the seriousness of U.S. intent. Moreover,

Central America had to be secured, and quickly, in order to free U.S. resources for use in theaters of greater inherent strategic or economic importance—notably, the Persian Gulf.

The new administration moved rapidly to provide the Salvadoran security forces with materials and advisors. The failure of the January 1981 offensive by the left had opened a possible window for a mediated solution, but the Reagan administration preferred to pursue a military victory; a political compromise seemed difficult, but, in any case, the administration preferred to illustrate U.S. willingness and capability to successfully project force in the Third World against revolutionaries. Moreover, a mediated solution could leave the left with considerable actual or potential influence, and any centrist solution in Salvador would be destabilizing in Guatemala. The United States did continue to support President Duarte and important elements of the agrarian reform, recognizing that they strengthened the government's domestic and international images.

Mutual distrust between the Reagan administration and the FSLN made conflict between the two nations almost inevitable.[38] The administration maintained the suspension on economic assistance flows because of intelligence reports of continuing Nicaraguan engagement in channeling arms to the Salvadoran guerrillas and the violation of other conditions placed by Congress on aid to Nicaragua.[39] By the fall of 1981, the administration had nearly written off Nicaragua as "lost" to totalitarianism.[40] The conflictive international and regional environment contributed to the deterioration of the internal coalition between the FSLN and the private sector and stimulated the Sandinistas to enlarge their security forces and restrict domestic dissent. The Reagan administration wanted to renew security assistance to Guatemala to help the military combat a growing insurgency, hoping to repeat the success of U.S. counter-insurgency programs against Guatemalan guerrillas in the late 1960s.[41] Congressional reaction to the systematic violations of human rights by the Guatemalan government, however, lessened the administration's maneuverability. In Honduras, the Reagan administration maintained Carter's policy of supporting the democratization process, albeit with less intensity.[42]

The Evolution of the U.S. National Interest

In the short span between 1975 and 1981, the U.S. government's definition of its national interest in Central America changed with remarkable frequency. These shifts in priorities resulted from rapid changes within Central America, altering perceptions of global trends, lurches in American public opinion, and variations in the relative power of individuals and agencies both within and between administrations.

In the early and mid-1970s, Central America normally received low-level attention while the permanent bureaucracy concentrated on fostering economic growth and regional stability as the best antidotes against the entrance of forces hostile to U.S. influence. In 1977, the Carter administration's assertion of its concern for human rights automatically provoked a rift in U.S. relations with formerly friendly regimes. U.S. involvement in Central America during this period was tempered by the region's relatively low visibility, the Latin American Bureau's protection of its traditional client governments, and the noninterventionist scruples of some Carter administration officials. By mid-1978, however, the administration became anxious that U.S. influence in the region was potentially threatened by political unrest unguided by the United States. The existing concern for human rights and the heightened security interest both caused the United States to favor political change in Nicaragua and Salvador, although security interests increased U.S. caution and involvement. Moreover, whereas human rights had initially been viewed primarily as an end in itself, increasingly the advancement of human rights and democracy was seen as an instrument whereby U.S. security interests could be pursued.

The Sandinista victory offered an opportunity for the United States to redefine the limits of its tolerance in the region. The presence of a leftist, nationalist government, while never welcome, was judged potentially not threatening to U.S. economic, political, or even security interests.

In apparent contradiction to the policy of accommodation with the Sandinistas, the United States worked hard to preclude a leftist victory in Salvador. In fact, both policies were derived from the same objectives: to work within each reality for nonradical outcomes and to contain the spread of Cuban influence. A policy of cooperation with Nicaragua was considered the best method to preserve pluralism and to lessen the Nicaraguan incentive to invite Cuban assistance. In Salvador, it was still possible to assure that Marxist-oriented parties and Cuban influence were precluded altogether. The two policies did, however, face a potentially real contradiction: escalating foreign involvement in Salvador threatened to undermine the U.S.-Nicaraguan entente.

As U.S. interests evolved from an emphasis on human rights to an emphasis on regional security and containing Cuban influence, the degree of U.S. activism increased dramatically. The U.S. decision to launch a mediation effort in Nicaragua signaled a sharp increase in

U.S. direct involvement, but the administration was still careful to multilateralize the mediation effort, gain an OAS mandate, and secure the support of the hemisphere's democracies. By 1981, the United States was prepared to act alone in playing an extremely activist role in El Salvador, although the support of other governments was encouraged.

On the surface, the Reagan administration represents a return to a traditional definition of U.S. security interests in the region—that the region ought to be denied to any hostile powers. A public human rights policy was rejected as threatening to the coherence of military institutions considered the most reliable partners in the defense of these interests. New, however, was the administration's public emphasis on viewing Central America as a testing ground for East-West competition in the Third World. This prism elevated Central America to a theater of high priority; however, the intention was to quickly secure the isthmus so that U.S. attention could be directed to more distant trouble spots of greater inherent importance. By the fall of 1981, it was clear that this scenario was overly optimistic. During the last decade, the political dynamics in Central America had become significantly more complex and difficult to control.

NOTES

1. For a more detailed description of these developments, see chapter 1 in this book by Francisco Villagran Kramer.

2. For example, following the watershed 1972 Salvadoran presidential elections, the United States made no public statements or even private representations to protest the fraud; nor were ongoing security and economic assistance programs suspended. Moreover, when the defrauded candidate, Napoleón Duarte, led a contingent of military officers in a "constitutionalist" rebellion, the United States not only opposed the attempt as reckless but immediately provided the president-elect, Colonel Fernando Molina, with a U.S. Air Force jet to rush him back to San Salvador. Molina had been traveling in Taiwan.

3. At least some officers in the Latin American Bureau of the State Department had actually hoped that the election of a non-Somoza Liberal in 1971 could begin a gradual transition away from Somoza rule. However, in late 1970 President Nixon appointed Turner Shelton as envoy to Managua. Shelton, apparently acting on White House instructions, acquiesced in Somoza's rewrite of the constitution, which allowed Somoza to remain in office.

4. This view, of course, differs from those that argue that Central American societies had remained, essentially, static and traditional, and that it was the shift of U.S. policies under Carter that generated instability. See, for example, Jeane Kirkpatrick, "Dictatorships and Double Standards," *Commentary* (November 1979), pp. 34–45.

5. Secretary of State Cyrus Vance, "Human Rights and OAS Reform," speech before the General Assembly of the OAS, St. George's, Grenada, June 14, 1977, Bureau of Public Affairs, Department of State.

6. The immediate cause was the executive branch's issuance of the *Country Reports on Human Rights Practices,* required at the time by Congress on all nations receiving U.S. security assistance.

7. For a detailed listing of human–rights-related actions by the United States in these countries, see the forthcoming book by Lars Schoultz on U.S. human rights policies in Latin America (Princeton University Press); and Washington Office on Latin America, *Update,* monthly bulletin.

8. This view was most frequently expressed by Cyrus Vance. For example, in reviewing progress toward democracy in Latin America, Vance argued: "These moves toward more democratic and open societies in Latin America are distinctly in our interest. The great strength of democracy is its flexibility and resilience. It opens opportunities for broadly based political and economic participation. By encouraging compromise and accommodation, it fosters evolutionary change." Address before the Foreign Policy Association, New York City, Sept. 27, 1979.

9. The most complete public presentation of this interpretation of the Central American problematic can be found in Viron P. Vaky, "Central America at the Crossroads," *Hearings,* U.S. Congress, House, Subcommittee on Inter-American Affairs, Committee on Foreign Affairs, 96th Congress, 1st sess., Sept. 11, 1979. pp. 9–20. This testimony drew heavily on a major internal study prepared in the spring of 1979 for the Policy Review Committee (PRC) of the National Security Council.

10. The Carter administration never questioned that a leftist accession to power in Central America was contrary to U.S. interests. For example, the idea of supporting, or even possibly accepting, a process leading to a Sandinista-dominated government in Nicaragua was never seriously considered as an option for U.S. policy (until it became virtually inevitable). A full explanation for this deep-seated U.S. opposition to leftist political movements, especially in the Western Hemisphere, is beyond the scope of this chapter.

11. This rendition of Carter administration attitudes and policies differs sharply from that presented by some conservative critics, who have argued that the Carter administration persisted in carelessly destabilizing friendly governments, and was not altogether unhappy when revolutions followed. See, for example, Jeane Kirkpatrick, "U.S. Security and Latin America," *Commentary* (January 1981), pp. 29–40.

12. This military aid was also intended to strengthen the Honduran ability to police its borders with Nicaragua and El Salvador.

13. *Keesing's Contemporary Archives,* Sept. 26, 1980, p. 30483.

14. Similarly, U.S. efforts to encourage a transition from authoritarian to democratic rule were more successful in those South American nations where important internal forces were already moving in that direction. See Richard E. Feinberg, *U.S. Human Rights Policy: Latin America* (Washington, D.C.: Center for International Policy Monograph, vol. 6, no. 1, 1980).

15. Viron P. Vaky, "Central America at the Crossroads," *Hearings,* p. 16.

16. "Controversy Looms over Bid to Aid Guatemala," *Washington Post,* Mar. 11, 1979.

17. The complete documentation of these negotiations can be found in "Report to the Secretary of State on the Work of the International Commission of Friendly Cooperation and Conciliation for Achieving a Peaceful Solution to the Grave Crisis of the Republic of Nicaragua" (Washington, D.C.: Organization of American States, 1979, mimeo). Critical accounts include William Leo-Grande, "The Revolution in Nicaragua: Another Cuba?" *Foreign Affairs* 58, no. 1 (Fall 1979): 28–50; and Jorge Lawton, "Crisis de la hegemonia; la politica de Carter hacia Nicaragua: 1977–79," in *Cuadernos Semestrales* (Mexico City: Centro de Investigacion y Docencia Economicas, 1979), no. 6., pp. 59–114. In his own account, Anastasio Somoza published edited versions of tapes of some of the conversations between himself and U.S. officials, in *Nicaragua Betrayed* (Boston: Western Islands, 1980).

18. This decision reflected several factors including a desire to allow the National Guard to recoup from its losses during the September insurrection; an intention to reserve the cutoff as an instrument of future leverage against Somoza; and a hesitancy to raise the issue with the Israelis and complicate the more important Camp David peace process then under way.

19. The policy of working with Romero was reaffirmed in congressional testimony as late as September 11, 1979. See Vaky, "Central America at the Crossroads," *Hearings,* p. 16.

20. This pattern was noticed in an Associated Press story, "U.S. Planning to Appoint New Envoy to Guatemala," *Washington Post,* June 28, 1980.

21. Some of the civilian resignees published an open letter to their former military colleagues explaining the reasons for their resignations: "We do not believe it is possible for the armed forces to continue analyzing the situation of the popular movement in terms of 'extremists' or as enemies to whom the sole response is confrontation." The civilians hoped to differentiate among the leftist groups and incorporate some of them. A review of this period can be found in a two-part series by Karen D. Young, *Washington Post,* March 8–9, 1981. See also William Leogrande and Carla Anne Robbins, "Oligarchs and Officers: The Crisis in El Salvador," *Foreign Affairs,* Summer 1980, pp. 1084–1103.

22. See T. S. Montgomery, "El Salvador: U.S. Policy and Revolutionary Process," May 1980 unpublished paper, p. 15.

23. According to the *New York Times,* DOD had not changed its assessment by February 1981. "Military Aspects of Crisis Are Underlined by Haig and a Pentagon Study," Feb. 21, 1981, p. 1.

24. Interview by the author, in Washington, D.C., February 1980.

25. Ambassador Robert White later commented: "When I went down to El Salvador one year ago, there was not one intelligence analyst in Washington who said there was a prayer of the present government lasting more than a month or two." "Arms Aid and Advisers: Debating the New Policy in El Salvador," *New York Times,* Mar. 8, 1981.

26. For details, see U.S. AID/El Salvador, *El Salvador Agrarian Reform Sector Strategy Paper,* July 12, 1980. For a critical assessment, see Lawrence

Simon and James Stephans, Jr., *El Salvador Land Reform, 1980–81, Impact Audit* (Boston: Oxfam, 1981).

27. T. S. Montgomery, "El Salvador," p. 6.

28. See chapter 8 in this volume by Robert Bond.

29. According to calculations of the Catholic church in San Salvador, approximately 80 percent of the 10,000 violent deaths recorded in 1980 were at the hands of the government and rightist forces.

30. For a discussion of this term, see Tom Farer, "Searching for Defeat," *Foreign Policy* 40 (Fall 1980): 155–174.

31. The Sandinistas were also more disposed to working with the Carter administration because its human rights policy had ended the long history of close U.S. association with the Somoza family.

32. Some officials, notably in DOD, disagreed with the accommodationist policy from the beginning, not only because they believed that the FSLN was intent upon creating a "second Cuba," but because even a radical nationalist regime was seen as intolerable in Central America. See "Aid for Nicaragua the Focus of Fierce Internal Policy Dispute," *Washington Post,* Aug. 8, 1980.

33. For example, in May 1980, Assistant Secretary of State William Bowdler stated that "The revolution's course . . . is still compatible with an open, pluralist society with a mixed economy." *Hearings,* U.S. Congress, House, Subcommittee on Inter-American Affairs, Committee on Foreign Affairs, 96th Congress, 2nd session, May 20, 1980.

34. See John Dizzard, "Why Bankers Fear the Nicaraguan Solution," *Institutional Investor,* November 1980, pp. 53–62.

35. The rather critical 1980 human rights report on Nicaragua was written from this perspective. Department of State, *Country Reports on Human Rights Practices,* submitted to the U.S. Senate, Committee on Foreign Relations and the U.S. House, Committee on Foreign Affairs, Feb. 2, 1981, pp. 489–498.

36. The Reagan administration first announced its intention to make El Salvador a demonstration case in a "backgrounder" for reporters. See "El Salvador: A Test Case," *New York Times,* Feb. 14, 1981, p. 1. The State Department later released a white paper detailing alleged Cuban and Soviet support for the Salvadoran guerrillas. "Communist Interference in El Salvador," U.S. Department of State, Bureau of Public Affairs, Feb. 23, 1981.

37. See chapter 4 in this book by Margaret Daly Hayes.

38. For a description and assessment of the Reagan administration's approach to Nicaragua and Central America, see Richard E. Feinberg, "Central America: No Easy Answers," *Foreign Affairs,* vol. 59, no. 6, summer, 1981, pp. 1121–1146.

39. The law required that the president certify "prior to releasing any assistance . . . that the Government of Nicaragua" was not "aiding or abetting or supporting acts of violence or terrorism in other countries." The president was also required to terminate aid if the Nicaraguan government violated freedom of speech or of the press, or inhibited labor union organization. The Carter administration had disliked the rigidity these amendments imposed on U.S. policy, but had accepted them in order to muster the necessary votes to pass the aid package.

40. "Anti-Nicaragua Action Not Ruled Out, Haig Says," *Washington Post,* Nov. 13, 1981, p. 1.

41. In congressional testimony that was friendly to the Guatemalan government and failed to even mention its human rights record, Acting Assistant Secretary John Bushnell stated: "Endemic violence is on the upswing [in Guatemala], spawned in considerable measure by communist exploitation of traditional social and political inequities." U.S. Congress, House, Subcommittee on Inter-American Affairs, Committee on Foreign Affairs, March 5, 1981.

42. Ibid.

4. United States Security Interests in Central America in Global Perspective

Margaret Daly Hayes

W hy is a region of underdeveloped countries whose populations live in rural impoverishment, and whose principal items of exchange with the world economy are coffee and sugar exports, considered important to the security of the United States? Historically, Central America and the Caribbean have attracted considerable attention as an element of U.S. security interest.[1] The region was of concern when the Monroe Doctrine was announced in 1823. Central America was the focus of concern that led the United States and Great Britain to negotiate the Clayton-Bulwer treaty limiting each country's right to exclusive control of a Central American canal. By the end of the nineteenth century, and especially in the aftermath of the Spanish-American War, Alfred Thayer Mahan's theories of the importance of sea power renewed interest in an isthmian canal that would link the Atlantic and Pacific coasts and provide a more rapid route to newly acquired U.S. possessions in the Philippines. The 1901 Hay-Pauncefote treaty abrogated Clayton-Bulwer and gave the United States exclusive freedom to build a canal. Once the canal was built, U.S. interest in its effective defense led to an expansion of security interests to include the entire Caribbean basin. The Panama Canal served primarily a military function up to and through World War II. The whole Caribbean basin became an important focal point of U.S. security interest immediately prior to and during World War II, as defense planners sought to defend not only the continental United States but also other nations in the Western Hemisphere from the advances of the initially technologically superior German forces. As

European powers fell before the onslaught of the German army, the defensive positions in the Caribbean gained importance.

Today U.S. security interests in Central America and the Caribbean are being discussed on the front pages of the nation's newspapers because the region is in turmoil, not because there is a new, clearer realization of profound U.S. interest in the region. Though the level of attention focused on the region has varied over the years, the assumption that the United States has security interests in the region has never been questioned by the defense community. Simply stated, the Caribbean basin constitutes the U.S. southern flank, a southern perimeter that is assumed to have undeniable security importance. While U.S. security interests in the Caribbean basin are not on the same plane with our interest in the Persian Gulf, in NATO, or in Japan, they *are important*. Were conditions different in the Caribbean basin, U.S. security could be seriously threatened, or made to be much more costly to defend than at present. In the present turmoil in Central America and some of the outer islands, the United States' most important and difficult task is to ensure that the risks to and costs of security in the region are not increased.

The pages that follow outline U.S. security interests in the Caribbean basin—what they are, how important they are, and why they should be defended. The analysis is presented from the perspective of the national security policy community. It is an effort to explain how an individual concerned with security issues would perceive events in the Caribbean and would react to them. While I am, for the most part, sympathetic to this community's basic assumption that the United States has clear security interests in the Caribbean basin, I am not always sympathetic to the recommended means for promoting and defending these interests.

In the aftermath of World War II, U.S. attention turned away from the Caribbean basin. The decimation of enemy (and allied) forces in the war meant that U.S. military power in the region went unchallenged. Only recently has Soviet blue–water-fleet development been such as to give the Soviet Union the mobility to have a presence in the Caribbean basin. As Europe and Japan began to recover from wartime ravages, trade expanded, enhancing the commercial value and importance of the Panama Canal and changing its primary function from a military asset to an economic asset. Only cold war issues seemed to attract attention to the Caribbean basin—in 1954 in Guatemala, in 1959, 1961, and 1970 in Cuba, and in 1965 in the Dominican Republic. After 1965, with the exception of continued antagonism with Cuba and the scrutiny given the region during the discussion of the Panama Canal treaties, the United States largely ignored the Caribbean basin. Indeed, the fact that the Panama treaties were able to gain support in the Congress was one measure of confidence that security was not threatened.

United States security interests in the post-World War II era have focused almost exclusively on the strategic balance of power between the United States and the Soviet Union, particularly the balance in Europe. More recently, concern over access to energy resources in the Middle East and Africa has been factored into the equation, but even there the threat to U.S. security is assumed to come from the Soviets. In this context of strategic balance, Latin America has been only marginally important. The countries in the region have had little power, the region has been relatively isolated from global political and military conflicts, and the Latin American states, with few exceptions, traditionally have been firmly in the U.S. camp. U.S. defense planners' attentions concentrate in the area of the North Atlantic and Pacific oceans. Of necessity, the NATO sphere of interest includes the Mediterranean, North Africa, the Canary and Azores islands, but excludes the Caribbean Sea-Gulf of Mexico and the entire South Atlantic Ocean. As a result, "little western strategic attention has been given to the areas south of the southern NATO boundary."[2] Until Soviet activities began to increase off the coast of Africa and in the Caribbean in the mid-1970s, there was little need for closer attention to Latin America.

The presence of a Communist regime in Cuba was (and remains) a profound irritant, but Cuban adventurism in this hemisphere had been contained in the later years of the 1960s and in the 1970s without great effort on the part of the United States. By the mid-1970s, the aura of stability in the Caribbean basin increased our sense of security there and permitted attention to focus elsewhere. Serious discussion of rapprochement with Cuba was conducted by scholars, political commentators, and more importantly, presidential candidates. At the beginning of his term, President Jimmy Carter made important overtures to the Castro regime. Interest sections were established in Havana and Washington under the aegis of third-country embassies; certain trade restrictions were lifted. A dialogue began.

Distant events spoiled the deal. Ongoing Cuban involvement in the Angolan civil war, which Castro refused to curtail even after seemingly clear demonstrations of U.S. restraint against supporting the threatened governments, angered U.S. officials. More importantly, in the aftermath of Angola, Castro sent troops and support immediately to Ethiopia, a context that U.S. policymakers feared would invite face-to-face confrontation between the United States and the Soviet Union. The "lack of good faith" shown by the Cubans in these two highly visible instances reconfirmed the worst suspicions of those Americans willing to see a trick behind every Cuban move and a Russian bear behind every Cuban. It also chastened many of Castro's liberal supporters in the United States.

Revolutionary turmoil closer to home in the Caribbean and Central America is inevitably compared with the revolutions in Cuba, Vietnam, Angola, or Ethiopia. While each of these cases is unique, the important similarity, one increasingly pointed out by conservative examiners of macroglobal politics, is that each resulted in a Communist government, hostile to the United States and friendly to the Soviet Union and its allies or surrogates. Each resulted in a "loss of face" for the United States, which had been committed to the losing side. Each afforded U.S. critics at home and abroad an opportunity to speculate about a "decline of America" that was both embarrassing and threatening. In short, U.S. nerves were already raw when the Sandinistas began seriously to threaten the long-standing Somoza regime in Nicaragua. When that regime fell, and later when the Sandinista coalition took increasingly decisive turns to the left, it was inevitable that a negative U.S. reaction would be quick and intense.

U.S. Security Priorities in Latin America

Not only because of current turmoil in Central America, but also for reasons of long-standing Latin American and North American tradition and treaty agreements, the United States has security interests in Latin America. First and foremost, the United States has a major, crucial interest in the friendliness and tranquility of the region.

To better understand the special position in this security picture that Central America and the Caribbean occupy, it is necessary to examine the role that has traditionally been ascribed to Latin America in the global security picture. As in other parts of the world, U.S. security interests in Latin America, narrowly defined, are conditioned by political and economic relations as well as purely military considerations. Some areas of the world have a security importance almost exclusively because of their economic importance—the Persian Gulf or southern Africa, for example. Others—Poland, Yugoslavia—are also important because of their geographic locations. An invasion of Poland or Yugoslavia would exacerbate perceptions of threats to Western Europe and the NATO alliance, whether or not the invaders intended to cross the border into NATO territory.

Although Latin America has played only a minor role in postwar U.S. strategic planning, the United States does have clear interests within the hemisphere that are often overlooked in assessing its importance. Foremost among these are economic and political interests. As a region, Latin America is today the most developed of developing world regions. By 1985 the regional economy will be the size of Europe's in 1970. The United States is still the single largest trading partner for the region, while Latin America provides approximately 14 percent of both U.S. imports and exports. It also provides a number of important raw materials to the United States and receives over 18 percent of all U.S. private investment abroad, far more than any other developing region. U.S. banks are committed to tens of billions of dollars of loans in the region.

The United States also has compelling political interests in maintaining good relations with the nations of Latin America. As part of the Western Hemisphere, and in the immediate U.S. geographic sphere of influence, Latin America has long been perceived as a key element in the U.S. political following in the world. While the inter-American system is not as closely knit today as it once was, and Latin American states are on record as seeking to diminish their dependence on the United States, the hemispheric community still figures importantly in our own and others' perceptions of the East-West balance. The Soviet Union has always recognized the importance of Western Hemispheric solidarity and has taken advantage of every opportunity to embarrass the United States when cracks appear. The United States has demonstrated a less clear understanding of the importance of the hemispheric community in measuring its own relative weight on a world scale. In the last decade it engaged in a number of actions, including arms control, trade, nuclear energy, and human rights policies, the perhaps unintended consequences of which were to undermine hemispheric cooperation and lessen Latin American commitment to the inter-American system. Nevertheless, though the Latin Americans at times resist the conclusion, and at other times use it as leverage against the United States, they continue to figure importantly in the global assessment of U.S. political weight in the world. Failure to achieve their support and collaboration represents a net loss in U.S. weight in the international balance of power. This applies whether one speaks of Southern Cone countries like Chile or Argentina, or of Mexico or Panama, which are nearer to home.

On closer examination, at least three separate areas of U.S. security interest in Latin America can be identified—the Caribbean basin and Gulf of Mexico, east coast South America and, finally, west coast South America. The intensity of U.S. interest in each region is determined in large part by proximity to the continental United States, proximity to other areas of security concern, and the political, military, and economic capabilities of the member states.

The focus of security interest in each area is quite different, reflecting the different objective political and economic conditions in the regions. In the Caribbean islands and in Central America, the United States is intensely concerned that political instability will result in the emergence of hostile, possibly Communist, states that could provide shelter to a more adventurous Soviet fleet, harbor offensive weapons aimed at the United States, or serve as listening posts to monitor our military movements in the area. A repetition of the Cuban Revolution of 1959, of the Cuban missile crisis of 1962, or the Cienfuegos submarine base incident of 1969 is clearly in the minds of defense planners and policymakers when they observe present instability in Nicaragua, El Salvador, and elsewhere in the Caribbean basin.

In the South Atlantic, policymakers are also concerned with defense of U.S. interests from Soviet offensive actions. In this arena, the potential targets of Soviet action are important sea lines of communication around the Horn of Africa. Because of the importance of such supply lines to the industrial economies of Europe, the South Atlantic plays an important role in scenarios for the defense of Europe in a prolonged conventional war. U.S. defense planners are concerned that the greatly expanded size of the Soviet blue-water fleet challenges Western ability to defend these important supply lines.

Finally, domestic instability and border conflicts are the factors that attract attention to the west coast South American countries. While their role in global security strategy is less salient, they again could play an important role in logistic support to the U.S. fleet in time of war.

U.S. Security Interests in the Caribbean Basin

Today U.S. attention is focused intensely on the Caribbean basin and especially on Central America, where first Nicaragua and now El Salvador have experienced wrenching civil turmoil resulting from leftist opposition to entrenched right-wing oligarchic regimes. Unrest is high and intensifying in Guatemala and Honduras. The future of the political processes unfolding in these countries is of intense interest to the United States.

As I noted, the Caribbean basin represents the United States' southern flank. The security community refers to it as the "vulnerable" southern flank. The current instability in Central America and the Caribbean islands has recalled the long-standing security concern for this region. Moreover, the intensity of present U.S. reactions to instability in the region is directly related to its perception and interpretation of security interests in terms of East-West conflict—the principal focus of U.S. security concern. At the same time, the Caribbean basin warrants security attention for its own reasons.

The Caribbean is militarily important to the United States in providing critical links in the network of U.S. listening posts monitoring ship and submarine activities in the Atlantic Ocean and approaches to the Caribbean. A variety of military training activities takes place at Panama, Puerto Rico, and Cuba that would be costly to move, or, in some cases, would be irreplaceable. Communications, tracking, and navigation facilities are located throughout the region and particularly in the eastern islands. The U.S. Navy's Atlantic Underseas Test and Evaluation Center in the Bahamas is critical to the development of antisubmarine warfare capabilities. The Panama Canal has become newly important in East-West trade, and would again be militarily important in any future prolonged conventional conflict.

The Caribbean basin is also economically important. A continuing high volume of interoceanic and hemispheric trade moves through the Caribbean on north-south trade routes, and to and from the Panama Canal. Lightering operations in the Antilles will be critical to the supply of U.S. crude petroleum imports until port facilities are developed to handle supertankers. Refineries in the Antilles supply over 50 percent of U.S. petroleum products made from Middle Eastern and African crude.

The Caribbean basin is also the principal source of U.S. raw materials imports from the Western Hemisphere. Mexico is, after Canada, the United States' second most important supplier of critical raw materials and the principal supplier of silver, zinc, gypsum, antimony, mercury, bismuth, selenium, barium, rhenium, and lead. With new petroleum wealth, Mexico could supply up to 30 percent of U.S. petroleum import requirements or up to 2 billion cubic feet of natural gas per day by the mid-1980s. Venezuela provides 28 percent of U.S. iron ore imports, 23 percent of its petroleum products, and 8 percent of its crude petroleum. Nearly 50 percent of U.S. bauxite imports come from Jamaica today. For the most part, the availability of such mineral imports from the Caribbean-basin countries represents a *convenience* to the United States. Only in the event of a major global conflict would their access be critical. At the same time, the cumulative "conveniences" of ready availability and long-standing commercial relations represents a real *interest* that is lost on neither the United States nor the regional governments.

So far, the U.S. interests identified in the Caribbean basin have been military and economic and largely confined to the island states of the West Indies—the English-speaking Caribbean. Political interests in the region are far less tangible, and more open to debate and discussion. Nevertheless, U.S. political interests are being challenged in the current instability of Central America.

From the traditional U.S. point of view, recent political instability in the Caribbean basin is especially unsettling because it reflects badly on the solidarity and viability of the Western Hemisphere community. This challenges the long-held U.S. security assumption that political stability and strongly pro-American governments are essential for the United States' security and well-being. As long as this assumption is a key to the U.S. interpretation of its own security, the Caribbean basin will be a gnawing problem for the United States.

The presence of a Soviet-backed regime in Cuba is a profound irritant to the United States both because it represents an undeniable crack in hemispheric solidarity and because it provides a base of operation for Soviet fishing, naval and satellite intelligence, and other activities. Moreover, Cuba is an unabashed source of support for anti-American movements in the Caribbean basin and elsewhere in the world. While Cuba kept a low profile in the region in the 1970s, its activism in other world regions threatened U.S. interests abroad, increased the opportunities for U.S.-Soviet confrontation, and suggested what could occur closer to home. The establishment of militant Communist regimes in Angola and Ethiopia are constant reminders of the possibility of Communist regimes in Nicaragua, El Salvador, Grenada, or Jamaica.

U.S. concern in the Caribbean basin currently focuses precisely on the possibility that unstable political situations there could provide an entree for further Soviet encroachment in the hemisphere. This concern is both justified and sometimes exaggerated. The Soviets recognize the psychological victory that Cuba represents and have exploited it. However, as the 1962 missile crisis and 1970 Cienfuegos submarine base incident suggest, the Soviets seem not to be willing to confront the United States directly in its sphere of influence.

Indeed, it would be difficult for the Soviets to make important inroads in the region. The Central American and Caribbean economies are extremely dependent on the United States for markets, investment, and replacement parts. They would be hard-pressed to maintain economic activity if they were to break relations with the United States or if the United States chose to embargo them. They could survive only if the Soviets were to underwrite their economies substantially, as in the case of Cuba. The experience of Chile under Allende demonstrated that this is unlikely. Cuba's dependence on the Soviets is well known. Few political leaders in the Caribbean or Central America desire to trade one overlord for another if a better alternative exists. Cuba itself has limited tangible resources—though important psychological ones—to offer these countries. Soviet support would be required for the Cubans to underwrite Caribbean and Central American economic development. This appears unlikely today when Soviet interests are occupied elsewhere.[3]

At the same time, it is both plausible and logical that the Soviets would encourage low-cost Cuban harassment of the United States by supporting and funding Cuban adventures in the Caribbean and Central America. Hence, it is not surprising that massive and persuasive documentary evidence that Cuba, other Communist bloc countries, and the Soviet Union were supplying arms and training to Salvadoran guerrillas has emerged.

The Caribbean-basin countries are able to contribute very little to their own domestic defense or to regional defense—a responsibility that consequently falls to the United States. Most Central American and Caribbean countries have poorly armed, poorly trained forces. The countries of the eastern Caribbean do not have the equipment to enforce their own fishing and antidrug-trafficking laws in their own waters. The Salvadoran navy is listed in a recent *Military Balance* as consisting of eleven ships.[4] We have learned, however, that "two are capsized hulls, four have been stripped for parts, and of the rest, only three are operational. . . . Only one has working radar."[5]

A direct consequence of poor training is lack of order and discipline, especially when units are actually put to a test. It is plausible that some of the violence that presently plagues Central America results from the sheer fear and lack of discipline that poorly trained peasant troops experience. Only Venezuela and Mexico have the population and economic wherewithal to support a sizeable military capability in the Caribbean basin, but it is in the interests of neither of these two countries to replicate capabilities available under the United States' umbrella.

Because the area has had such a low military profile, and has effectively served as a relatively easily controlled buffer zone for the United States, escalation of irregular military activity is especially alarming to U.S. defense strategists accustomed to focusing their attention on other world areas, confident that the neighborhood was safe. When a hostile enemy power is perceived to be behind the widespread instability, terrorism, and guerrilla activity, alarm is intensified. Thus Jeane N. Kirkpatrick, to be named U.S. ambassador to the United Nations, hit a raw nerve when she wrote that "the deterioration of the U.S. position in the hemisphere has already created serious vulnerabilities where

none previously existed and threatens now to confront this country
with the unprecedented need to defend itself against a ring of Soviet
bases on and around our southern and eastern borders."[6] Neither the
historical inaccuracies nor the obvious hyperbole of this statement can
disguise the simplified view of the world as a reduction of East-West
power interests.

Rationale for Reactions in Central America

Given the belief in the buffer functions of the Caribbean and Central
America, the United States has always been inclined toward a pessimistic interpretation of events there. Some Americans, like Ambassador Kirkpatrick, view each political upheaval in the highly unstable
area with alarm, suspecting that "The Russians are coming, the Russians are coming." Our attitudes are rooted in the tradition of Teddy
Roosevelt's "Big Stick" and the World War II experience when German submarines did patrol the Caribbean frontier as well as our own
eastern coast. They are rooted, too, in the cold war experience of the
1950s and the 1960s, and in our reaction to the Cuban Revolution,
perhaps the most nettlesome political setback we have ever experienced.

The tone with which policymakers react to events,[7] especially
negative events, in Central America and the Caribbean, antedates by
many years the current "Russians are coming" cry of neoconserva-
tives. In the 1970s it was not in vogue to wave the cold war banner. It is
much more acceptable today, and this explains some of the rhetoric of
our reaction to events in Central America. Moreover, it is a fact that
Cuba has been more active in the region in the past two years than
previously, that other extrahemispheric actors—Libya, the PLO, the
European Social Democrats, and others—are all getting involved in a
region to which few of them previously paid any attention. At the same
time, sober analysis shows that the United States has traditionally
reacted strongly, even viscerally, to Caribbean-basin crises. It is a
response that results from at least three different considerations, all of
which have applied in the evolution of our reactions to unrest in Central America and the Caribbean basin. The first consideration has been
our ill-founded overconfidence in the stability and placidity of this
region and in the United States' ability to control events there. A
second factor influencing our reactions is the nature of the long-range
strategic planning process with its tendency to drive all conflict toward
an East-West military confrontation. Finally, the crisis management
process also tends to focus attention on the East-West element of a
conflict, even when they may be minor components of the situation.

The Overconfidence of Past Security

In the long historical perspective, the Caribbean basin has been relatively secure in the sense initially conceived in the Monroe Doctrine. It has been free of outside influence. Until World War II, the United States was principally concerned with economic opportunities in the area. These were shared, by treaty and de facto, with the European colonial powers that had interests in the eastern islands, and there were relatively few issues over which conflict might arise. The Europeans maintained little military capability in the area, certainly not sufficient to challenge the United States. European interests were elsewhere, in Asia, Africa and the subcontinent, and thus the Caribbean was effectively left to the United States. The Rainbow plans developed by the U.S. in the interwar period for the defense of the region indicate that the United States had a clear vision of its critical need to retain control of the Caribbean basin—not only the islands, but the Central American isthmus as well—in time of war.[8] A number of incidents involving German submarines in the early days of World War II confirmed the need.

In the period after World War II, no other world power had the desire or capability to maintain a major military presence in the Caribbean basin. Over time the Europeans were going to pull out, confident that the United States would defend their remaining interests. Until the mid-1970s, the Soviet Union did not have the ability to maintain a sizeable force in the region, nor did it provide Cuba with such a force.

Under such circumstances, the United States became perhaps overconfident of the stability of the region. We relied heavily on predictable dictators or on our British and French allies. We failed to note the changes taking place in the regional societies and economies that could give rise to domestic unrest. As aid and military assistance budgets diminished, we had fewer and fewer people in the region to report back through channels on development. We failed to be prepared for the exodus of the British in the eastern Caribbean, or for the fall of Central American dictatorships.

The Planning Process and East-West Confrontation

The strategic security planning process requires planners to deal, on a day-to-day basis, with the unthinkable, the worst case, the least likely—and therefore most dangerous—probabilities. The defense planner must prepare for the maximum test of capabilities. Strategists' war games lead to the brink of nuclear war or global conventional conflict with few hesitations along the way. In spite of the fact that in the post-World War II period, the United States has used its armed forces most frequently for political purposes short of war,[9] it is war that tests the "readiness" of the defense machine. The planner, by the nature of his job, is interested in war, or the uses of military power short of war—show of force, for example. There is no long-range, nonmilitary strategic planning.

The security analyst can readily envision such threatening scenarios resulting out of the current turmoil in Central America, and earlier instability in the Caribbean island communities. The threats to U.S. security that might result from Central American unrest might include any or all of the following elements short of conflict:

• The emergence of a hostile nation backed by a hostile foreign power able to support a hostile Caribbean-basin nation economically and politically. Cuba is the obvious example.

• The presence of enemy ships able to patrol the Caribbean Sea and possibly the Gulf of Mexico at will.

• Enemy ship access to Caribbean-basin deepwater port facilities at which they would dock for extensive repairs, refueling, and so forth, thus effectively providing hostile power a naval "base" in the region.

• Access to air base facilities with long runways for jets and equipment for sophisticated reconnaissance (such as the listening posts the United States already has in Europe and the Near East).

Given the real security that derives from a politically quiescent Caribbean basin "buffer zone," any one of the imaginable consequences can be conceived as posing a direct and costly threat to U.S. national security. In any one of the circumstances, the United States would have to allocate substantial resources—manpower, ships, aircraft, and intelligence assets—to monitor the activities of the hostile neighbor so as to be prepared for a deteriorating set of contingencies—a possible attack on the United States, or more likely on a U.S. ally. To respond to such a contingency would likely entail a change in force allocations, cutting down support for contingencies in Europe, Korea, or other troubled areas—all areas that are already thinly held by units of uncertain degrees of military readiness.[10] Once forces were reduced in these other areas where the United States is accustomed to standing eyeball-to-eyeball with the Soviet Union, the Soviets might be tempted to test U.S. strength and resolve. Even if they weren't, prudence dictates that we be prepared to meet the challenge.

One obvious remedy to this difficult situation would be to increase the size of U.S. forces, expending large sums of money to obtain a truly two-ocean navy, building installations to monitor ship and air movements better in the Caribbean basin, and increasing the size of the standing armed forces to a point that forces would be available for several military frontiers. The cost of such a build-up would be formidable, however, and far beyond the nation's need or willingness to pay. Moreover, conditions much less extreme than those imaginable in hypothetical worst-case scenarios would also demand substantial reinforcements of the very low levels of manpower and resources now engaged in monitoring events in the Caribbean basin. In short, a crisis of nearly any proportion is likely to, and has, triggered a reactive and escalatory response in the Caribbean area.

Crisis Management and Crisis Escalation

During a crisis, whether it be a full-blown crisis, or a crisis-brewing, as we have had in Central America since 1978, the locus of government situation analysis, response formulation, and decisionmaking tends to shift away from those levels of the bureaucracy that routinely handle the affairs of our relations with the country or countries in crisis. The national command authority—the White House—becomes involved. Decisionmakers tend to be less informed about the country and situation in question simply because they have not been intimately involved in the details and nuances as the crisis was building. Frequently, detailed background information is not available to these decisionmakers or cannot be communicated in time. Decisions and interpretations tend to be made on the basis of whatever incomplete information is available.

In addition, though the individuals assembled for dealing with the crisis or crisis-brewing are likely to include the nation's most experienced commanders and bureaucrats—persons who should be less prone to overreaction to crisis—they are also the persons most likely to deal with strategic, East-West and balance of power dimensions of U.S. relations with the world. They are more likely to interpret—or overinterpret—a Central American revolution in terms of its East-West dimensions and its impact on the balance of power, rather than in terms of its domestic political origins. They are likely to have less confidence in the ability or integrity of unknown local leaders than credence for the long-range goals of the Russians and their "surrogates." Moreover, decisionmaking in crisis conditions is conducted much closer to the political sensitivities of the nation as perceived by the politicians in the White House. Depending on the national political mood, this also profoundly affects decisions taken.[11]

The three processes described above—the undoing of our confidence in the stability and predictability of the Caribbean basin region, the nature of the defense planning process that lead to emphasis on meeting the most extreme challenge, and the crisis management process that tends to cast events in global East-West terms—are all responsible for the ways in which the United States reacts to revolutionary instability in Central America and the Caribbean. Little high-level attention is given to problems until they reach proportions that hint at East-West balance questions. Therefore, resources are not easily available to tend to the problem until it becomes one that requires a military as well as a diplomatic and economic response. These are difficulties inherent in a system that must be attuned to events around the world. Another factor, not a domestic political factor, also influences reaction to Central American and Caribbean events. That is the fact that the region has become infinitely more permeable in the past ten years than had previously been imagined possible. Not only are Cubans and Americans active, but so are Russians, Europeans, other Latin American powers, Libyans, and so forth. Even the benevolent or benign participation of these many actors contributes to perceptions of diminished U.S. ability to maintain control over unraveling situations. Such perceptions also heighten feelings of insecurity.

New Approaches to the Caribbean Basin

How, then, should the United States deal with Central America and the Caribbean basin? The region is undergoing dramatic change. The old order cannot last, and we should not seek to maintain what remains of it at any cost. The first question we must ask is what do we want in the Caribbean basin? A fair answer is, we want stable, friendly, prosperous states and freedom of movement of goods and services inside and outside the region. We also want no hostile powers in the region; thus an expanded Cuban-Soviet military presence in the region is intolerable. In short, we want a situation that will require little attention from us, precisely the state of affairs that has existed from time immemorial. Unfortunately, in the 1980s the United States cannot impose such a state of affairs but, rather, must work to promote its evolution.

In promoting this state of affairs, the United States might take the following steps:

• Make a long-term commitment to the development of at least minimal economic and political conditions conducive to stability, and

• State clearly what behaviors in the region are not tolerable and what the consequences of intolerable behaviors are—and be prepared to impose these consequences when challenged.

A policy for the Caribbean basin must combine the tactic of isolating domestic crises from outside forces with a strategy of long-term commitment to economic development. The first is a short-term response to limit the crisis; the second attacks the underlying cause of crisis.

Crisis Isolation—the Short-Term Tactics

There is nothing absolute and definitive about political change. In the 1950s the countries of South America experienced leftist-led social and political agitation similar to the turmoil of the Caribbean in the 1980s. Beginning in 1964, nearly every revolutionary government in South America was replaced by a conservative military dictatorship. In the petroleum-poor Caribbean-basin countries, continuing economic problems have been exacerbated by oil price increases beginning in 1973 and by the subsequent recession in the developed world. The region's problems have also been intensified by the inexperience, inefficiency, and underdevelopment of current domestic institutions.

The United States—once a revolutionary society itself but now a supporter of the status quo—can do absolutely nothing about the social and political evolution of these Caribbean-basin societies once violence becomes endemic. Revolutions, coups, and shifts to the left and right are inevitable; we just waste considerable national energy trying to forestall them. Once a country is in the throes of civil war, as has occurred in Nicaragua and El Salvador, the probability of our halting the inevitable social convulsions is infinitesimal.

The U.S. national interest is best served if the United States can remain outside such disputes, carefully monitoring the evolution of controlling forces and preparing to deal with the survivors. At the same time the United States should make it clear to Cubans and Soviets and others that they, too, must stay out of the domestic affairs of the Caribbean and Central American countries. In short, every effort must be made to *isolate* domestic revolutions so that domestic solutions can be found to them. Both the United States and the antagonists must resist the temptation to become involved. It is when outside forces are perceived to be involved in serious domestic crises in Central America that U.S. security concerns are most stimulated.

Determining *how* to isolate such domestic upheavals, how to resist the temptation to become involved ourselves, and how to convince our political antagonists not to become involved is an enormously difficult task. It is, nevertheless, possibly the most important challenge confronting the policy community today. Earlier in this chapter I suggested that there is no long-range, non-military strategic planning. This is a gap that must be filled if the United States is to meet the challenge posed by the political crisis of Central America today, of other small states on the U.S. Caribbean Basin flank, and indeed of the Third World in general.

Economic Commitment for the Long Term

Other chapters in this book argue persuasively that at the root of political instability are poverty, illiteracy, frustrated aspirations, unequal income distribution, and inadequate economic opportunities for the people. Such conditions provide a friendly sea in which the fishes of dissent can swim. The political crisis in the Caribbean basin is likely to continue until the economic crisis is solved.

If the United States' long-range goals for the Caribbean basin can be agreed upon—that it be less crisis-ridden, demand less of our security attention, and be more self-sufficient—then considerable economic aid, along with increased private investment, becomes the logical remedy for both the near term and the long term.

A U.S.-sponsored economic development program for the Caribbean basin[12]—tailored, of course, to be responsive to the real economic differences in the region—would tell the people of the region that the United States has an interest in the fate of its neighbors, and is committed to their well-being. In addition, such a program would provide innumerable channels for enhancing communication and cooperation among the twenty-five or more nations that constitute the region. Such a development program for the Caribbean basin should include the following features:

• Provision of grants and low-interest, long-term loans, with emphasis on the latter so that repayment obligations are recognized,
• Promotion of practical, economically efficient projects with maximum local input,
• Promotion of energy conservation; development of domestic energy resources,
• Emphasis on efficiency and self-sufficiency in agriculture; exploration of cooperative marketing techniques,
• Emphasis on education at practical levels and on services that meet minimal basic human needs.

To avoid costly duplication of efforts, the planning for such a program should involve all the countries in the region. Other countries in the hemisphere should be asked to participate. The oil-exporting countries, Venezuela and Mexico, should provide further financing for petroleum purchases by the poorest countries. Brazil should be persuaded to help develop programs among the sugar-producing nations to convert sugar to fuel. In short, the Caribbean development program should not only strengthen the region economically but also engage with the more-developed Latin American countries in solving regional problems. Nevertheless, the United States must also engage actively and enthusiastically in bilateral assistance efforts, both as a sign of its confidence in the region and as a means of retaining influence in individual countries.

In implementing the proposed economic development program, the rules of the game must be explicit. It must be understood that the United States would not make program investments in countries experiencing civil war, or in countries supporting turmoil abroad. Decisions to rescind aid have to be swift, firm, and indisputable, based on clear evidence. Decisions would, of course, be revocable if behaviors changed.

The proposed strategy is a possible solution to current and future waves of political instability in Central America and the Caribbean basin and to the enormous appeal of the left as an alternative to traditional political systems that have failed to meet the social, economic, and political demands of regional populations. It is in the United States' interest to help the local government meet the people's demands, thereby minimizing the ideological appeal of the extreme left and expanding the pragmatic center in which compromises can be achieved: this policy is based on the principle that economic stability is a regional interest, shared by the United States and its neighbors, and that economic stability contributes positively to political stability and military security.

The United States should not expect gratitude for a development program such as this. Nor should our policymakers expect either economic development or stability to lead to a lining up of Caribbean states behind U.S. leadership. Our history of involvement in the region evokes too much emotion for such responses. But a well-orchestrated diplomacy of regional development and stability would contribute to a more desirable state of affairs in this now volatile, impoverished region. Regional energies could then be mobilized to attack regional problems, and national energies to attack internal problems. Neighbors would not meddle in the affairs of neighbors, and an evolving regional stability would allow the United States to turn its attention once again from its backyard.

NOTES

1. I use the term *Caribbean basin* because, from the security perspective, the entire region is important. The Caribbean basin includes the Central American nations (Guatemala, Belize, Honduras, El Salvador, Nicaragua, Costa

Rica); Panama; Colombia and Venezuela (although these countries have problems quite different from those of most Central American nations); and the island republics of the Greater and Lesser Antilles. Guyana and Surinam should also be included because of the similarity of their political, economic, and social problems. Depending on the issue, Mexico also is often included. Focus on the Caribbean basis as a region does not mean that there are not great differences in political and economic conditions within the region. The national security community's attention must focus first on the *region* and then on the subregions within.

2. Adm. W. H. Bagley, USN (Ret.), *Sea Power and Western Security: The Next Decade* (London: International Institute of Strategic Studies (IISS), Adelphi Papers, no. 139).

3. Jiri Valenta argues the position in chapter 6 of this book. In contrast, Robert Leiken maintains that the Soviets have embarked on a major economic and political offensive in the Western Hemisphere. See "Eastern Winds in Latin America," in *Foreign Policy* 42 (Spring 1981).

4. International Institute of Strategic Studies, *The Military Balance: 1980* (London: IISS, 1980).

5. Edwin Schuhmacher, "Salvadoran Navy, Down to 3 Boats, Tries to Halt Arms Flow," *New York Times,* Mar. 7, 1981.

6. Jeane Kirkpatrick, "U.S. Security and Latin America," *Commentary* 71, no. 1 (January 1981): 29.

7. *Policymakers* as used here refers especially to security policymakers, who may be either military or civilian personnel.

8. See John Child, "From 'Color' to 'Rainbow': U.S. Strategic Planning for Latin America, 1919–1945," *Journal of Inter-American Studies and World Affairs* 21, no. 2 (May 1979).

9. Barry M. Blechman and Stephen S. Kaplan, *Force without War: U.S. Armed Forces as a Political Instrument* (Washington, D.C.: Brookings Institution, 1978). Of 215 uses of armed forces for political purposes between 1946 and 1975, over one-fourth took place in the Western Hemisphere and virtually all of these in the Caribbean basin.

10. See the *New York Times* series of seven articles, "Defense: Is the U.S. Prepared," September 1980. Defense planning documents assume that, in a global conflict, the United States would have to protect the Persian Gulf oil fields, as well as maintain commitments in Europe and Korea. The present size and status of U.S. forces would make it difficult to meet the one and one-half or one and two-half war (e.g., one major and two smaller wars) preparedness targets. Reserve units would not likely be available for 90–120 days, and then their readiness would be problematic.

11. This process is described in detail in chapter 3 of this book.

12. The Caribbean Basin Initiative under discussion by the Reagan administration is a step in the right direction, but to date lacks the important component of a U.S. economic commitment that properly reflects the importance of the Caribbean Basin to U.S. national security.

5. The Perceptions and Interests of U.S. Business in Relation to the Political Crisis in Central America

John F. H. Purcell

The history of U.S. business in Central America is long and controversial. In particular a few major U.S. companies involved in
export agriculture and natural resource extraction have dominated the
economies and often the political systems of the five Central American
countries plus Panama for most of the twentieth century. Historical
descriptions and analyses of this dominance abound, and it is not my
intention to repeat them here.[1] Nor do I attempt to discuss the *impact*,
either past or present, of U.S. banks and companies on Central American economies and societies. Certainly the impact has been and still is
tremendous in terms of defining the models of development, relationships to the international economy and social and political structures of
these small countries.

Instead this chapter analyzes the point of view of large U.S. multinational companies with business interests in Central America (primarily Guatemala, El Salvador and Nicaragua, and to a lesser extent Costa
Rica and Honduras) faced with a regional political crisis threatening
the end of U.S. hegemony there. My focus, then, is the perceptions
and interests of U.S. business in the aftermath of the Nicaraguan Revolution.

Perceptions are discussed at two levels: The first is the assessment
of "country risk" by managers and analysts within the company or
bank, as well as the mechanisms by which this assessment is translated
into an "institutional" assessment; the second is the ideological level—
the unexamined "truths" perceived by decision-makers in the company
about how society does and should work—which form the context of
the country or regional assessment.

Interests, or the stakes, both ideological and material, which a company holds in the region, include not only the amount of exposure or investment in the country, but also the degree to which it appears to be at risk, how profitable it may be, and how significant a part of the company's total exposure or investment it represents. Perceptions and interests are therefore closely intertwined and will be discussed in terms of the *strategies* of companies—a concept which translates perception and interest into action, which is, after all, the final test of these two concepts.

The perceptions, interests, and related strategies presented here are based on interviews with a number of middle-level managers and analysts from companies and banks involved in Central America in a wide range of operations.[2] While most of the interviews represented the view of "headquarters," the often wide divergence in views between headquarters and the field and the multipronged nature of strategies undertaken by large, complex multinational companies is also highlighted.

Perceptions

The Economic Situation in Central America

While the focus of this chapter is perceptions of the political crisis, much of the strategy of U.S. banks and, to a marginally lesser extent of U.S. companies, is derived from their own assessments and projections of the *economic* situation. These economic assessments, gathered by the author in interviews, tend to be fairly uniform, unlike political perceptions, and can thus be presented in capsule form for each country with the understanding that banks will pay particular attention to them while other companies will do so to a varying degree depending on how they affect company operations in that country.

Guatemala   The Guatemalan government is traditionally extremely conservative in its fiscal policies, and its external economic situation is favorable. The debt service ratio is low by Latin American standards, and reserves are relatively high, though declining rapidly. While the economy has grown rapidly in the past, low coffee prices suggest only modest growth in 1981–1982. The extremely unequal distribution of wealth means that a high proportion of the population has not benefited from the expansion of economic activity over the past twenty years. The economy, depending as it does at present on the export of a few agricultural commodities, remains highly vulnerable to both political unrest and world market prices. The discovery of significant amounts of petroleum announced in mid-1981 by Texaco may, however, radically improve the economic picture. Capital flight for political reasons and because of government interest-rate policy is a significant concern.

Costa Rica International financial concern focuses mainly on Costa Rica's economic rather than immediate political situation. In September, 1981, Costa Rica was forced to enter into a debt renegotiation with its external creditors. The government has traditionally financed public spending by international borrowing and high levels of middle-class consumption by imports. The oil shock of 1979 and the collapse of the Central American Common Market have made these traditional methods appear less and less viable. External debt has expanded rapidly, and international reserves are dangerously low. The government has been unable either to cut spending significantly or to increase revenues. Inflation is a serious problem for all but the very wealthiest individuals. Few bank economists see any likelihood of immediate improvements in the external economic situation since world market prices are depressed for major traditional exports, and productivity is low. Most banks pin their short-term hopes on an International Monetary Fund (IMF) agreement but as of September 1981, after months of negotiation, a successful agreement had eluded the negotiators. In spite of these problems, some U.S. banks continue to be hopeful that a new government in 1982 will enact economic measures necessary to restore confidence. Considerable confidence remains in the technical and political skills of the Costa Rican leadership.

Honduras The Honduran economy is the least developed in Central America. While balance of payments pressures are expected to intensify during the 1980s, there are realistic hopes of diversifying the export base beyond coffee and bananas. Honduran development plans are considered realistic and will be financed largely on concessional terms. International confidence is strengthened by the Hondurans' having negotiated an extended fund facility with the IMF on softer terms than an ordinary stand-by agreement. Fiscal and monetary policy are regarded as prudent. The factor that has shaken bank confidence in Honduras somewhat is the collapse of a private bank, Banco Financiera Hondureña (BANFINAN), and the refusal of the Central Bank to make good on BANFINAN's debts to external lenders. While losses were not extremely large, it has become clear that government oversight of the banking system is not effective.

Nicaragua The lack of accurate data on Nicaragua's economic situation makes assessment difficult. Nevertheless, the destruction wrought by civil war reduced the Gross National Product (GNP) by at least a third between 1979 and 1980. Since renegotiation of the debt with commercial banks was still under way in mid-1981, Nicaragua is unlikely to receive financing from that source in the immediate future. The medium-term prospects for economic recovery depend very heavily on political factors including the *modus vivendi* worked out between the Sandinistas and the private sector and the attitude of Western aid donors. The reaction of U.S. businessmen and bankers to government economic policy is mixed though many give high marks to some government planning and economic officials.

El Salvador   Until the outbreak of sustained guerrilla fighting, El Salvador, like Guatemala, was considered a good economic risk, with a strong export base relative to the rest of Central America, conservative fiscal and monetary policies, strong reserves, much of them in gold, and a reasonable balance of payments situation. In 1980 all this changed, largely for political reasons. Capital flight accelerated, capital and financial inflows virtually ceased, and at the present moment most U.S. banks fear that El Salvador may not be able to pay even existing short-term debts regardless of how the political situation evolves. An economic "bail-out" by the Reagan administration could partially restore confidence, however.

Political Assessments of Central America

The most common attitude among respondents was that the political situation simply could not be predicted with any certainty. None of them were willing to state unequivocally that their company or bank had an assessment any more defined or articulated than "cautiously negative" (an insurance company) or "all this will pass" (an oil company).

In terms of assessments of how to interpret what was happening in Central America, even those who viewed themselves as optimistic in terms of future stability believed that major, even revolutionary, changes were taking place and could not be reversed. All respondents spoke of the choice between major economic and political reforms or revolutionary change even more sweeping than that in Nicaragua. Virtually all saw these events as internally generated and not the result of Cuban or Soviet interference, though several expressed concern about outsiders exacerbating the situation. At the same time, the largest companies with significant investments in the region appeared to feel that, no matter what happened, there would still be the possibility of doing some kind of business there.

Nicaragua The most varied and thoughtful views were expressed about Nicaragua. The revolution there appears to have evoked a great deal of interest and ambivalence among U.S. businessmen. No one espoused the view of some right-wing observers in the United States that Nicaragua has "already gone Communist." The closest to this view was from a U.S. banker born in Cuba, who felt he saw all the same trends taking place as had occurred in Cuba. At the same time he believed that the Sandinistas would eventually be overthrown. However, respondents divided nearly equally between those who felt that "it is not yet proved that the National Directorate is Marxist-Leninist" (a chemical company executive) and those who felt the situation is moving *toward* a Cuban model. One executive who had visited Nicaragua also made the analogy with the 1968 Peruvian "revolution."

In addition to companies, business organizations have shown a great interest in Nicaragua. The Council of the Americas in late 1980 sponsored a trip by U.S. businessmen to Costa Rica and Nicaragua to meet private-sector representatives, journalists, and government officials including members of the junta and the National Directorate. The Inter-American Committee of the New York City Bar Association traveled to Managua in February 1981 to discuss approaches to Nicaragua's foreign investment law scheduled to be drafted in mid-1981. Both groups, while not fully endorsing the political process, showed themselves sympathetic to the need for social change and perceived most Sandinista government officials as "genuine and sincere." Another member of one of these groups stated that "All evidence indicated that the Nicaraguans are relatively pragmatic and willing to listen."

While one or two respondents indicated that they doubted the Sandinistas would last, most believed them to be firmly in power and regarded the issue as whether the private sector would be allowed enough autonomy to continue doing business. If this happened, they believed, economic "realities" would gradually moderate their views toward a still mixed but less state-controlled economy.

Bankers' views of Nicaragua were very influenced by the experiences of renegotiating the first phase of the Nicaraguan government debt, a process that continued during most of 1980 and ended in August of that year.[3] Two major issues in the assessment that the thirteen banks on the steering committee had to make of Nicaragua were, first, whether the government was "serious" about negotiating its debt and, second, whether the Nicaraguan situation was sufficiently singular to avoid setting a precedent for other debt renegotiations. After considerable discussion and analysis of many sources of information, the consensus was affirmative on both questions, though a number of banks had serious doubts at first. Two respondents declared themselves "very surprised" that the Nicaraguans were willing to negotiate at all.

El Salvador   Assessments of El Salvador were also quite mixed but not nearly so ambivalent. No respondents expressed any particular sympathy for the guerrillas. A small handful of respondents reported that, while they personally believed that some kind of negotiated solution (i.e., political rather than military) was necessary, their senior managements appeared to sympathize with a hard-line military solution (though not necessarily direct U.S. involvement). Most respondents reported that both they and their senior managements believed that reforms, particularly land reforms, were absolutely necessary for any lasting solution.

Personal predictions tended toward the optimistic, usually with the caveat that it depended on actions of the U.S. government. Most felt that the left was not strong enough to "win" unless serious policy blunders were made, such as reversing the land reform. Nevertheless, all reported that their company or bank did not feel the situation was predictable enough to assume a stable outcome in the near future. One respondent raised the analogy with Vietnam, saying that U.S. public opinion would not allow the U.S. government to follow through on its commitments to the junta. All others dismissed the Vietnam analogy as inappropriate. The "optimists" generally painted a scenario of an eventual moderate-to-left civilian government incorporating some elements from the Democratic Revolutionary Front (FDR).

Guatemala   Most respondents regarded Guatemala as an extremely dangerous situation. One local manager for an oil company active in Guatemala, after expressing optimism about Guatemala's future, stated: "I really don't pay much attention to politics but have to be optimistic—I live here." An executive of another oil company not deeply involved in Guatemala expressed a more common view: "It's a really bad situation, the right-wing finances terrorism when what they need is social reform." Among most respondents, very little sympathy was expressed for the Guatemalan military and the violent approach of the right wing to eliminating the left.

Most bankers declared that they and their institutions believed that Guatemala was stable only in the short term, though one declared that he saw no problems even in the medium term (up to five years). There was considerably less willingness among respondents to discuss Guatemala in detail than was the case for El Salvador and Nicaragua. A representative of a large insurance company said, "Guatemala is a much larger market for us [than other Central American countries] and we're very concerned about it." He and other respondents seemed at a loss when asked to paint a more detailed scenario, however.

Honduras and Costa Rica   Most respondents indicated that while they felt it was relatively stable, Honduras was so small and poor as not to be particularly interesting. Representatives from companies with large investments in both Honduras and Costa Rica expressed more concern about Costa Rican labor problems than about Honduran political stability. One oil company executive said, "Honduras has a very weak military, and that's negative, but nevertheless I think they will stabilize." Bankers are less concerned about political issues in Honduras than they are about a recent bank failure and the lack of government regulation of the private banking system.

Most respondents believe that Costa Rica "is different" and will remain so, though bankers worried at length over the country's economic difficulties. One banker said: "They have always lived beyond their means but basically I think they will muddle through. They will probably have to reschedule their debt." The representative of one large U.S. bank gave the most pessimistic comments, saying, "It's a very dangerous situation given their economic problems and the fact that it would be so easy to take over the government."

Sources of Information

In general, the firms with significant investment or exposure in Central America use a wide variety of information sources. Common sources of information are personal contacts of senior and middle management in the country, regional representatives and managers who make frequent trips to the country, and organizations (such as the Council of the Americas and the Fund for Multinational Management Education) that sponsor trips to the region or hold seminars or meetings in Central America. Finally, the largest companies and banks have internal units that analyze economic and political risk.[4] It is very seldom that a company with significant interests in Central America has only one or two information sources. While local businessmen or bankers are often an important source, they are almost never the sole or even the most credible source.

Analysis of Information

While the data are too scanty to be definitive, an impression emerges about the way these various sources of information are used by companies. The Central America situation is quite unusual for most companies since it is an intense political crisis in an area that is for most of them fairly marginal in terms of investment or exposure. This produces a situation where some middle-level managers and analysts (the "experts") spend a great deal of time thinking about Central America, while the senior executives spend very little time. In most cases this leads to a divergence of opinion within the company in which the higher one goes, the more hard-line the views become. Several respondents reported that their superiors were more willing than they to endorse military solutions and to accept the "domino theory" espoused by some senior officials in the Reagan administration. Often the analysts and middle-level operational people had a more complex view of events.

For most companies, the institutional perception of each country appears to incorporate the views of the country experts in spite of the more purely ideological reactions of some senior management. An analyst for a large insurance company, for example, noted that while the senior management reacted very favorably to the Haig-Reagan posture on El Salvador and believed that was the solution to the political crisis, they listened to other views when it was explained that the policy could fail for a variety of reasons related to the internal dynamics of the political system. This analyst noted: "They may be as right-wing as Attila the Hun but they are extremely pragmatic when it comes to business decisions." Several bankers noted that, while senior officers tended to take the domino theory more seriously than the account officers specializing in the country, they gave considerable weight to account officers' views.

The case of the Nicaraguan debt renegotiation is interesting because it illustrates the manner in which sophistication of perception increases as senior executives focus on a country and a business decision for a period of time. The thirteen-bank steering committee utilized a wide variety of contacts in Nicaragua and elsewhere in Central America, in Washington, D.C., information from their own analysts, and a number of information-gathering and negotiating trips to Nicaragua itself.

At first several banks, in the words of one steering committee member, "panicked" and "would have been willing to sign anything." Apparently this willingness derived from the belief that, if the negotiations were protracted, the Nicaraguans would simply walk away from it. Other banks took an extremely hard line and were unwilling to accept any but standard commercial terms. Over the months of negotiation, while differences in perception and proposed strategy certainly remained, the interaction on the steering committee produced much more of a consensus that: (1) the Nicaraguan government was committed to negotiating a settlement and would stick with the negotiating process; (2) the revolutionary rhetoric of some Nicaraguan negotiators was sincere at one level, but it did *not* imply that Nicaragua was unwilling to make some concessions for a settlement or that the Sandinistas were not prepared to continue to be pragmatic in their dealings with the U.S. financial community; (3) the Nicaraguan case really was unique in the degree of devastation of the economy and the unanimous hatred of the Somoza regime by the population; and (4) the Sandinistas were firmly in power and had considerable leeway to make concessions from their early proposals (such as the absolute 7 percent cap on interest repayment) without fear of attack by even more militantly leftist groups.

Because all decisions on the banks' steering committee were made by consensus rather than majority vote, there was constant airing of diverse opinions and a thorough analysis of differing assumptions. Interestingly, this process probably strengthened the hand of the banks proposing a fairly hard line because it resulted in a near consensus that fears of a breakdown of negotiations for political reasons were probably unfounded and that the harder the banks bargained, the more they would get. This view was ameliorated somewhat by economic analysis of the country, which showed that the final negotiated outcome probably represented the limit of Nicaragua's ability to pay and still generate foreign exchange needed for development goals.

Ideology

Most respondents prided themselves on being "nonideological." While it is true that ideology is usually something ascribed to other people, the word as used here means the underlying assumptions about how broad social, economic, and political processes that provide the framework for respondents' specific assessments of particular political situations should and do work. Such a discussion is necessarily impressionistic.

No respondent gave any indication of a belief that local or international capitalism was anything less than extremely beneficial for the people of Central America. One representative of a large agribusiness firm who noticed considerable hostility among plantation workers toward foreign managers expressed sincere puzzlement that this should be so when "we are really their only possibility for upward mobility." Both bankers and company executives not surprisingly expressed an "ideology of the international market"—the view that only through capitalist growth, including the financing of international trade and the integration of Central American economies into the world economic system, could the Central American population become prosperous.

Respondents also expressed the view that support for a country's economy and trade links could be separated from support for a repressive regime such as that of Guatemala or El Salvador. Those who disapproved of the Salvadoran military, for example, believed that, as long as loans financed imports of medical supplies or food as opposed to weapons, this did not constitute support for the regime. Most major U.S. banks do have very strictly enforced prohibitions against arms sale financing. These distinctions appear to be sincerely drawn and *not* simply a thin veneer of justification over a basic amoral cynicism. The basis for the sincerity appears to be an ideological outlook that elevates trade, finance, and investment into a general social good that should not be tampered with lest the tampering produce distortions that would be even more harmful than the original problem. It is an ideological outlook too, that separates politics and economics in a very basic way. Another intriguing suggestion by a banker was that a major reason for banks' prohibition on arms sale financing was that the worst situation from a banker's point of view is uncertainty and that arms sales, by feeding warfare, perpetuate uncertainty.

Another perspective on Central America with roots in the "ideology of the international market" was the view of some respondents that eventually Salvador would become more peaceful and democratic and that economic factors would eventually moderate the militancy of the Sandinista leadership in Nicaragua. One businessman expressed this in saying that "In Nicaragua time is on our side. They [the Sandinistas] will eventually see the importance of the free market." In addition, some respondents expressed a preference for democracy. As one businessman put it: "New York business and financial circles have a lot of closet liberals." Several respondents stated that very repressive military regimes were bad for business (though it is not clear how much this is a post-Somoza phenomenon) and that capitalism plus social reform is the long-term solution to the Central American crisis.

Thus, in the broadest terms, ideology appears to influence perceptions of the nature of the Central American conflict. One should be careful, however, about assuming that ideological perspectives often influence business decisions. In the case of Nicaragua, for example, virtually all businessmen disapprove of the political and economic model espoused by the Sandinistas. This does not affect companies' and banks' willingness to do business with the Nicaraguans when it will be profitable to do so. If anything, the liberal ideology of some businessmen has led them to visit Nicaragua and to express sympathy for certain *aspects* of the Revolution in spite of the fact that real opportunities for major business in the country are extremely scarce and risky by any reasonable calculation. From another perspective, the recent signing of an agreement for banana exports between Castle & Cooke and the Nicaraguan government illustrates a very pragmatic negotiating process overlaid by ideological posturing by a company senior executive once the agreement had been signed.[5]

In the case of the Nicaraguan debt renegotiations, it could be said that at first some bankers' ideological perceptions led them to believe that the Nicaraguans were not inclined to negotiate seriously. After their experience on the steering committee, however, a more pragmatic perception prevailed.

Interests

The Stakes

The precise interests of U.S. business in Central America are difficult to define. For companies, these include not only the absolute amount of direct investment but also the relative size and profitability of this investment in relation to the company's operations elsewhere in the world. Related factors are the size of the local market, both for imports and for domestically manufactured products, and the importance of the country as a source of raw materials, both for a particular company and in terms of world market supplies. The stakes involve both risk and opportunity and are very specific to the particular operations of the firm. For banks, the risks involve timely repayment of loans (the issue of *any* repayment almost never arises). Losses generally result from delayed repayment or, very infrequently, repayment on different terms than those originally contracted. In the Nicaragua case, both delay (a period without any interest or principal payments) *and* a revision of the terms occurred. Because each bank's exposure was relatively small, the actual losses in most cases totaled only a few hundred thousand dollars (assuming that the new repayment schedule is followed). A much more serious issue, however, is the precedent set by the final terms of the category I (Nicaraguan government) debt renegotiation.

If other countries, particularly large ones such as Brazil, regarded the Nicaraguan case as a precedent, the banks would consider this a disaster. While bankers indicated themselves able to live with the Nicaraguan settlement, this is really only true if one understands that they view Nicaragua as a unique case, both in terms of the small size of banks' exposure there, and the unusual circumstances leading to the renegotiation. A similar situation is unlikely to occur in El Salvador because U.S. bank exposure there has been reduced so drastically.

Tables 1 and 2 provide data on direct U.S. investment by country in Central America and on exposure of the eight largest U.S. banks.

Table 5.1   CENTRAL AMERICAN EXPOSURE OF EIGHT LARGEST
U.S. BANKS: 1978–1980
(Millions of dollars)

	Total Exposure		
	June 1978	*June 1979*	*June 1980*
Total Latin America/Canada	38,818.7	45,339.6	52,434.1
Honduras	320.8	337.9	225.8
Guatemala	267.7	242.7	331.9
Costa Rica	474.3	369.3	357.5
Nicaragua	338.8	265.9	221.8
El Salvador	205.0	238.1	95.1
Total Central America	1,606.6	1,453.9	1,232.1
Central America as Percentage of Latin America/Canada	4.1%	3.2%	2.3%

SOURCE: Federal Reserve
NOTE: The exposure of the top eight banks normally represents 75–80 percent of total U.S. bank exposure.

Table 1, showing total exposure for the composite of eight banks between June 1978 and June 1980, indicates that, while total international exposure in the Western Hemisphere climbed steadily, the picture for some Central American countries was more mixed, and total exposure in the region declined from 1978 to 1980. It should also be noted that the Central American exposure as a percentage of the Western Hemisphere international total was very small even in 1978. Table 2, showing total U.S. direct investment, indicates that Central American investment, too, was a very small portion of the total in Latin America. The data are not adequate to examine trends, and it should be noted that the data for 1980 probably would show the beginning of a significant stagnation of the level of investment for at least some of the countries.

Table 5.2   U.S. DIRECT INVESTMENT IN CENTRAL AMERICA: 1974–1979
(Millions of dollars)

	1974	1978	1979
Total Central America*	. . .	793	895
Total Latin America	. . .	32,662	36,834
Honduras	186	202	. . .
Guatemala	170	221	. . .
Costa Rica	161	143	. . .
Nicaragua	97	121	. . .
El Salvador	71	111	. . .
Central America as Percentage of Total Latin America	. . .	2.4%	2.4%

SOURCE: U.S. Department of Commerce
*Excludes Panama

Strategy

Business Strategy

Business strategy combined with related political strategy ought to provide a practical test of both perceptions and *perceived* interests. The briefest answer to the question what strategy are U.S. companies and banks adopting toward Central America is a strategy of "wait and see." Most respondents in the section on perceptions reported that the Central American political situation is essentially unpredictable and potentially extremely risky.

Nevertheless, many companies do not have the luxury of doing nothing. In some cases their investment or exposure is so large as to require some kind of decision. Many investments require continued capital to make them profitable. In some cases, such as petroleum companies in Guatemala, the potential return is high enough to balance out considerable political risk. In this and other cases (perhaps the banana companies, certain high technology manufacturers, and so forth), the importance of the investment to the country and the leverage the company has in any bargaining process make the company feel that, even under the worst of circumstances, it will be able to deal with a new government. (Note the case of Castle & Cooke in Nicaragua, in which the government proposed to market bananas itself and found that the company essentially controlled the distribution system for exporting bananas.) Leverage may derive from technology, control of markets or distribution systems, the need for international finance, or any one of a number of other factors.

Banks face not only the risk of increasing exposure in a situation that may lead to delays in repayment or renegotiation, but also of losing a profitable relationship if they act overcautiously. Short-term debt can be increased and decreased quickly, but longer-term money can only be gradually reduced. In general, U.S. banks' reaction to the Central American political crisis has been to move more and more to the short-term end of the spectrum in Guatemala and Honduras, to reduce or even eliminate all but cash-collateralized exposure in El Salvador, and not even to consider new money for Nicaragua until all old debts have been renegotiated. Even then it is doubtful whether Nicaragua will have an easy time borrowing even short-term very soon, given what one banker called the "sour taste" left by the recent negotiations. In Costa Rica, bankers are cautious mainly because of the country's economic problems and only secondarily for medium-term political reasons.

Within these general parameters a variety of different substrategies exist. One large American bank with a branch in Guatemala is reported by other bankers to be continuing to do business on a fairly regular basis. Another equally large bank, which describes itself as "slow to react to good markets and quick to react to bad ones," is cutting back in all Central American countries, including Costa Rica. Several banks with small representative offices in Guatemala City are reported to have moved them to Panama over the past year. One small U.S. bank, on the other hand, reported that it is going ahead with medium-term loans to Guatemala. In general the larger banks do not have the ability to move fast enough to react to monthly changes in the political and economic environment. They tend to take either a cautious or aggressive policy "line" over longer periods of time. Smaller banks with smaller exposures, particularly if they have considerable experience in Latin America, are more able to "fine tune" their business strategies in Central America. The larger banks, like the larger companies, have somewhat of an advantage in being able to exert some leverage over decisionmakers in the country to take financial and economic measures that the banks wish to see implemented. Nevertheless, this leverage is limited. For example, it has not prevented the nationalization of branches of U.S. banks, including Citibank in El Salvador. Insurance companies are in a somewhat similar situation. They are easy to nationalize and can be pointed to (incorrectly, they maintain) as net exporters of capital from the host country. While banks can withdraw their physical presence from the country yet continue to finance trade or even medium-term projects, insurance companies have had to re-think their presence in virtually all Central American countries, including those not immediately threatened by revolutionary change such as Panama.

Companies with large fixed investments in Central America are mostly taking a day-to-day approach. Their size allows them to deal directly with the government over each issue as it arises, and the general unpredictability of the area makes long-term strategic planning rather frustrating. In general, representatives of these companies reported that they hope to "ride out" whatever changes are in store and adapt to variations in the business environment on an *ad hoc* basis. One such company, for example, reported that it still had plants operating in Nicaragua. They had been closed but not damaged during the Revolution. The management distributed the existing stocks to the population during the period of fighting. After the advent of the Sandinista government, the company put in enough capital to reopen the plants and has since had no problems with the government. A similar situation was reported by an oil company with refining capacity in Nicaragua. Many of these companies are operating in Nicaragua and El Salvador with only domestic management and plan to continue as long as is feasible. Their experience in Nicaragua leads several of them to believe that, except for peak periods of revolutionary activity, they can more or less conduct business as usual.

Some of the natural resource companies have been less fortunate, though the final verdict is not yet in on the Nicaraguan experience. Mining companies such as Asarco and Rosario, which had operations nationalized in Nicaragua, are still conducting negotiations with the government about the terms of compensation.

No companies interviewed plan any major capital investment in Central America with the exception of Costa Rica and possibly some petroleum companies exploring in Guatemala. Even one large agribusiness firm, which claimed to have no strategic plan, asserted that it was exploring diversification outside Central America, probably in the United States. An oil company with considerable investment in several Central American countries said that it does have a detailed strategic plan for Central America and that its analysis "would make us look very hard at any major capital investment there." The same respondent stated that his company might reconsider a year or so *after* any apparently peaceful settlement of the current crisis in El Salvador.

Companies less locked into Central America but still able to do profitable business there plan to continue until the situation becomes too much of a nuisance to continue. The representative of one large multinational with a relatively small amount of investment in all Central American countries said, "We would just chuck [the investments] if they took too much of the time of our senior people." In the meanwhile, "We would rather be there than not, because we're making money and don't want to leave it all to the Japanese." His general categorization of his company's presence in Central America was "more of an irritation than an interest."

The adaptive and reactive character of U.S. multinationals in relation to the Central American political crisis means that they adopt different postures in different countries, though in all cases it is cautious and nonaggressive in terms of business strategy. In Nicaragua, companies attempt a low profile sympathetic to the Revolution. One high-technology firm still operating in Nicaragua refused to join a visit of U.S. businessmen to Nicaragua organized by the Council of the Americas, because it feared (incorrectly according to the council) that there might be criticisms of the Nicaraguan government expressed on the trip. In Guatemala, on the other hand, as one very frank executive put it, "We are tied in to the oligarchs—it's the only way we can do business." The practice of moving toward host-country nationals as managers and employees of local operations reinforces the adaptive character of each company's posture in the country. One respondent noted "All our employees there are nationals. This makes things difficult because they are not as well trained as we would like, but we have to do it that way."

Political Strategy

One of the confusing aspects of analyzing the strategy of large multinational companies is that these are many-faceted, and indeed sometimes quite different strategies are carried out at different levels at the same time. An area where this seems particularly true is in the political aspects of the strategy—that is, the company's relationship to the host-country government and various social and political groups in the country, its relationship to the U.S. government, and the activities of various business organizations to which the company belongs (local American Chambers of Commerce, groups like the Council of the Americas, and so forth). A major distinction appears to exist between the local operation and the headquarters. In some of the most well-publicized cases, local subsidiaries or franchises have taken actions that the headquarters or parent company subsequently disowned or did not take responsibility for. The most notorious occurred in Guatemala, where the management of a company with a Coca-Cola franchise apparently colluded with the Guatemalan police to harass and assassinate numerous leaders and members of the bottling plant union over a period of years in an attempt to break the union. Only after considerable pressure and a boycott on Coca Cola by the International Food Workers Union was the franchise sold and changes made in the local management to allow a contract to be signed with the union.[6] Subsidiaries of other U.S. companies have been accused of similar kinds of human rights violations in Guatemala.

The role of local American Chambers of Commerce has at times been regarded as supportive of repressive host governments. In Nicaragua the president of the American Chamber was declared *persona non grata* by the government because of anti-Sandinista testimony given before the U.S. Congress. Because the U.S. Chamber appears *not* to have been able to adapt to the revolutionary changes (unlike a number of U.S. companies), its future in Nicaragua is very much in doubt. The American Chamber in Guatemala is outspoken in favor of the current military government. In May 1980 the president of the Chamber was quoted as saying to corporate leaders in New York City, after noting the U.S. Department of State's opposition to privately financed and controlled right-wing death squads:

> There is another point of view that contends that the only feasible way
> to stop Communism is to destroy it quickly. Argentina and Chile are

demonstrated *(sic)* as nations which used this approach with considerable effectiveness and have gone on to become among Latin America's most stable and successful countries, in spite of the fact that they do not enjoy U.S. support on human rights grounds.[7]

This view cannot be generally ascribed to U.S. business without considerable further documentation, and it certainly contradicts the views expressed by respondents in this study. These and other less blatant cases do suggest, however, that views and strategies in the host country may not be the same as those at headquarters. It should also be noted that the cases cited are ones in which there is a fairly loose informal linkage between the local operation or group and companies in the United States.

With regard to political activity within the United States, there is a need for considerably more research than is available for this chapter. One or two respondents indicated that their companies had lobbied for or against various U.S. government policies in Central America. Some large banks and insurance companies, for example, complained to the administration about what they saw as Ambassador Robert White's condoning of bank nationalization by the Salvadoran junta.It has been reported, but not confirmed, that Guatemalan business interests with ties to U.S. business were active in the Reagan campaign and are promoting a sympathetic U.S. policy toward the Guatemalan government. There is no evidence as yet that major U.S. companies are involved, however. The U.S. banks on the Nicaraguan steering committee lobbied individually for the release of the $75 million of U.S. aid to Nicaragua for fiscal year 1980.

Groups such as the Council of the Americas are mainly information sources rather than lobbyists per se. Nevertheless, the council is a vehicle through which its members' views are focused on Washington policymakers. Under the Carter administration the council drew up a position paper called "Toward Realism in Western Hemisphere Relations—A U.S. Foreign Policy for Latin America and the Caribbean," which was formally presented to the U.S. Department of State for consideration. Most recommendations call for expanding opportunities for trade and investment, though some support increased military and security training and a response "to requests from Latin American and Caribbean nations seeking to purchase military equipment." The document also advocates "a sincere commitment to support concretely viable democracies in this hemisphere."[8]

The respondents' attitudes toward both the Carter and Reagan administrations' Central American policies were concern rather than full-fledged support or opposition. Several respondents were sympathetic to the human rights "policy" but felt it was a posture rather than a policy. The same was said about the Reagan administration position on El Salvador. One oil company executive said: "We have our fingers crossed that the U.S. won't go in with troops. That would be a real step backward. We need a political solution." While, as noted earlier in the chapter, there were indications that many senior executives were perceived as supporting a bellicose posture toward Cuba and the left in Central America, there was a stronger sense of worry that U.S. policy under Carter and possibly under Reagan was unpredictable and thus bad for business. While there was very little indication that respondents felt that they could formulate a better policy, it was simply the appearance of policy drift and wide swings back and forth that they found disturbing. Some executives felt that Carter's policies had fueled instability in the region, but these same respondents and others feared that Reagan's policy would polarize Central American society and make lasting stability impossible. One executive declared himself worried by "the simplistic analogy with the World Series and the idea that the U.S. would 'win' or 'lose' in Central America."

Conclusions

The perceived interests of large U.S. multinationals in relation to Central America are in general terms much the same as in relation to anywhere else in the world: profitability and predictability. It is the peculiar character of the current political environment and its interaction with companies' organizational characteristics that leads to business and political strategies that are considerably different from the stereotypical historical image of U.S. business in the region. One of the most interesting issues in this regard is whether U.S. business or significant segments of it will be willing to "follow the flag" into Central America—to join what some have referred to as an "interventionist coalition"[9] between U.S. business and government attempting to impose a capitalist and pro-U.S. outcome upon all the countries of Central America. There is little doubt that this is the preferred outcome for virtually all U.S. businessmen interviewed, and past experiences in Latin America suggest that U.S. business might be willing to lend itself to such a project. The role of International Telephone and Telegraph Corporation and other companies in Chile certainly points to such a possibility. Nevertheless, it is argued here that the Chilean case may be significantly different from that of Central America and that, given the interests and perceptions described in this chapter, U.S. business is unlikely to join such a coalition in spite of its ideological proclivities.

As several authors have pointed out in other studies elsewhere in the world, multinational companies are highly adaptable to the structure of power in *each* of the host countries in which they have a presence.[10] There are exceptions, but in general these companies are capable of taking on different styles, postures, and political positions depending on the political and social environment. The attitudes of management in at least two companies with a presence in both Nicaragua and Guatemala show these differences clearly. In one extreme case the Guatemalan manager expressed the view that it might be useful to drop poison gas on Indian villages that supported the guerrillas, while the Nicaraguan managment bent over backward to show its tolerance of and support for the Revolution.

In the process of adaption within the company, extreme views tend to get smoothed over—even when these are held by senior management. This takes place more rapidly when the company is forced to focus on the situation by making choices that are unavoidable. A similar process occurred among banks on the Nicaragua steering committee. The renegotiations forced bankers to learn about and think about the Revolution in a way they would never have had to if the Nicaraguans had either honored the debts immediately or repudiated them.

These characteristics of companies' behavior interact with particular elements within the Central American political environment to produce characteristic strategies (or lack of them) in the face of the current political crisis. In the first place, an apparently stable environment changed very rapidly into an obviously unstable and unpredictable one; second, the situation is fluid—it is not clear precisely how hostile even the Nicaraguan environment is for doing certain kinds of business; third, the depth of the social change taking place is clear to nearly everyone. There seems to have been the perception in some business circles that the Allende regime in Chile was "unnatural" and needed only a small push to get things "back to normal." A similar perception does not appear to be widely held about Nicaragua among the respondents interviewed. Most of the talk is of "moderating" rather than eliminating the Sandinistas. Many respondents are very much opposed to the cutoff of U.S. aid to Nicaragua, for example.

Finally, since interests are small in relative terms, most companies are likely to opt for withdrawal as more and more time and effort of senior management are required to keep abreast of the situation. This does not include companies that are locked into the region though even these are considering diversification. The suddenness of the change, the potential depth of the change, and the perceived unpredictability of the situation have made companies and banks reactive to the environment and ad hoc in their strategies. Companies perceive themselves as buffeted by events rather than leading them or molding them.

In conclusion, the factors mentioned make it unlikely that significant segments of the U.S. business and financial community would be likely to support the "interventionist coalition" mentioned. A combination of the relatively low level of material stakes held by U.S. business in Central America with the perception that business can be done within a broad spectrum of national ideologies makes a reactive posture seem less risky in Central America. This view is reinforced by the institutional sophistication of many large companies and banks in their analysis of the nature of the political crisis in Central America. Their analysis leads to the view that events in Central America stem from deep internal social processes and are not amenable to simple unidimensional solutions (such as military intervention).

On the other hand, should it appear that the Reagan administration policy in El Salvador were achieving political stability at whatever cost, U.S. business and finance would be likely to embark on a cautious reconsideration of their "wait and see" posture. Announcements in May 1981 of major oil discoveries in Guatemala are likely to convince many banks and some companies that the Guatemalan government can meet its international financial obligation for some time to come in spite of increasing guerrilla activity.

Because this chapter does not provide a historical treatment of U.S. business perceptions, it cannot be said with certainty that the picture painted here represents a significant change from past strategies and perceptions. As a concluding hypothesis, however, it is suggested that change has indeed occurred. The change stems partly from the often-noted decline of U.S. hegemony even in its traditional spheres of influence such as Latin America. This decline has been accompanied by increasing international competition with U.S. business from European and Japanese companies and banks. The result has been a higher level of insecurity and unpredictability, especially regarding business decisions and strategies with a political component. One reaction to this unpredictability has been the growth of a new field often called "political risk analysis," whereby companies and banks attempt to analyze more closely the political events affecting their international business. A parallel and perhaps partly related trend is the increasing realization by U.S. businessmen and bankers that intensified competition brings the need to examine business opportunities in a wider variety of political environments, including countries with "revolutionary" or socialist governments. These factors plus the perceived decreasing ability of the U.S. government to protect business investments overseas may be weakening the ties between U.S. government strategic-political interest and U.S. business interests in the international arena.

It would be premature, judging from the interviews conducted for this study, to speak of a significant divergence of interests between U.S. business and the U.S. government. However, in specific instances, possibly in Nicaragua if the internal political situation there should stabilize in the future, there may be an increasing willingness and capacity of U.S. banks and companies to deal with Socialist governments in Latin America even in the face of contrary U.S. policy.

NOTES

1. See, for example, the bibliography in NACLA reports on El Salvador (*A Revolution Brews,* vol. 14, no. 4 [July–August] 1980) and on Guatemala (1974) as well as Marc W. Herold, "From Riches to 'Rags': Finanzkapital in El Salvador, 1900–1980," manuscript, Feb. 29, 1980.

2. Interviews were conducted during January, February, and March 1981 with 15 representatives of large U.S. companies representing a broad range of business activities in Central America, including finance (banks and insurance companies), petroleum production and refining, agribusiness, mining, and manufacturing. In addition, nonbusiness groups, both supportive of and critical of U.S. business activity in Latin America, were interviewed. In general, those interviewed were not key decisionmakers in the corporation but did have access to the thinking of such decisionmakers and a thorough knowledge of the decisions themselves.

3. For one account of the renegotiation not fully endorsed by all bankers, see John Dizard, "Why Bankers Fear the Nicaraguan Solution," *Institutional Investor,* November 1980, pp. 53–62.

4. See Steve Blank et al., *Assessing the Political Environment: An Emerging Function in International Companies,* Conference Board Research Report, No. 794, 1980.

5. See, for example, "Castle and Cooke Unit and Nicaragua Agree on Banana Production," *Wall Street Journal,* Jan. 13, 1981; "Nicaraguan Minister Details Banana Pact," *Times of the Americas,* Feb. 4, 1981; and Ward Sinclair, "Slip in the Banana Trade," *Washington Post,* Jan. 31, 1981.

6. See the account by Robert Morris, "Coca-Cola and Human Rights in Guatemala," Interfaith Center for Corporate Responsibility brief, November 1980. See also *This Week—Central America,* Feb. 2, 1981.

7. Ibid., p. 3D. Morris cites his source for the quote as American Chamber of Commerce in Guatemala, Bulletin no. 162, May 23, 1980.

8. "Toward Realism in Western Hemisphere Relations—A U.S. Foreign Policy for Latin America and the Caribbean," Council of the Americas, July 1980.

9. See chapter 2 by James Kurth in this book.

10. An interesting example using mining companies in southern Africa is Richard L. Sklar, *Corporate Power in an African State: The Political Impact of Multinational Mining Companies in Zambia* (Berkeley: Univ. of California Press, 1975).

PART THREE

External Influences Other than the United States

6. Soviet and Cuban Responses to New Opportunities in Central America

Jiri Valenta

The Russians are the whip of reform. But these impatient and generous men, darkened as they are by anger, are not the ones who are going to lay the foundation for the new world! They are the spur, and they come in time as the voice of man's conscience. But the steel that makes a good spur will not do for the builder's hammer.
—*José Martí (1883)*

Because of the victory of the Sandinistas in Nicaragua in July 1979 and the ongoing civil war in El Salvador, both supported in varying degrees by the Cubans and Soviets, Soviet and Cuban strategy and tactics in Central America are being analyzed more seriously than ever before.* The revolution in Nicaragua, according to some observers, is transforming that country into a "second Cuba." Meanwhile the Reagan administration has presented an array of evidence about cautious yet active Soviet support relayed by the Cubans (armaments and military instruction), via Nicaragua, to left-leaning guerrillas in El Salvador.

Aside from their importance within a specific regional context, these latest developments shed new light on the even more crucial issue of Soviet-Cuban strategy in the Third World in general.[1] The Soviet-backed and Cuban-orchestrated support to left-leaning allies in Central America follows a decade of limited Soviet-Cuban military and security assistance to other Third World countries—Mozambique, Guinea, and Zambia in Africa, Syria and South Yemen in the Middle

*Parts of this study were prepared for the Secretary of Defense. I am indebted to Andrew Marshall for his and his staff's encouragement. I am also indebted to Virginia Valenta, Mike Clough, Richard Feinberg, Jerry Hough, Robert Looney, and William Leogrande (who disagrees with me on some basic points) for their comments, and to Linda Jenkins for her help with research.

127

East—and comes on the heels of Soviet-Cuban military interventions on behalf of revolutionary forces in Angola in 1975–1976 and Ethiopia in 1977–1978. These activities, along with Soviet support of the 1978 intervention on behalf of "true revolutionaries" in Kampuchea (Cambodia) conducted by the North Vietnamese ("Cubans of the Orient" as the Chinese call them) and the Soviets' own military intervention in Afghanistan in 1979 on behalf of the Parcham faction of the Afghan Communist party, are perceived by U.S. policymakers as fitting into an overall Soviet plan. Secretary of State Alexander Haig views developments in Central America in particular as part of "a very clearly delineated Soviet-Cuban strategy," the clear objective of which is "to create Marxism-Leninism in Central America—Nicaragua, El Salvador, Guatemala, and Honduras."[2] In Haig's view the Soviet-sponsored interventions in Central America are "an extension of the 'Brezhnev doctrine' [once only applied to Eastern Europe] outside the sphere of Soviet hegemony." This school of thought was echoed by President Reagan himself, who explained that "the terrorists aren't just aiming at El Salvador," but "at the whole of Central and possibly later South America, [and] I'm sure, eventually North America."[3] The Reagan administration has apparently decided to counter what it sees as Soviet implementation of the Brezhnev doctrine by acting on the principle of the Monroe doctrine, wherein the U.S. government announced its intention to oppose outside interference in the Americas. Thus the crises in Central America in general and El Salvador in particular have become a crucial test of this administration's determination to challenge Soviet-Cuban designs, whatever they may be, in the Western Hemisphere and perhaps in other areas of the Third World as well. This analysis will be limited to Cuban and Soviet perceptions and strategies with regard to Central America and the Caribbean region with emphasis on specific tactics employed in Nicaragua and El Salvador.

A brief statement must be made about the complex beginnings of the ongoing conflict in the region and the reasons for the revolutionary transformation occurring there. The present crises in Central America cannot be attributed solely to Cuban and Soviet interference. What is occurring in El Salvador and to varying degrees in other Central American countries, particularly the northernmost, is the rapid decay of *anciens régimes*.[4] This process has been witnessed already in other Third World countries such as Ethiopia. The decay of outmoded political and economic structures and social orders is the result of the dynamic interaction of a number of factors internal to the countries themselves. The societies of Central America are polarized by antagonism between a small upper class and a very poor majority; in most of these countries the middle class remains weak and underdeveloped. Socioeconomic polarization and the past and existing oppressive regimes have contributed significantly to the rise of internal and interregional conflict in these countries.

Though internal and regional forces have provided the central impetus for radicalism in the area, the last several decades of U.S. hegemony and policies, ranging from intervention to benign neglect, contributed to the development of nationalist reaction in the region. The prevailing feeling of many nationalists and radicals south of the Rio Grande regarding the United States resembles the traditional attitude of the Poles and Hungarians regarding the Soviets. This view was well articulated by prerevolutionary Mexican President Porfírio Díaz, who once lamented, "Poor Mexico, so far from God, so near the United States." More recently the tension has been exacerbated by Cuba, the USSR, and some other Communist and Third World states that have sought to exploit radical currents and capitalize on the tides of revolution.

In examining the various aspects of Soviet-Cuban strategies and tactics in Central America, the following questions will guide the discussion; How and why did the Soviets and Cubans become involved in Central America? What have been their ties with both the more traditional Communist parties as well as with the guerrilla groups of the region? How does Central America fit into the Soviets' overall global strategy? To what degree does Cuba have its own strategy in the region? Are Cuba, the USSR, and their allies competing with the United States for influence in Nicaragua and El Salvador, as they have done for several years in Africa, particularly Angola and Ethiopia? If so, are they prepared to risk further deterioration of U.S.-Soviet relations in order to accomplish this? Are the Soviets motivated simply by the desire to cause problems for the United States or by more complex desires? Do Soviet and Cuban commitments in Angola, Ethiopia, and South Yemen and the Soviet preoccupation with the war in Afghanistan, the crisis in Poland, and the Iran-Iraq war limit their ability to become heavily involved in Nicaragua and El Salvador?

A Historical Perspective

Unlike Cuba, which is an integral part of the Caribbean basin, the Soviet Union has no long-standing cultural, political, or commercial ties with the countries of Central America. It only began to develop such ties in the 1960s. Unlike in Europe and Asia, Soviet interaction in Central and South America has been until recently rather modest. This was primarily because of the area's geographic remoteness and, therefore, marginal importance to the USSR, and to the traditional hegemony there of the United States.

The element of geographic remoteness, however, has been an asset to the Soviet Union in its efforts to become gradually involved in the region from the 1960s onward. Like the United States in Eastern Europe, the USSR does not have a strong imperial record in Central and South America. Like the American image in Eastern Europe, the Soviet image in some Central American countries, particularly Mexico, has been a favorable one in the minds of many people. The Bolsheviks, as "enemies of American imperialism," were viewed after the October Revolution of 1917 as natural allies by revolutionary and patriotic circles in Mexico. Despite U.S. intervention in favor of revolutionary forces in 1916, two years later the military boss of a Mexican region said: "I don't know what socialism is but I am a Bolshevik, like all patriotic Mexicans—The Yankees do not like the Bolsheviks. They are our enemies; therefore the Bolsheviks must be our friends and we must be theirs. We are all Bolsheviks."[5]

Although there was sympathy for the Bolshevik Revolution and the Soviet regime among Central American revolutionary elements, the Soviets were ostracized for several decades by the ruling elites of Central America and handicapped by the absence of diplomatic relations. With the exception of Mexico, Soviet relations with the countries of the Caribbean basin up to the 1960s were limited to relations with their respective Communist parties. In fact, until the Cuban Revolution, the USSR had diplomatic relations with very few Latin American countries, namely, Mexico, Uruguay, and Argentina. Thus firsthand Soviet knowledge of the Caribbean basin was limited primarily to Mexico.

Before World War II, Mexico was the principal center for the dissemination of the publications of the Third International (the Comintern) to Spanish-speaking countries in the region. With the help of Mexican Communist party officials, the Comintern was able to supervise the founding of the Communist party of Guatemala and assist with the founding of other Communist parties in the region. Unlike Cuba, however, where the Communist party was at times a legitimate mass party, the Communist parties of Central America have been illegal, their memberships ranging from several dozen to a few hundred. In Cuba, with Soviet encouragement, the party even entered into a coalition with the government of Fulgencio Batista during the Popular Front era of the 1930s and again briefly in the 1940s. The Central American parties, on the other hand, with the notable exception of the Communist party of Costa Rica, have traditionally operated in a conspiratorial or semilegal fashion. Even in Costa Rica the Communist party is weak and has participated in only a limited fashion in the politics of the nation.

Comintern officials have traditionally discounted the prospects for communism in Central and South America, displaying, like Marx and

Engels, a certain Eurocentric disdain for Latin American people and viewing the countries within the framework of a colonial context in which the United States was firmly in command. Until the victorious Cuban Revolution, the Communist party of the USSR (CPSU) had had only sporadic contacts with the Latin American Communist parties through individual party and Comintern officials. Soviet financial subsidies to these parties have been small, though regular.[6]

There were some unsuccessful insurrections in Central America in which the local Communist parties were involved. One was the 1932 uprising in El Salvador, which was crushed by government forces. In Guatemala in 1953–1954 the nationalist regime of President Jacobo Arbenz attempted a swing toward radicalism with the backing of the Communist party of Guatemala, a small but influential party that was in control of the labor movement. Available evidence suggests that the Soviets provided Arbenz's regime with financial and political support and even shipped 2,000 tons of Czech-manufactured weapons to Arbenz and his supporters. Yet this support was marginal, and there is little evidence pointing to direct Soviet involvement. The meager level of support was in part determined by the Soviets' then limited capabilities and by the fact that the United States treated Guatemala as a major issue, thus warding off further Soviet involvement. With covert support from the Central Intelligence Agency, anti-Arbenz forces launched an invasion from Honduras and soon overthrew the regime.[7]

The turning point in Soviet relations with Central America came in 1959–1960 after the Cuban Revolution. When U.S.-Cuban differences became unbridgeable and the United States withdrew from Cuba, the Soviets, after a period of hesitation, tried to fill the political and economic vacuum thus created. After the Bay of Pigs invasion Nikita Khrushchev and his colleagues painstakingly went about building a major alliance with Cuba. Despite ups and downs and even great tension in 1966–67 resulting from disagreements about strategies in the Third World in general and Latin America in particular, the alliance begun at that time has remained solid.

Initially, at least until the Cuban missile crisis in 1962, the Soviets were quite exuberant about the success of the Cuban Revolution. The revolution spurred Soviet research in Latin American affairs, and in 1961 the Soviet leadership established a new Institute for the Study of Latin America. For a brief time during this period of euphoria Moscow seemed to believe that the Cuban style of revolution could be exported, with Soviet backing, to Central America. Thus in 1959 and 1960 respectively the Communist parties of Nicaragua and El Salvador tried to overthrow their countries' regimes. The Cuban missile crisis, however, which the Chinese describe as the "Caribbean Munich," soon reminded the Soviets of the limits of their power in the area. Khrushchev's decision to remove the Soviet missiles had some repercussions for the USSR in Cuba. In the aftermath, marching militia in Havana chanted *"Nikita mariquita, lo que se da no se quita"* ("Nikita, you little braggart—what one gives, one doesn't take away").[8] Castro naturally was worried at that time about the degree of Soviet commitment to protecting Cuba from the United States. Like many others, he did not realize what would become clear only in the 1970s. Though humiliated, Khrushchev achieved at least one of his objectives during the missile crisis: while agreeing to remove the missiles from Cuba, he was able to extract an American pledge not to topple the revolutionary Cuban regime. In retrospect, considering the success of joint Soviet-Cuban operations in the Third World in the 1970s, it appears that Nikita Khrushchev and not John Kennedy was the winner in the 1962 confrontation.

The resolution of the Cuban missile crisis had a sobering impact on Soviet perceptions of the potential for revolution in the Caribbean basin. So did U.S. intervention in the Dominican Republic in 1965, when the motto "Never a second Cuba" became the imperative for U.S. policy in Latin America. The failure of Cuban-backed guerrilla revolutionaries in the 1960s in Guatemala, Nicaragua, and in South America (Bolivia, Peru, and Venezuela) further ingrained this Soviet attitude, which Castro did not share, at least not immediately. In the 1960s there were indeed profound differences between the Soviets and Cubans about what strategies to pursue in Latin America. As a result of doctrinal differences, Soviet-Cuban relations were in 1966–1967 strained almost to the breaking point. It was not just their pessimistic assessment regarding "revolutionary potential" in the Caribbean basin nor their realistic appraisal of the U.S. response to Soviet-Cuban-supported guerrilla revolution that restrained the Soviets; there were other internal and external factors as well. Because of their preoccupation with the power struggle after Khrushchev's dismissal in 1964, the course of the Vietnam war, and the deepening of the Sino-Soviet dispute, the Soviets in the late 1960s were unwilling and unable to sponsor Castro's call to create "two or three" and even "four or five more Vietnams" for the United States in Latin America. Castro, who was in favor of a "genuine revolutionary road," criticized the USSR for dealing with capitalist governments in Latin America. He even clashed over the issue with pro-Soviet leaders in some Central American parties, such as those of Guatemala and Venezuela, where young, pro-Castroist elements resisted Soviet advice to proceed gradually and with caution.

After the death of Ernesto "Che" Guevara in 1967, however, when most of the guerrillas were wiped out, the Cubans soon came to realize the need for overcoming their differences with Moscow and coordinating their policies with those of the Soviets. As Castro saw it, there were no immediate revolutionary opportunities in Latin America in the 1970s (the case was otherwise in Africa). Thus, he grudgingly approved the Soviet policy of employing diplomatic, commercial, and cultural channels (in addition to revolutionary tactics where feasible) in order to expand relations with "progressive forces" in Latin America. Until very recently, the Soviets and Cubans have been less successful in dispelling traditional anticommunist hostilities from the Caribbean basin than from the South American continent. Besides those in Mexico and Jamaica, prior to the revolution in Nicaragua the USSR had only one other ambassador in the Caribbean region, stationed in Costa Rica. In some other countries of the area, however, the Soviets were able to accredit nonresident ambassadors (Panama and Honduras) and negotiate trade representation (El Salvador).[9] The Soviets were also able to promote better economic cooperation with a friendly Mexico by helping to bring about a new cooperation treaty between Mexico and the Council for Mutual Economic Assistance (COMECON) in 1975.

Soviet diplomatic initiatives in Latin America in the 1970s engendered some political payoffs, helping among other things to invalidate the political and economic blockade of Cuba. Subsequently, Cuba was able to normalize relations with many Latin American countries. Cuba exchanged consuls with Costa Rica, established diplomatic relations with Panama, and extended her influence to the Caribbean countries of Jamaica, Guyana, Barbados, Trinidad, and Tobago.

It is misleading to suggest, because of these trends, that the USSR and Cuba had given up the notion of supporting revolutionary movements in the region. Although their posture was realistic, it was not one of acquiescence. Neither the Soviets nor the Cubans entirely renounced the efficacy of revolution as a means for overthrowing unfriendly, anticommunist governments. In the mid-1970s, when conditions were not ripe for revolution in Latin America, the Soviets and Cubans were busy supporting their allies elsewhere, particularly Africa. This situation changed dramatically with the successful revolution in Nicaragua in 1979, and the upswing in guerrilla warfare in El Salvador in 1980.

The USSR and Central America: A Strategic Perspective

The behavior of the Soviets and Cubans in the Third World is not motivated solely by their respective historical experiences and available opportunism. Both the USSR and Cuba have developed a coherent strategic vision with regard to the Third World. Theirs is an integrated, though flexible, plan of action aimed at achieving specific long-term objectives. What are they, and how does Central America figure in them? As far as Soviet strategy is concerned, these are four distinct components that can be verified with Soviet sources: ideology, politics, security, and economics. In terms of ideology the Soviet objective is to create Marxist-Leninist regimes in the Third World (though in the long run this does not always work to the benefit of the USSR, as was the case with China). While it is misleading to assume that the Soviets support revolutionary political movements in the Third World primarily because of claimed unselfishness and ideological affinity with such movements, ideology cannot be discounted.

The Soviets believe that at least some radical Third World nations will someday embark on a path toward truly Socialist development, as Cuba did in the 1970s. Meanwhile, because of Moscow's experience in the 1960s and 1970s—when revolutionary or radical regimes were overthrown and/or more moderate regimes substantially reduced the Soviet presence and influence in the countries in question—the Soviets feel impelled to exercise caution and prudence in making commitments to the variety of Socialist and would-be Socialist regimes in developing countries.

Indeed, with few exceptions, the Soviets in the early 1980s hardly view the radical regimes of the Third World as truly Marxist-Leninist in the Soviet understanding of the term. Thus Soviet officials in the Central Committee responsible for dealing with Third World revolutionary regimes refer to them as "progressive," "anti-imperialist," "revolutionary-democratic," and at most (when referring to Angola and Ethiopia) as having a "socialist orientation" and pursuing "noncapitalist" (but *not* "socialist") development. Soviet experts on Latin America, such as M. F. Kudachkin, who is responsible for the Latin American section of the Central Committee of the CPSU, appreciate the diversity and unevenness of economic and political development in Latin America and recognize that the region holds a special place in the Third World because of its success in throwing off the Spanish colonial yoke in the nineteenth century, and because, unlike in Africa and most of Asia, capitalism has reached a high state of development in part of Latin America—particularly Argentina and Chile and, to a certain degree, Mexico.[10] In these countries there also exist a significant working class and in Mexico and Chile (before the anti-Allende coup) large Communist parties. In the Soviet view the situation in the Caribbean basin is different, not only because of a lower level of capitalist development, but also, as stressed, because of a weak Communist movement and more pervasive U.S. hegemony.

The Marxist inclination of new regimes in such countries as Nicaragua and Grenada, however, cannot but be appreciated and applauded by the Soviets. Because of it they are better able to justify to Soviet domestic constituencies the aid extended to these countries. By the same token, as demonstrated by Jerry Hough, there exists an evolving debate among Soviet experts about the prospects of revolution in Latin America.[11]

The USSR also has political objectives in the Third World. These appear to be primarily the fomentation and furtherance of "progressive" anti-American and anti-Chinese regimes. By exploiting growing anti-American currents, the Soviets hope to win influence at U.S. expense without projecting direct military power. They also try to counter the activity of another major rival, China, particularly in such areas of the Third World as Asia, East Africa, and the Middle East; China's influence in Latin America is minimal. Though some Marxist groups in the region have identified with Maoism, most of the Communist parties have taken a pro-Soviet position in the Sino-Soviet conflict, identifying Maoism with Trotskyism and adventurism.

Since the Soviets view Central America as being the "strategic rear" of the United States,[12] until recently they have exercised caution in forming policy regarding the region. However, from the Cuban Revolution onward they have believed the Monroe Doctrine to be no longer viable in Central America. Already in 1960, Khrushchev declared that "the Monroe Doctrine has outlived its times." U.S. acceptance of the Cuban Revolution was proof that the Monroe Doctrine had died "a natural death."[13] In spite of this new attitude, Soviet strategy in Central America during the last two decades has been refined and subtle. It provides for revolutionary transformation that can use violent methods and/or follow a "peaceful road," that is, a prolonged political process during which anti-American "progressive forces" build national coalitions to challenge U.S. hegemony. As pointed out in the Havana Declaration adopted at the 1975 regional conference of Latin American and Caribbean Communist parties:

> The utilization of all legal possibilities is an indispensable obligation of the anti-imperialist forces. . . . Revolutionaries are not the first to resort to violence. But it is the right and duty of all revolutionary forces to be ready to answer counter-revolutionary violence with revolutionary violence.[14]

The formulation of Soviet strategy in the 1960s was affected significantly by the Soviet-Cuban dialogue and even by Soviet-Cuban disputes. In this period, the Cubans decided to promote revolution when the Organization of American States undertook sanctions against them. They favored and originally even insisted on Soviet-Cuban support of revolutionary guerrilla movements in Latin American countries, with the exception of such friendly states as Mexico. By adhering to Che's and Regis Debray's concept of guerrilla-peasantry insurgency (see Debray's *Revolution in the Revolution?*), Castro's strategy in Central America in the 1960s contradicted and even challenged the Soviet doctrine allowing for diversified roads to socialism. Yet, as Herbert Dinerstein notes, in the late 1960s the Soviets and Cubans arrived at a kind of compromise strategy by making mutual concessions. Thus, the Soviets approved support for guerrilla activities in some Latin American countries with extremely pro-American and anti-Communist regimes, while the Cubans gave their blessing to the pursuit of diplomacy with others.[15] Overall, however, the Cubans basically accepted the Soviets' more gradual and realistic "anti-imperialist" strategy.

Thus in the 1970s diplomatic channels were pursued in Panama (where the late Omar Torrijo Herrera's dictatorial yet "progressive" regime was avidly courted by the Cubans and Soviets), in Costa Rica to a certain degree, and even more so in Mexico—both the latter being (in the Soviet view) liberal-democratic regimes. In the Caribbean proper, the Cubans courted the "progressive" Jamaican regime of Michael Manley. Available evidence suggests that the Soviets and Cubans have dissuaded the Communist parties and other leftist groups from trying to overthrow these regimes, encouraging them rather to expand their influence and work toward the greater goal of building "anti-imperialist" coalitions.

The Soviet and Cuban strategy in Central American countries having pro-American, anti-Communist regimes—that is, Nicaragua, El Salvador, Guatemala, and Honduras—has been to encourage revolutionary struggle though not necessarily by fostering terrorism. In the late 1970s more emphasis was placed on revolutionary struggle than on peaceful coexistence. Yet even at that time the party's role was designated as one of gradual coalition-building among all revolutionary forces and as the leader of their struggle (inasmuch as possible). In the Soviet view the "correlation of forces" in the 1970s was shifting on a worldwide scale because of the U.S. defeat in Vietnam. In Central America, this was manifested in a growing wave of radical anti-U.S. sentiment. This and the Soviets' greater military and economic capabilities paved the way for a more mature, assertive globalism in the Third World. Moreover, the 1973 ouster of Allende in Chile illustrated that peaceful and revolutionary strategies could not be mutually exclusive. At the same time, however, it seemed to increase Soviet doubts about the feasibility of a "peaceful path" toward socialism in Latin America.[16]

Another important component of the Soviet strategic vision regarding Central America and the Caribbean is security concerns. Soviet security objectives in the region fit into the Soviets' overall "anti-imperialist" strategy in the Third World. This strategy includes gradually securing access to and maintaining naval and air facilities in the basin so as to better project Soviet influence, while undermining the influence of the West—particularly the United States and its allies. The basin—whose confines have grown out of a geopolitical concept—constitutes a key transit zone for oil and vital raw materials enroute from Guatemala, Venezuela, and the Caribbean islands to the United States, as well as for all seagoing vessels approaching the Panama Canal. In an extreme case, such as during wartime, a substantial Soviet military presence in the basin would endanger logistic support for U.S. allies in Europe and the delivery of oil and other strategic materials to the United States. During such times Cuba, though highly vulnerable, nevertheless might serve as a forward submarine base. The Soviets recognize the strategic importance of the basin and that it is an area of special security concern for the United States, much as Eastern Europe is for them. Soviet writers recognize that in military-strategic terms, the Caribbean is a sort of hinterland on whose stability freedom of U.S. action in other parts of the globe depends.[17] Thus the Soviets remained passive throughout U.S. intervention in the Dominican Republic in 1965 and the U.S.-supported anti-Allende coup in Chile in 1973. Likewise the United States took no action during the Soviet interventions in Hungary in 1956 and Czechoslovakia in 1968. So far Soviet military presence in the region is limited by a lack of facilities necessary for permanent deployment. At present, the Soviets do not have sufficient strength in the region to be able to disrupt the flow of oil to the United States, a scenario feared by some analysts. Moreover, they would probably attempt such action only in case of all-out war.

Despite these limitations, the Soviets were able to establish a military presence in Cuba after 1961 that has grown considerably in the past two decades. As of the present, thanks to Soviet financial and advanced technical assistance, the Soviets are permitted to use modern docking facilities, (potential) submarine facilities in Cienfuegos, air facilities for reconnaissance aircraft, satellite stations, and sophisticated intelligence facilities for monitoring U.S. satellite and microwave conversations and also NATO advanced weapons testing in the Atlantic. Since 1978, Soviet pilots have been flying MIG-27s on patrol missions in Cuba while Cuban pilots serve in Africa. Meanwhile, Soviet TU-95s conduct regular reconnaissance missions monitoring U.S. naval activities in the Atlantic. Cuba is also a center for close Soviet-Cuban coordination in gathering intelligence information in the basin itself.

Though proceeding with caution, the Soviets would undoubtedly like to see their military presence in the Caribbean basin expanded. This has been suggested by the increasing number of Soviet submarine visits to Cuba since 1969, an indication of Soviet plans to make permanent use of the facilities at Cienfuegos, which were partly shelved in 1970 because of vociferous U.S. protests. The Soviets are trying to establish other strategic footholds in the area. In revolutionary Grenada, for instance, Soviet equipment and financial assistance from the USSR and Libya have enabled the Cubans to commence building a new international airport capable of handling all types of jet aircraft, including the Soviet Backfire bomber. As the Cubans work to build a revolutionary army the Soviets assist in developing and promoting a fishing industry on Grenada. After Commander-in-Chief of the Soviet Navy Fleet Admiral Sergei Gorshkov's visit to Grenada in 1980, there were unconfirmed reports about the Soviet intention to build naval facilities there as well.[18] The Soviets may be seeking similar facilities in Nicaragua.

Up to the present time, given the Soviets' awareness of the basin's paramount importance to the United States, Soviet naval activities in the area seem to have been designed to establish the legitimacy of a Soviet naval presence with regular visits by warships. There have been twenty such visits to the Caribbean in the last twenty years. During the visit in April 1981, the group included a cruiser equipped to carry small nuclear weapons. The Soviets deploy not only warships, however, but also intelligence, fishing, and merchant vessels. The Soviets have also sponsored joint Soviet-Cuban marine cruises for the purpose of conducting fishery and oceanographic research as well as gathering and establishing future channels of information. Soviet naval deployment is designed to help encourage long-term political and economic transformation of the area along the lines of what Gorshkov refers to as "progressive changes" offshore. In this respect the security, political, and economic aspects of Soviet strategy in the region are mutually complementary, since Soviet naval visits to the Caribbean are facilitated by the establishment of diplomatic and economic relations. As the Soviets see it, "progressive changes" offshore make the environment more amenable to Soviet interests in the region.

Economic calculations also play a role in Soviet strategies in Central America. Soviet trade and investment in the region, though growing, are limited primarily to Costa Rica, where the Soviets are apparently running a large deficit, as they are everywhere else in Latin America. Since they generally have to pay for imports in hard currency, it seems the Soviets would not tend to view Central America as a priority interest in strictly economic terms. Soon, however, one can expect the Soviets to establish regular trade relations with the new regime in Nicaragua.

There is little doubt, however, that the discovery of natural resources—particularly in Guatemala, Mexico, and the Caribbean proper—have spurred increasing interest in the basin. Thus the Soviets are working with the Mexicans on long-term cooperation in oil matters and may be interested in similar cooperation with other oil producers in the region. (Mexico has also agreed to supply crude oil to Cuba, assist with Cuba's oil exploration efforts, and help expand Cuban oil-refining facilities.) Soviet-bloc trade and economic aid to such "progressive regimes" as the one in Nicaragua encourage the Soviets' overall "anti-imperialist" strategy in the area. In the long run, the Soviets may calculate, Central America may offer a more lucrative potential for COMECON trade than do many of the African and Asian countries now courted by the Soviets. Cuba, since 1972 a full COMECON member, can play a key role in this effort. The Soviets view Cuba as a useful instrument in restructuring the economic base of the Caribbean basin by reducing the preponderance of U.S.-based multinational corporations. Thus the Soviets applauded Cuba's important role in founding the Caribbean Free Trade Association (CARIFTA) and the Latin American Economic System (SELA) cosponsored by Mexico and Venezuela. In 1975, with Cuban help, COMECON was able to work out a special agreement with Mexico, which may be followed in the not too distant future by a similar agreement with Nicaragua.

Cuba and Central America: A Strategic Perspective

There are two extreme views regarding the Soviet-Cuban alliance in the Third World. The first views Cuba as a surrogate of the USSR, simply implementing Soviet orders. The second depicts Cuba as an almost totally unconstrained, autonomous actor, having its own independent strategic vision. As I have argued elsewhere, Cuba is neither of these.[19] The view that Cuban policy is necessarily subservient to that of the USSR is unsophisticated and obscures the existence of mutual constraints and leverages in the alliance. While the USSR plays the dominant role and exercises great influence upon Cuban foreign policy, Cuba in turn provides certain inputs into Soviet decisionmaking regarding the Third World. The degree of Cuban autonomy in the Third World seems to vary according to the area of involvement. Whereas in Africa Cuba appears to enjoy only a small degree of relative autonomy, in the Caribbean basin Cuba's autonomy seems to be significant.

Even Soviet African policy, however, has been dependent to some extent on the willingness of Fidel Castro and his colleagues to provide ground forces for joint enterprises in Africa. In Angola and Ethiopia, unlike Afghanistan, the Soviets were cautious about committing their own troops in direct military fashion. The use of Soviet combat units might have elicited a firmer response from the United States, with resulting detrimental consequences for the USSR. Furthermore, the similarity of the physical environment of Africa, particularly Angola, to that of Cuba and the presence in the Cuban forces of a substantial number of blacks and mulattos, who share a racial and cultural affinity with the black Africans, make the Cubans much more suitable for the task than the Soviets. Soviet strategic decisions regarding the Third World thus reflect, at least marginally, Cuba's desire to support revolutionary operations there and its willingness to supply the necessary manpower. Castro, who is currently president of the nonaligned movement, has exercised some influence on the USSR both directly (by consulting with Soviet leaders) and indirectly (by serving as a broker between Soviet and Third World leaders, many of whom admire Castro's courage, self-confidence, and personal charm). As in Africa, Castro can serve as a useful mediator between the USSR and the Central American leaders since he is viewed by many radicals and revolutionaries in the region, if not as a second Bolivar—a modern continental liberator, then at least as a type of new *caudillo socialista* worthy of being emulated and followed.[20]

Although Castro's foreign policy cannot be viewed as totally subservient to that of the USSR, it would be far-fetched to think of Cuba as an independent or even semi-independent actor. Cuba's emergence as a major player in the Third World in the 1970s and early 1980s has been possible mainly because of growing Soviet military and economic power and Soviet willingness to exploit changes in the international system. More specifically, Cuban ascendancy in the Third World and particularly Africa and the Middle East in the 1970s and more recently in the Caribbean basin has been possible because of Soviet military-strategic cover and Cuba's expectation that Soviet support and protection will be forthcoming in the event of an attack on the island. Moreover, the Soviets subsidize the Cuban economy with an estimated $7 million per day. Without this help, Cuba's faltering economy could never have absorbed the cost of the military interventions in Africa. Certainly in Africa the major portion of these expenses has been picked up by the Soviets or by the recipient countries, who in turn have received the money from the USSR. The basic subordination of Cuban foreign policy to that of the Soviet Union seemed to be acknowledged at the First Cuban Party Congress of December 1975.[21] Another important factor suggesting Soviet preponderance in the Soviet-Cuban alliance is the growing Soviet military, security, and economic presence in Cuba in the 1970s. At the onset of the 1980s there were 2,700 Soviet soldiers in Cuba as well as several thousand intelligence personnel, technicians, and other specialists. In addition to protecting sophisticated communications facilities, the Soviets train the Cuban armed forces.

Cuba's dependence on the USSR in carrying out military and security operations in Africa was first demonstrated during the Angolan crisis of 1975–1976. The view that the Soviet role was confined primarily to the supply of weaponry is mistaken. It is true that, because of initial uncertainties regarding the U.S. response, the Soviets were cautious about committing themselves in direct military fashion in Angola. Nevertheless, in early November 1975 they took over the Cuban air- and sea-lift, transforming the Angolan campaign into a massive operation during which both the Soviet air force and the Soviet Navy were operationally active. A small yet effective Soviet naval task force provided physical and psychological support to the Cuban combat troops, protected the Cuban staging areas against local threats, served as a strategic cover for established sea and air communications, and worked as a deterrent against possible U.S. naval deployment. It is quite possible that if Moscow had not become so involved in Angola and if the South Africans had been encouraged actively by the United States to continue their blitz campaigns, the Cubans would have been defeated.

The alliance between the Soviets and Cubans was even tighter in the case of the intervention in Ethiopia in 1977, where four Soviet generals ran the entire operation from start to finish. While during the original stage of the operation in Angola the Cubans temporarily functioned independently, Cuba functioned as a very subordinate actor, if not a Soviet proxy, during the conflict in the Ogaden between Somalia and Ethiopia. Clearly the Soviet leadership determines the limits of Cuban options in Africa. Although Cuba could choose *not* to get involved in a large-scale military operation with the USSR (the war in Eritrea), Cuba could not undertake a substantial military operation not approved of or supported by the Soviets. Cuba is also highly vulnerable to Soviet politico-economic coercion, which the Soviet leaders used to their advantage in the late 1960s, when they slowed down the supply of oil and arms to Cuba to make Castro more amenable to the subtleties of Soviet "anti-imperialist" strategy. The Soviets are likely to use this leverage again should the need arise.

There exists a basic agreement between Cuba and the USSR regarding the joint coordination and implementation of strategy so as to promote Soviet global interests and policies. Some Cuban strategic priorities, however, are not necessarily identical with those of the

Soviets. As a result, there are often subtle and not so subtle emphases and nuances that differentiate Soviet and Cuban policies. This is more true in the Caribbean basin than in Africa. Although the basin is of marginal geopolitical importance to the USSR, its importance is paramount to Cuba. The USSR is a superpower with global interests, responsibilities, and capabilities; Cuba, not withstanding its copious rhetoric, is basically a regional power.

What are the perceived ideological, political, security, and economic payoffs that Cuba expects to receive for helping to promote a joint anti-imperialist strategy? Though Castro has never been renowned for his theoretical conceptualization of Marxism-Leninism, it seems that his ideological commitment to the revolutionaries in Africa and Central America has been more genuine than that of the USSR. The Cuban Revolution is young in comparison with the Soviets' 1917 October Revolution. Soviet strategic priorities are now forged under the shadow of Central Committee bureaucrats, whereas Cuban strategic vision arose out of the revolutionary was against Batista. Cuba maintains a strong ideological affinity with the Third World nations that has been conditioned by common Latin and African ancestries, colonial legacies, and exploitation by outside powers resulting in wounded national sentiments. Thus, in Castro's words, Cuban support of revolution comes as a natural "result of our principles, our convictions, and our own blood."[22] Castro, himself a sort of Red Robin Hood, has been a vehement and long-standing supporter of various revolutionary movements and a close friend of the leaders who have spearheaded them. Cuban support of revolutionary groups in Africa and Latin America has been consistent in most cases since 1960, without the ups and downs characteristic of Soviet support for some of these organizations.

The joint strategies pursued in Central America are important to Castro's regime for reasons other than ideology and cultural affinity. Though more ideologically motivated than the Soviets, Cuba has already witnessed the passing of an initial revolutionary exuberance and enthusiasm (aptly dubbed "socialism with the *pachanga*" [a Cuban dance] by Che Guevara). Today Castro has some very pragmatic security, political, and economic interests in pursuing a joint anti-imperialist strategy with the USSR. His objective in being closely associated with the USSR is to ensure the survival of the Cuban Revolution, preserve Cuba's political independence, and secure further security guarantees for his state in the face of continuous U.S. hostility. Further, Castro's regime hopes to rebuild bridges to Central American countries, all of which supported the expulsion of Cuba from the Organization of American States in 1962.

In political terms, Castro wants now, more than ever, to increase the prestige and influence of his regime in the Third World. Since the unpopular Soviet invasion of Afghanistan, many Third World countries have become less willing to accept Castro as leader of the nonaligned world and defender of progressive Third World regimes. They realize that "natural alliance" with the USSR, as advocated by Castro, can also lead to "unnatural death," as in the case of Afghan President H. Amin. Indeed, Afghanistan has had a detrimental political effect on Cuba's standing in the Third World and on Castro's ambitions about refurbishing the prestige of his regime and his personal image as recognized leader of the nonaligned movement. Proof of this was the withdrawal of support by the nonaligned nations for the election of Cuba, and the subsequent selection of Mexico, as Latin America's nonpermanent representative to the United Nations Security Council in 1980. It is not surprising, given this turn of events, that Cuba voted against the UN resolution condemning the USSR while at the same time signaling frustration over Soviet policies in Afghanistan and making little effort to support or defend the Soviet rationale for the invasion. The Cuban leadership, obviously displeased with the invasion, decided, as in the case of the Czechoslovak invasion of 1968, to give only qualified support to the USSR. Unlike other Soviet allies, the Cubans did not object to the United Nations' right to deal with the Afghan question. This is a good illustration of Cuba's dilemma as both titular leader of the nonaligned movement and Soviet ally. Cuban aid to Nicaragua and support of the rebels in El Salvador in 1980–1981 have provided Castro with new opportunities for improving his image as an independent and fearless defender of revolution in the Third World.

Cuba also receives economic payoffs in the Caribbean basin itself for its pursuit of an "anti-imperialist" strategy. Though economic relations with the Caribbean and Central American countries are modest, Cuban leaders, like their Soviet counterparts, may hope for more substantial relations in the future, similar to those now in effect with Mexico.

More important than the promise of future dividends are the actual economic payoffs awarded to Cuba for her support of "anti-imperialist" strategies. Because Cuban willingness to deploy regular troops in Africa and support the revolutionary forces in Nicaragua and El Salvador became indispensable to the implementation of Soviet "anti-imperialist" strategy in those regions, Cuba gained the status of a privileged ally and was able to insist on adjustments in Soviet-Cuban economic relations, though these are difficult to specify. Thus in the aftermath of the invasion of Angola in 1975, and again after the intervention in Ethiopia in 1978, the Cubans obtained even more favorable agreements from the USSR. This and Cuban support for the Nicaraguan Revolution and the guerrillas in El Salvador may have ensured continuation into the 1980s of Soviet subsidies of Cuban sugar and nickel production and of prices paid for petroleum. One source estimates that the USSR paid $0.44 a pound for Cuban sugar when the world market price for this commodity was about $0.10. (In 1979 alone Cuba sold four million tons of sugar to the USSR.) The price Cuba pays for oil is estimated to be about half that prevailing on the world market.[23]

One can speculate that Castro is expecting that new instances of his country's "internationalism" in El Salvador will be rewarded, as previously in Africa and Nicaragua, by increased economic aid from the USSR such as a rescheduling of the repayment of the enormous Cuban debt, new credits, and an increase in commerce with the USSR. The USSR ensures a continuously stable market for a large part of Cuban output. It is noteworthy that the trade agreement signed in Moscow during the Cuban-orchestrated arms transfer to El Salvador provides for trade between Cuba and the USSR in 1980–1985 amounting to 30 billion rubles—a significant increase over the trade level of 1976–1980. The USSR has apparently pledged to supply all Cuba's oil during this period. To further facilitate the solution to Cuba's energy problem, the Soviets plan to build a nuclear power plant in Cuba from 1981–1986.

Another payoff for Cuban assistance in implementing the USSR's Third World policies has been the Soviet modernization of Cuba's armed forces with sophisticated weaponry. The Cuban forces (190,000 men and 60,000 reservists) are now more formidable than any other in the basin, including those of Mexico. In the whole of Latin America they are second in size only to the armed forces of Brazil. Of the USSR's Warsaw Pact allies, only Poland, which is four times larger than Cuba, has greater forces. Thanks to Soviet-supplied MiG-21s and MiG-23s, Cuba has the best-equipped air force in Latin America. Moreover, the Soviets have helped to build a small but very modern and efficient Cuban coastal navy and merchant fleet. In the last few years, they have equipped the Cubans with seven guided-missile patrol boats, more than a dozen Turya-class patrol boats, several landing craft, one Foxtrot and one Whiskey-class submarine, with another expected. The Cuban army meanwhile has been equipped with T-62 tanks of Soviet origin. The Soviet arms transfer to Cuba is relatively advanced in the overall context of the Soviet arms aid program.

In spite of various past disagreements and existing differences, the Soviets and Cubans in the 1970s discovered that their strategies in the Third World, which were a subject of disagreement in the 1960s, were inexorably linked. Moscow has made enormous ideological, political, economic, and security investments in Cuba. To turn its back on Castro's regime now would seriously undermine Soviet strategies in Africa and in Central America. Likewise, Soviet strategic, economic, and political support are essential to Cuba. Cuba is too dependent on the USSR to try to alter the relationship and, furthermore, is still too committed to revolutionary change to do so.

Soviet and Cuban Tactics: The Nicaraguan Revolution

For the jubilant Soviets and Cubans, the triumph of the Sandinistas in Nicaragua in 1979 signaled an important juncture in the revolutionary transformation of the Caribbean basin, equal in importance only to the victory of the Fidelistas in Cuba twenty years earlier. In both cases the United States was perceived by the Soviets as suffering humiliating political defeat. In the view of such Soviet officials as Deputy Head of the International Department of the Central Committee V. Zagladin, the Nicaraguan Revolution was one of the "starlets" of the anti-imperialist movement in Latin America. Zagladin, at least implicitly, has tried to link the "victory of Nicaragua" with Soviet–Cuban-supported, anti-imperialist strategy and has expressed the hope that Nicaragua will "have its continuators."[24] As during the Allende period of 1971–1973, revolutionary change in Latin America has become a favorite topic in Moscow.

Was the triumph in Nicaragua indeed the result of coordinated Soviet-Cuban strategies and tactics in Central America, or more the result of a complex interplay of internal and regional as well as external forces? Like the Cuban Revolution in 1959, the revolution in Nicaragua was conditioned by various internal forces: the unpopularity of the Somoza regime, underdevelopment, unequal distribution of wealth, enormous poverty, and other deep social and economic cleavages. Nicaragua has been dominated for a long time by military dictators *(caudillos)*, Anastasio "Tacho" Somoza (1936–1956) and his son Anastasio "Tachito" Somoza (1967–1979) being the most recent. Also, the great powers have traditionally played a role in national policymaking.[25] The fact that Nicaragua holds a promising site for an interocean canal and lies in close proximity to the existing Panama Canal has caused Nicaragua's foreign policy to be of some concern to the United States. Thus U.S. strategic interests were largely the motivating force behind the U.S. intervention in 1912 and in 1927 when, except for a brief interlude from 1926–1927 until 1933, Nicaragua was virtually a U.S. protectorate.

U.S. interventionism in Nicaragua gave rise to Yankeephobia characterized by resentment of and even violent resistance to the United States. The symbol of this resistance in 1927–1933 was Augusto César

Sandino who, like Castro in the 1950s, was a staunch radical nationalist and opposed both the corrupt dictatorship in his country and what he saw as U.S. interference. Though exalted as an "anti-imperialist" hero by the Soviet press in the early 1980s, in the 1930s the Soviets and Comintern denounced his "rebel bands." Although the USSR condemned the U.S. intervention of 1927, the Soviets failed to display much admiration for Sandino and his original Sandinistas. Though Sandino had cooperated with the Communists in the 1920s, he later denounced their activities. After the withdrawal of U.S. troops from Nicaragua, Sandino actually made peace with the Nicaraguan government. The Comintern meanwhile accused him of "capitulation . . . over to the side of the counter-revolutionary government."[26]

Communism in Nicaragua, as elsewhere in Central America, traditionally has been a weak movement. In the last two decades, there have been three Marxist parties in Nicaragua, all of them illegal and clandestine, or semiclandestine groups: a very small Maoist group, the anti-Soviet Communist party of Nicaragua, and the pro-Soviet Socialist party of Nicaragua (PSN), a semiclandestine organization founded in 1937 of never more than 250 members. Though some members of the PSN had links with the Sandinistas in the 1960s and 1970s, the PSN was not the main force behind the Revolution. The Sandinista National Liberation Front (FSLN) was founded in 1961 by radical, left-leaning nationalists led by Carlos Fonseca Amador, who, though not a Communist, had visited the USSR in 1957. The Sandinistas, from the very beginning inspired and supported by Castro, tried to overthrow the Somoza regime but were soon crushed by the National Guard in 1961. In time the FSLN evolved into a conglomerate of heterogeneous Marxist and non-Marxist elements united under an anti-Somoza banner, yet still separate from the PSN. Though Amador died later while fighting Somoza, the Sandinistas continued their struggle in the 1970s, with only limited support from the USSR and Cuba. (Cuba actually sent material aid to the Somoza regime following the earthquake in 1972.) Although the revolutionary struggle in Nicaragua coincided with Soviet-Cuban "anti-imperialist" strategy, geographic remoteness and general pessimism about the prospects for revolution in Latin America following the anti-Allende coup of 1973 caused the Cubans and Soviets to be rather pessimistic about the prospects of the Sandinista struggle. Additional probable reasons for the Soviets' low-key support up to 1979 were Soviet and Cuban military involvement in Angola, Ethiopia, and elsewhere in the Third World as well as events in Afghanistan, all of which occupied the greater part of Soviet attention from 1975 to 1979. Soviet support of the FSLN continued to be modest even as of 1978, when a unified FSLN directorate brought together in one coalition all guerrilla factions, whose struggle had begun to assume a genuinely revolutionary character. Even during this high point the PSN's role was limited mainly to propaganda support, clandestine radio broadcasts, and some financial aid.

Although by 1978 the Soviets probably knew about Somoza's critical situation, they might have thought that President Carter, despite his human rights rhetoric, would not let Somoza fall. Nevertheless, in the 1970s the Cubans, with Soviet blessing and perhaps even financial help, were training the FSLN in Cuba and providing it with arms (primarily rifles) and money.[27] However, the FSLN was securing weapons from elsewhere as well. Athough we do not have enough evidence at this time to suggest that the Soviets and Cubans coordinated arms transfers for the Sandinistas, as they did for the guerrillas in El Salvador in 1980, we do know that some weapons flowed from Cuba to the FSLN via such Third World countries as Costa Rica and Panama. We also know that the FSLN used weapons coming from Venezuela, Panama, the Middle East, and, as the Sandinistas maintain, Mafia sources in the United States and Europe. Though many guerrillas were trained in Cuba, there is no evidence to the effect that Cubans were involved in command and control functions for the Sandinistas prior to early 1979. Though the Cuban factor was important, it was not crucial. The Sandinistas also received active political, economic, and moral support from various groups in Venezuela, Panama, and Mexico, and found sanctuaries and a place to train on the territory of democratic Costa Rica. The Costa Rican capital of San José was the site of the FSLN government in exile. Leftists from other Central American countries, such as the Victoriano Lorenzo Brigade from Panama and various groups from Costa Rica, fought alongside FSLN forces in Nicaragua.[28]

The Cubans and particularly the Soviets exercised considerable caution prior to the Sandinista victory of 1979. Indeed, the Soviets published few analyses of the Nicaraguan struggle and only in 1978 did the Soviets and Cubans begin to reassess the chances for a successful revolution. In early 1979 the Cubans finally decided to set up intelligence headquarters in Costa Rica to monitor the anti-Somoza struggle and to send military personnel to advise the Sandinistas. Within several months of the Sandinistas' assumption of power on July 19, 1979, Castro sent a large number of Cuban specialists to help with the reconstruction of Nicaragua: 1,200 teachers, 250 doctors and health personnel, technicians, some security and propaganda experts, and a large number of construction workers to build a road uniting Nicaragua's east and west. At the same time Castro reportedly cautioned the Sandinistas not to push their socialist program too far or too fast. The Cubans perceived the victory of the Sandinistas as a great opportunity for them to pursue their own strategic objectives in Nicaragua as well as in other countries of the region. Unlike in the 1960s, the risks of Cuban involvement seemed to be low, both because of apparent U.S. inability to intervene and because the U.S. basically opposed Somoza and promptly recognized the Sandinistas.

In contrast to the Cubans, the Soviets, who opened an embassy in Nicaragua in October 1979, were typically guarded in their willingness to make commitments to the new Sandinista regime, as they were originally in 1959 in Cuba. The only Soviet initiative at this time was the decision to provide a variety of emergency donations in the weeks following the overthrow of Somoza. These were much smaller, however, than U.S., Mexican, and Venezuelan donations and deliveries during this period. Only after a gradual reassessment of their options did the Soviets decide to become more assertive in Nicaragua. This "new chapter," as the Soviets called it, commenced in March 1980 during the first high-level visit of Sandinistas to the USSR since the overthrow of the dictator Somoza.[29] Subsequently the Soviets concluded a variety of economic, technical, and trade agreements, mainly in the areas of fishing and marine affairs, water power resources, mining and geological surveys, communications and air traffic. The FSLN and the CPSU also agreed on future party-to-party contracts, apparently along the same lines pursued by the Soviets with other revolutionary organizations—such as the regimes in Angola and Ethiopia—whom they consider reliable, long-term partners. By the spring of 1981 the Soviets, Cubans, and East Europeans (particularly the East Germans and Bulgarians) concluded with Nicaragua several other new related agreements for economic aid (including the donation of 20,000 tons of wheat), scientific and cultural cooperation, and technical assistance in telecommunications, agriculture, transportation, and other fields. There were also signs of some sort of future military cooperation, as evidenced by the Soviet loan or gift of a few helicopters to the FSLN, who were trained how to use them by Soviet pilots, and East Germany's credit sale to the FSLN of 800 military trucks. As the crisis in neighboring El Salvador began to mount in late 1980, there were also unconfirmed reports about the influx into Nicaragua of additional Cuban military officials (who were supposedly running training camps) and about the arms transfer of tanks and helicopters, possibly for use in El Salvador. Western reports that the Soviets were building naval facilities in Nicaragua were denied by Soviet ambassador to Nicaragua, G. Schliapnikov. The Nicaraguan government, however, has confirmed that the Soviets' floating workshop, designed for repairing ships, will be operating off the Pacific coast of Nicaragua.[30]

Soviet and Cuban Tactics in El Salvador

How do Soviet and Cuban perceptions of the crisis in Nicaragua (before the overthrow of Somoza) and the ongoing crisis in neighboring El Salvador compare? What were the similarities and differences in Soviet and Cuban tactics with regard to these two countries? The victory of the Sandinistas in Nicaragua prompted the Soviets to anticipate a chain reaction of leftist upheavals and revolutions throughout Central America. Thus, in an important speech on October 20, 1980, candidate Politburo member and a secretary of the Central Committee of the CPSU B. Ponomarev added the countries of Central America to the list of states in Africa and Asia that could be expected to undergo revolutionary changes of "a socialist orientation." Ponomarev described the revolution in Nicaragua as a "major success" and compared it with the revolutions in Angola and Ethiopia.[31] President of the Soviet Association of Friendship with Latin American Countries Professor Viktor Volski assessed the Nicaraguan Revolution as a "triumph for the people of Latin America and the Caribbean" and a "model for all peoples fighting for liberation."[32]

After Nicaragua, the Central American country singled out by Soviet writers as being most pregnant with revolutionary opportunities was of course El Salvador, which the Soviets see as occupying "an important strategic position in the region."[33] Like Nicaragua, El Salvador has a strong heritage of instability caused by a rigid class structure, unequal distribution of wealth, and 30 percent or more unemployment. In El Salvador, the smallest yet most densely populated country in Latin America (400 people per square mile), the socioeconomic life has been dominated by an oligarchy of wealthy families while military strongmen have run the politics of the country.

In El Salvador, as in Nicaragua, the Communist movement has been very weak. The pro-Soviet Communist party in El Salvador (PCES) was founded in 1930 and was actively involved in a massive peasant insurrection in 1932 which was crushed by the military and resulted in 30,000 deaths. Since that time, the PCES has been an illegal, clandestine organization. As late as 1979, it had only 225 members. In the 1960s and 1970s, however, the PCES, like the PSN, had to compete with more radical and relatively larger groups such as the Maoist-leaning People's Revolutionary Army (ERP), the Trotskyite Popular Liberation Forces (FPL), and other groups. The latter organizations, and not the miniscule PCES, were responsible for the organized terrorism and guerrilla activities of the 1970s. In fact, with Soviet blessings the well-known secretary-general of the PCES, Shafik Jorge Handal, published a severe critique of these groups in the Soviet journal *Latinskaia amerika* in early 1979, *before* the fall of Somoza. He accused them of violence and nihilism.[34] Unlike those in Nicaragua, the various guerrilla factions have not yet united, in spite of rhetoric to the contrary. In El Salvador there is no Sandinista legacy. In contrast to the meager support given the Nicaraguan party, the Soviets have given strong public support to the PCES, particularly its leader Handal, who seems to be following the tactical advice of the Soviets. With the Sandinista victory in Nicaragua and the increase in political violence in El Salvador, the PCES and the Soviets have become more optimistic than ever before about the revolutionary potential of the region in general and El Salvador in particular. These changing perceptions certainly have been shared by the Cubans. Although in their public reports the Cubans continue to be somewhat more cautious than the Soviets, they nevertheless began to support directly the various competing guerrilla factions and in late 1979 and early 1980 played an important role in minimizing their differences and in trying to unite them.[35]

The Soviets, unlike the Cubans, however, continued to proceed with caution, at least for some time. Though initially they promised to supply weapons to the guerrillas during a meeting organized by Castro in Havana in December 1979, only in the spring and summer of 1980 did the Soviets decide to switch to supporting the guerrillas. They agreed to provide the military training of a few dozen Salvadoran youths. This decision became evident when the pro-Soviet PCES endorsed violent revolution at its Seventh National Congress in May 1980. Up to that time, the PCES, though committed to revolution, opposed armed struggle and terrorism as revolutionary means in El Salvador. In the fall of 1979, Handal, though jubilant about the victory in Nicaragua, was cautious about making comments regarding the prospects for revolution in El Salvador. In April 1980, however, he became much more optimistic and, according to Soviet sources, expressed "confidence" in the "defeat of internal reaction, despite the fact that the latter is backed by imperialist forces."[36]

Although the example of Nicaragua was very important, it was not the only motive for the changing perceptions and tactics of the PCES and the Soviets in the spring of 1980. Both the Soviets and Cubans probably feared that if the PCES did not use violence to implement its "anti-imperialist" strategy it would soon be outdone and overshadowed by its more radical rivals, who were quickly gaining popular strength. The PCES, they reasoned, should not be suddenly surprised by a success of the non-Communist guerrillas and deprived thereby of responsibility for the victory, as happened in Nicaragua to the PSN, who were outshone by the Sandinistas. Thus Cuban and Soviet tactics since the spring of 1980 were directed at transforming the numerically small PCES into a leading force in the guerrilla struggle in El Salvador.

The Soviet assessment of the U.S. ability to maintain hegemony in the region also seemed to have changed. In spite of the Cuban Revolution, the Soviets continued to believe throughout the 1960s and 1970s that the United States had the ability and will to challenge outright revolution in Central America. In Nicaragua, however, the U.S. administration made one mistake after another. It failed to break completely with Somoza, and it tried too late to modify the outcome of a Sandinista victory. A Soviet analyst, quoting an anonymous official in Washington, wrote in July 1980 that the Carter administration was "too late and too indecisive" with its intervention in the Nicaraguan crisis, that it therefore could not prevent the complete victory of the Sandinistas, and that "a different course of action" must be taken by the United States in El Salvador.[37] According to this analyst, the situation in El Salvador, which was arousing the "anxiety" of American strategists, was even more "tense" than in Nicaragua before the fall of Somoza.

Developments in El Salvador may have been linked to Soviet-perceived changes in Soviet-American relations in the wake of the Iranian and Afghan crises in late 1979. In the Soviet view, as I have argued elsewhere, the U.S. administration was veering toward a dangerous new cold war by encouraging a semialliance with China, threatening Iran, and sabotaging SALT II negotiations.[38] Most grievous in the Soviet view was U.S., Chinese, and Egyptian "allied" support of the Afghan rebels with Soviet-made weapons. (Whether this was true in 1979 is still a matter of speculation; the Soviets profess to have believed it was so, and sometimes the perceptions of policymakers are more important than the facts.) The Soviet invasion of Afghanistan, a matter of necessity as the Soviets saw it, was met with retaliatory policies by the zigzagging Carter administration aimed at further punishing the USSR. The Soviets may have thought, after Nicaragua, that El Salvador provided an easily exploitable opportunity in the same geographic proximity of the United States as Afghanistan is to the USSR. The idea of making El Salvador an "American Afghanistan" in retaliation for perceived Egyptian-U.S.-Chinese support for the Afghan rebels, and/or using the issue as a bargaining chip in future negotiations may have played a part in the Soviet decision to back the Cuban orchestration of support for the guerrilla struggle.

Though we can only speculate on the motives for the Soviet decision, the facts of the story are well known. Unlike what happened in Nicaragua, the Soviet-backed Cuban orchestration of the supply of armaments from Soviet-allied countries has been significant. It appears that the involvement of Cuba backed by the USSR has significantly strengthened the guerrillas in El Salvador. Handal's search for arms in the East, which seems to be well documented by the U.S. administration, began around the time of the Seventh Congress of the PCES, during which a passive line was radically exchanged for one of organized violence intended to topple a regime. After the congress the Cubans took charge of the clandestine operations in El Salvador, and Castro actively assumed the role of broker in attempting to unify the various revolutionary groups. In June and July, with the assistance of Soviet officials responsible for Third World affairs in the Soviet Secretariat, such as K. Brutens and his deputy Kudachkin, Handal visited the USSR and certain East European countries and obtained American-made weapons (M-14 and M-16 rifles, M-79 grenade launchers) from Vietnam and Ethiopia both of which hold large stocks of U.S. weapons. Thus the USSR (initially unwilling to transport arms from Vietnam by air) could, by proceeding with caution, deny its involvement if accused. The East European allies (minus Poland and Romania) promised to provide communications equipment, uniforms, and medical supplies while the Soviets helped to arrange for the transportation of the weapons to Cuba in the fall of 1980. In Cuba they were reloaded and transported to Nicaragua and from there directly by ship or air to El Salvador or by surface through Honduras to El Salvador. Following the U.S. presidential elections, Cuban experts, with cautious Soviet backing, played a key role in the arms transfer and the preparation of the "final" guerrilla offensive. As concluded by a U.S. State Department report, "the political direction, organization, and arming of the insurgency are coordinated and heavily influenced by Cuba—with active support of the Soviet Union, East Germany, Vietnam, and other Communist states."[39]

Conclusions

The joint strategy for dealing with Third World countries worked out by the USSR and Cuba in the late 1960s and 1970s is not necessarily designed to create Marxist-Leninist regimes in these countries but rather to achieve a variety of "anti-imperialist" political, ideological, security, and economic objectives. Soviet and Cuban strategic visions have not always been identical, particularly in the 1960s, when there were some rather serious disagreements regarding doctrine and tactics. As recent Soviet-Cuban policies in Africa and Central America attest, however, most of these differences have been overcome in the last several years. Although Cuba is not subservient to the USSR, for a variety of reasons its foreign policies are basically dependent upon Soviet support (Africa) or linked to Soviet foreign policy (Central

America). Both the Soviets and Cubans happen to have linked strategic visions regarding Central America. Though the Soviets are newcomers, with Cuban help they have been able to exploit the socioeconomic malaise and anti-U.S. sentiment characteristic of the region. In doing so, they have employed a variety of tactics: peaceful and legal, violent, often a combination of both.

Undoubtedly deep socioeconomic cleavages are the main source of the ongoing crisis in Central America, particularly in the countries located in the region's northern tier: Nicaragua, El Salvador, Guatemala and, to a certain degree, Honduras. Though the more southern countries of Costa Rica and Panama do not have such pronounced social problems, they face severe economic difficulties (particularly Costa Rica) and are not immune to revolutionary change. The civil war in El Salvador could escalate into a regional war, perhaps even leading to the involvement of Mexico and Venezuela, with Guatemala and Honduras assisting the regime, and Nicaragua and Cuba assisting the guerrillas.

Internal forces were the main impetus for local insurgency and revolution in Nicaragua in 1979; the Soviets and Cubans were deeply involved in Africa prior to 1978–1979, when it peaked, and their involvement in Nicaragua was marginal. Afterwards, however, the Nicaraguan Revolution became an inspiration to other revolutionaries in the region and a catalyst in changing the perceptions and tactics of the USSR and Cuba. Both seemed to believe that the Nicaraguan "example" could be repeated soon in "strategically located" El Salvador. The dramatic change in Soviet and Cuban tactics in the spring of 1980, *after* the Nicaraguan Revolution, is proof of their flexibility in the implementation of "anti-imperialist" strategy.

Though the socioeconomic problems in Nicaragua and El Salvador are similar, there are some profound differences between the situations in both countries. Nicaragua's revolution was genuine, in that it expressed the will of a majority of the people in overthrowing the hated dictatorship of Somoza, while El Salvador's revolution is less genuine, having significant Cuban support while cautiously being backed by the Soviets. Both of the latter supported, if not encouraged, a dramatic change in the tactics of El Salvador's Communist party in May of 1980 and facilitated an impressive arms transfer in the fall of the same year. In late 1980 the guerrillas in El Salvador announced the creation of a united liberation front—the Farabundo Martí People's Liberation Front—whose general command includes Handal. Although the so-called final offensive in early 1981 failed, El Salvador may still develop into a "second Nicaragua." However, the guerrilla offensive in El Salvador has failed so far to spark a popular insurrection as in Nicaragua. As of mid-1981, the majority of the people did not appear to support the leftist guerrillas. One can "spur" revolutionary struggles, but one cannot sustain them without genuine popular support.

The Soviet and Cuban vigorous support of Salvadoran leftists and their new closer relationship with Nicaragua since last year were the result of more than preconceived strategy. They also illustrate Soviet and Cuban tactical skill in implementing this strategy in exploiting available opportunities. In the case of Nicaragua, such an opportunity was the hesitancy of the U.S. Congress in providing aid to that country and U.S. failure to assume a more active role.

In El Salvador there might be additional reasons for the Soviets' position other than the desire to exploit revolutionary opportunities. Though the Soviets will not tell us, it may be that the USSR, by taking a tough stand on that country, was trying to tie down the United States and eventually be in a position to bargain on other issues, such as Afghanistan and Poland. The internal situations in both of these countries that border the USSR are causing serious problems, which the Soviets have attributed to outside provocation and assistance. Does the USSR want to bargain with the United States? It may be, as suggested by some Central American observers, that Soviet tactics in El Salvador are being used to divert Western attention from Soviet domestic failures and the problems faced in Poland and Afghanistan in order to prepare a hardening of Soviet policies in these countries, including perhaps some kind of intervention in Poland. In exchange for U.S. acquiescence to such hard-line policies, the USSR would change its tactics in El Salvador. The Soviet leadership appears to link the crises in Poland and Central America. While delivering an important speech on the Polish crisis on April 7, Brezhnev unexpectedly concluded his remarks by stressing the Soviets' role as protector of Cuba's security.[40]

As of the summer of 1981, any firm conclusions about the outcome of the struggle is El Salvador are, of course, premature. Indeed, a number of internal and external constraints could mitigate against assertive Cuban and Soviet implementation of "anti-imperialist" strategy in the Caribbean basin. First, the Cuban economic situation is the worst it has been since the Revolution, despite massive Soviet economic support. The economic malaise, to which the costly African adventures have certainly contributed, led to a radical reorganization of the Cuban government in early 1980 and the rationing of essentials.

Public resentment was further fed by the soaring cost of living. This culminated in open dissent in the spring of 1980: more than 10,000 Cuban dissidents sought asylum in the Peruvian embassy in Havana and subsequently emigrated to the United States. Cuban economic difficulties, however, failed to elicit any kind of major antiwar movement, or, for that matter, any visible opposition or even political debate. Despite the difficulties arising from its alliance with the Soviet Union, Cuba in 1980–1981 succeeded in maintaining its overseas commitments and somehow was able to expand them, as seen in Nicaragua and El Salvador.

Local conditions in the Caribbean basin, however, may not always favor revolutionary upheaval and its exploitation by the Cubans and the Soviets. A crucial setback for Cuba was the defeat of the left-leaning regime of Manley in Jamaica and the election in October 1980 of the more pro-Western Edward Seaga. In the last few years, Soviet economic backing allowed the Cubans to expand their influence in Jamaica. Like Nicaragua and Grenada, Jamaica was offered financial credits by Cuba (perhaps with Soviet help) and the assistance of several hundred Cuban civilian teachers, technicians, and construction workers as well as some security officials to train the Jamaican security forces. The fall of Manley's regime was a setback for Cuban and Soviet policies in the Caribbean basin. So were the electoral defeats of other parties with close Cuban ties on the small Caribbean islands of Saint Vincent, Dominica, Antigua, and Saint Kitts and Nevis.

Vigorous Cuban involvement in Africa and the Caribbean basin can also be constrained by the Soviets themselves, whose support determines the limits of Cuban assertiveness in the Third World. Indeed, in the future Soviet leaders may be less willing to back Cuba's role in Africa and the Caribbean basin because of Soviet economic difficulties at home and because of new developments having greater importance. Given Soviet preoccupation with the Polish crisis, the continuing resistance of Muslim rebels in Afghanistan, and the ongoing war between Iran and Iraq, Soviet concern in 1981–1982 may be directed at Eastern Europe and the strategic "arc of instability" to the south of the Soviet borders in Asia (e.g., Afghanistan and Iran). A significant shift in Soviet priorities could have a significant effect on Cuban foreign policy. Hence Castro reportedly believes that the USSR is being too "patient" with Poland; he has repeatedly assaulted the Polish free trade unions whose activities, he says, are prompted by "imperialist provocation."[41] This should come as no surprise. Continuous Soviet preoccupation with Poland and Afghanistan could impose some hard choices on the Soviet leadership with regard to its strategy in the Third World, including Cuba. What effect will all this have on Soviet-Cuban commitments in other parts of the Third World, particularly Angola and Ethiopia but also Central America? How long can Soviet-backed

Cuban deployment in Angola and Ethiopia be maintained and how effectively? These questions, for which there are no pat answers, are probably being posed by foreign policy experts in the Soviet Union, who may feel that Caribbean and Central American anti-U.S. nationalism simply cannot be exploited as vigorously as the Cuban leaders believe, at least not in the foreseeable future.

The most important factor affecting Soviet-Cuban strategy in Central America is the future course of U.S. policy vis-à-vis the USSR and Cuba. In the wake of the Vietnam debacle, Cuban and Soviet activities seemed hardly constrained by the United States because of the unwillingness of the American public and Congress to support a forceful response to their assertive behavior. This point was well demonstrated during the Angolan and Ethiopian interventions. It seems that the political mood in the United States is now changing, as had been demonstrated to some degree by the election of Reagan, who back in 1980 suggested a naval blockade of Cuba as a response to the invasion of Afghanistan. In early 1981 Reagan and his advisors repeatedly warned that the United States would take all measures necessary to stop the arms transfer to El Salvador, not excluding actions against Cuba. These threats were taken seriously by the Cubans, who in late 1980 decided to organize a territorial militia defense system. One thing is almost certain. The Soviets themselves are not going to undertake a direct military intervention in Central America. They still do not have the capability to do so effectively, in spite of what they see as a "weakening of U.S. hegemony" in the region.

NOTES

1. See my earlier work on Soviet-Cuban alliance in the Third World: "The Soviet-Cuban Intervention in Angola, 1975," *Studies in Comparative Communism* (Los Angeles), Spring/Summer 1978, pp. 3–33; "Soviet Decision-Making on the Intervention in Angola," in David Albright, ed., *Communism in Africa* (Bloomington: Indiana Univ. Press, 1980); "The Communist States and the Conflict in the Horn of Africa," in J. Valenta and D. Albright, eds., *Communist Countries and Africa* (Bloomington: Indiana Univ. Press, forthcoming); "Comment: The Soviet-Cuban Alliance in Africa and Future Prospects in the Third World," *Cuban Studies/Estudios Cubanos* (Pittsburgh) (July 1980): 36–43; "The Soviet-Cuban Intervention in Angola," *U.S. Naval Proceedings,* April 1980, pp. 51–57, and for an expanded version of the same article, see Steven Rosefielde, ed., *World Communism at the Crossroads: Military Ascendancy, Political Economy and Human Welfare* (Boston: Martinus Nijhoff, 1980).

2. *Time,* Mar. 16, 1981, pp. 24–25.

3. Ibid., p. 10.

4. See chapter 1 by Francisco Villagran Kramer in this book.

5. M. N. Roy, *Memoirs* (Bombay: Allied, 1964), p. 154.

6. For studies dealing with early Soviet relations with Latin American Communist parties, see Rollie E. Poppino, *International Communism in Latin America: A History of the Movement, 1917–1963* (Glencoe, Ill.: Free Press, 1964); Robert J. Alexander, *Communism in Latin America* (New Brunswick, N.J.: Rutgers Univ. Press, 1957); Karl M. Schmidt, *Communism in Mexico: A Study in Political Frustration* (Austin: Univ. of Texas Press, 1965); Ronald M. Schneider, *Communism in Guatemala 1944–1954* (New York: Frederick A. Praeger, 1959), and Robert J. Alexander, "The Communist Parties of Latin America," *Problems of Communism,* July–August 1970, pp. 37–46.

7. Cole Blasier; *The Hovering Giant: U.S. Responses to Revolutionary Change in Latin America* (Pittsburgh: Pittsburgh Univ. Press, 1976).

8. K. S. Karol, *Guerillas in Power: The Course of the Cuban Revolution* (New York: Hill & Wang, 1970), p. 272.

9. Cole Blasier; *Soviet Relations with Latin America in the 1970s* (Washington D.C.: National Council for Soviet and East European Research, 1980).

10. M. F. Kudachkin, *Velikii Oktiabr; i kommunisticheskie partii Latinskoi Ameriki (The Great October and Communist Parties of Latin America)* (Moscow: Progress Publishers, 1978). The "anti-imperialist" strategy has been also argued for in many articles published in *Latinskaia amerika* in the 1960s and the 1970s. There were of course some significant disagreements in making this strategy. These were well analyzed in the forthcoming book by Professor Jerry Hough, and I am indebted for his comments.

11. For a very perceptive analysis, see Jerry F. Hough, "The Evolving Soviet Debate in Latin America," *Latin American Research Review* 10, no. 1, pp. 124–143.

12. S. Mishin, "Latin America: Two Trends of Development," *International Affairs* (Moscow), July 1976, p. 450; and Leon Gouré and Morris Rothenberg, *Soviet Penetration of Latin America* (Miami, Fla.: Miami Center for Advanced International Studies, 1973).

13. *Tass* (Moscow), July 12, 1960.

14. *Declaration of the Conference of Communist Parties of Latin America and the Caribbean* (Havana, 1975), p. 42.

15. For an excellent analysis, see Herbert S. Dinerstein, *Soviet Policy in Latin America* (Santa Monica, Calif.: Rand, May 1966), pp. 28–30.

16. Kudachkin, "The Experience of the Struggle of the Communist Party of Chile for Unity among Leftist Forces and for Revolutionary Transformation," *Voprosy Istorii KPSS,* no. 5 (May 1976), pp. 72–76.

17. For a discussion, see L. I. Kamynin, *International Affairs,* no. 2 (1967), pp. 27–33.

18. Radio Paris, Jan. 15, 1981, in *FBIS—Latin America,* Jan. 21, 1981.

19. See my "Soviet-Cuban Alliance in Africa," *Cuban Studies* 19 (July 198): 36–43.

20. Edward Gonzales, *Cuba under Castro: The Limits of Charisma* (Boston: Houghton Mifflin Company, 1974), p. 220.

21. Jorge I. Dominguez, *Cuba: Order and Revolution* (Cambridge, Mass.: Belknap Press of Harvard Univ., 1978), p. 149.

22. Castro's speech at the Congress of the Cuban Communist Party, Radio Havana, Dec. 22, 1975.

23. "Failure of the Cuban Economy" (editorial), *La Prensa* (Buenos Aires), Jan. 15, 1981.

24. Vadim Zagladin, "On the Threshold of the Eighties," *New Times,* Jan. 1, 1980, pp. 5–7.

25. Charles W. Anderson, "Nicaragua: The Somoza Dynasty," in Martin C. Needler, ed., *Political Systems of Latin America* (New York: Litton Educational Publishing, 1978), pp. 108–131.

26. Compare "USSR-Nicaragua: Building Cooperation," *New Times,* no. 13, March 1980, pp. 6–7 with "Struggles of the Communist Parties of South and Caribbean America," *Communist International* 12, no. 10 (May 20, 1935), pp. 564–576. Also see Robert Alexander, *Communists in Latin America,* pp. 347–378.

27. See a statement by W. H. Duncan, a vice-president with the American Chamber of Commerce of Latin America in Nicaragua, in U.S. House Committee on Foreign Affairs, *Central America at the Crossroads: Hearing before the Subcommittee on American Affairs,* Sept. 11–12, 1979, p. 47.

28. James N. Goodsell, "Nicaragua," in R. F. Starr, ed., *Yearbook on International Communist Affairs, 1979* (Stanford, Calif: Hoover Institution Press, 1980), pp. 369–371.

29. See "USSR–Nicaragua: Building Cooperation."

30. *Prela* (Havana), April 26, 1981 in *FBIS–Latin America,* April 29, 1981, *Baltimore Sun,* Feb. 26, 1981; *News Gazette* (San Salvador), Feb. 1–7, 1981 and *Managua Radio,* March 27, 1981 in *FBIS–Latin America,* March 30, 1981.

31. Ponomarev's report can be found in *Kommunist,* no. 16 (November 1980), pp. 30–44.

32. Moscow Radio, July 17, 1980.

33. V. Korionov, "El Salvador: The Struggle Sharpens," *Pravda,* Dec. 30, 1980 and Ruslan Tuchnin, "Reign of Terror," *New Times,* no. 14 (April 1980), pp. 9–11.

34. Thomas P. Anderson, "El Salvador," In R. F. Starr, ed., *Yearbook on International Communist Affairs, 1979* (Stanford, Calif.: Hoover Institution, 1979), pp. 347–348. See also Anderson's analysis in Starr, ed. *Yearbook in International Communist Affairs, 1980,* pp. 354–355.

35. "Communist Interference in El Salvador" *Special Report no. 80,* Washington, D.C.: U.S. Department of State, Bureau of Public Affairs, Feb. 23, 1981.

36. An interview with Handal. *Tass* (Moscow), Oct. 22; and V. Dolgov, "Mounting Struggle," *New Times,* no. 14 (April 1980), p. 11. In November of the same year the leading theoretical journal of the CPSU published a lengthy article by Handal in praise of the guerrilla struggle. See "Na puti k svobode (On the Road to Liberty)" *Kommunist,* no. 17 (November 1980), pp. 94–103.

37. Ye. V. Mitiaieva, "The United States Interference in El Salvador," *SShA: Ekonomika, politika, ideologia,* no. 7 (July 1980), pp. 60–64.

38. See J. Valenta, "From Prague to Kabul," *International Security,* vol. 6, no. 2 (Fall 1980), pp. 114–141.

39. "Communist Interference in El Salvador," *Special Report,* no. 80, Feb. 23, 1981. Though various critics have rightly pointed to inconsistencies in this report, none has proved it is a forgery or that the USSR and other Communist countries did not actively support Cuban assistance to the guerrillas of El Salvador. For a critique of the report, see T. Segel, *Washington Star,* May 18, 1981, and James Petras, *Nation,* vol. 232, no. 12 (Mar. 28, 1981).

40. See Brezhnev's speech delivered at the Sixteenth Party Congress of the Czechoslovak Communist Party, Prague, in *Pravda,* Apr. 8, 1981.

41. Radio Madrid, Dec. 5, 1980, in *FBIS-Latin America,* Dec. 5, 1980, and Castro's speech at the twenty-sixth Party Congress of the CPSU in Moscow, *FBIS-Latin America,* Feb. 24, 1981.

7. Mexican Foreign Policy and Central America

René Herrera Zúñiga and Mario Ojeda

Mexican policy toward Central America is based on three fundamental premises: first, that Mexico will maintain a general
position in accord with the principles of self-determination and
nonintervention; second, that Mexico will favor—and support if
invited—political solutions through negotiations of the involved parties; third, that Mexico's dissent with respect to U.S. positions on
regional politics should not be allowed to adversely affect bilateral
relations.

None of these premises are new to Mexican foreign policy. Thus
most assumptions by Washington officials and U.S. political observers
about Mexico's political attitudes and political role—both actual and
potential—are exaggerated to some degree. Some observers see Mexico as a simple object of the global dispute between the superpowers,
while others take the opposite position: Mexico is a key actor in regional politics and may even be considered as the main rival of the
United States in the near future. We believe both views are grossly
overstated. Mexico's foreign policy in the region is not new, and
neither is Mexico's dissenting position with respect to the United
States in regional matters. Three cases in particular can be cited to
substantiate this assertion: Guatemala in 1954, Cuba from 1959 to the
present, and the Dominican Republic in 1965. Moreover, Mexico's
adherence to the principle of nonintervention has been applied, not
only with regard to United States actions, but also with regard to Cuba,
as was the case in 1967 with respect to the Organization of Latin
American Solidarity, and with regard to the Soviet Union in the case of
Afghanistan.

What is, in fact, new with respect to Mexico is oil. This resource has been the basis for a more active presence of Mexico in the region and in the world at large. Oil in itself brings political influence. In this sense the name of an old Broadway musical parody could be applied to Mexico: "How to Become an International Power without Trying."

It should be noted that this more active presence in the region has applied to countries with all kinds of political regimes, from revolutionary Nicaragua to conservative Guatemala. There is, however, a recent case that can be considered as a deviation from the Mexican policy of self-determination and nonintervention. In an effort to help accelerate the downfall of Somoza in Nicaragua, Mexico broke off relations with his government. Many considerations could be forwarded to explain and justify this action; however, the fact remains that Mexico deviated from a long-standing tradition by terminating relations with an established government.

But the point to emphasize here is that precisely because of this deviant case Mexico is returning rapidly to traditional foreign policy as a safer ground, a safer ground with regard to both international and domestic politics. Not to break with tradition but to maintain continuity and consistency is the way for developing countries to give strength to their foreign policy.

Finally, in this chapter we want to emphasize the different perceptions that Washington and Mexico City have with regard to the Central American crisis. While Washington tends to see it mainly as a result of Communist-oriented agitation, Mexico perceives it mainly as the consequence of long-standing social injustice and political illegitimacy. While Washington's objective is to contain Soviet-Cuban expansionism, Mexico's objective is to achieve the stabilization of the region through negotiation and democratization.[1]

The Washington Perception of the Crisis

The change of administration in Washington in January 1981 was important, not only because it signified a replacement of the Democrats by the Republicans, but mainly because it brought to Washington the right wing of the latter party under a political program that promised to bring about a conservative revolution in the United States. The Reagan administration came to power with the strong belief, not entirely incorrect, that the Soviet Union and its allies had taken advantage of the power vacuum in world politics left by the United States in the wake of the traumas of Vietnam and Watergate by intervening in various ways to increase Soviet influence. Angola, Ethiopia, Afghanistan, and Nicaragua are glaring examples of Soviet expansionism, according to this view. This interpretation does not take into account cases such as the war between China and Vietnam, the Israeli-Egyptian peace treaty, and changes of political regimes such as those that occurred in Chile and Jamaica and that, from a cold-war perspective, should count positively for the United States. However, despite the fact that Reagan's government is more pessimistic about U.S. foreign policy than facts warrant, it goes even further. The new government believes that the United States has lost its will to act decisively as a great power and has allowed itself to be defeated even by small countries such as Iran. This show of weakness is believed to have serious consequences for American interests and for the credibility of its leadership even among its own allies.

Given that in politics the actor's perception is often as important as the reality itself, this interpretation of the U.S. position must be taken seriously, regardless of its relation to reality. There is no doubt that the principal objective of Reagan's foreign policy is to regain the U.S. image as a major world power determined to defend and promote its interests, and to check any new Soviet expansionist adventure. However, a geopolitical global perspective of the present world suggests that different regions and countries do not have the same strategic importance for the United States. A global strategy perspective suggests that, because of high U.S. dependence on foreign oil, magnified by the "loss" of Iran, the Persian Gulf has become an area of primary interest for the United States. Europe, with which the United States shares the leadership of the Western world, is also important, mainly since it borders the USSR directly. Today, however, the Atlantic alliance is not as critical as the Persian Gulf in terms of urgency. Japan, for almost the same reasons as in Europe, is also important but not critical. Canada and Mexico are also important because of their geographic contiguity, the intensity and complexity of their bilateral relations with the United States, and their energy resources. Nevertheless, they are not important in the present confrontation with the Soviet Union. Central America and the Caribbean retain strategic importance because of conventional concerns of national security, but also because of the highly emotional significance they have as the symbol of U.S. traditional hegemony in the Western Hemisphere. The Caribbean basin has been the traditional backyard of the United States. All in all, the real primary and objective concern of U.S. foreign policy and the major area of confrontation with the Soviet Union in 1981 are undoubtedly in the Persian Gulf, both for its strategic importance and its overwhelming urgency.

Nevertheless, in order to meet this challenge intelligently, Washington must act cautiously though urgently, and for her own sake avoid direct confrontation with the Soviet Union in the most sensitive political region (the Persian Gulf) for the time being. First, it is necessary to prove through a showcase that the new hard-line policy is serious and that the *Pax Americana* has not died but is coming back with new vigor, though with a different face. What better place then for this demonstration of power and political will than the Western Hemisphere, where traditional American influence reduces the risk of a confrontation and assures success from the start? The revolution in El Salvador represents an ideal case for the armchair policy analyst. Once again the United States takes the line of least resistance, as with President Carter's human rights policy, in preparing to test its foreign policy.

In what seems to be a campaign to prepare public opinion for an interventionist action in the region, the U.S. government and other interested parties have given disproportionate emphasis to the revolution in El Salvador, its connections with Havana and Moscow, and the actual and potential role of other actors. Within this portrayal of events, Mexico becomes a potentially important actor because of its geographical proximity, its traditional historical and cultural ties, its new petroleum wealth, and its recent presence in the region, principally with respect to Nicaragua.

U.S. Perception of the Role of Mexico in the Region

There are two different sets of interpretations of Mexico's role with regard to events in El Salvador in particular and Central America and the Caribbean in general. Some observers tend to see Mexico as a simple object of, rather than actor in, world politics because of its recently acquired oil wealth or as a passive tool of Communist designs; others see it as a major actor in regional politics, and some go as far as assigning it a key role in the future. Among the first group is a previous director of the Defense Intelligence Agency, who stated the following: "The primary objective of the Communist maneuver in Central America today is Guatemala. Why? Because of Guatemala's proximity to Mexico's oil which is so important to them."[2] (And to the United States, it should be added.)

Furthermore, others see Mexico as trying to gain Communist neutrality in its own internal affairs through the means of appeasement. Ronald Yates, from the *Chicago Tribune,* has written the following:

> The dictionary defines appeasement as the process of buying off an aggressor by concession, usually at the sacrifice of principles. Probably the most infamous example of this kind of ill-fated diplomacy was in

1938 when Britain's Prime Minister Neville Chamberlain agreed to allow a militant Adolf Hitler to occupy a portion of Czechoslovakia. By giving Hitler what he wanted (the Sudetenland) Chamberlain and other European leaders hoped to head off war.

The world well knows the result of that bit of wishful strategy. Today, yet another example of diplomatic conciliation is occurring in America's backyard. Some diplomats and military experts argue that the results in 1981 could very well parallel those of 1938.

This time the disciple of Chamberlain is none other than Mexican President Jose Lopez Portillo—a man who seems intent on indulging Cuban- and Soviet-backed guerrillas in Central America in the hope that if they get what they want (support, recognition and ultimately power) they will stop fighting and allow political and economic stability to replace revolution. . . .

In return for such lavish personal praise . . . one assumes Lopez Portillo has elicited some kind of promise from Castro that the Cuban- and Soviet-backed insurgencies currently raging in Central America won't spill over into Mexico.[3]

Among those observers who see Mexico as a major actor in regional politics, there are three types of interpretation. First are those who think that the Mexican position in the region is only part of a broader policy of internal political stability, designed "to persuade the more leftist elements of the ruling party to accept the pragmatic and partly conservative domestic program which has brought economic growth and increasing inequalities of income distribution . . . and to placate the large leftist constituency in the opinion-shaping politics of Mexico. . . ."[4]

A second interpretation claims that Mexico now demands full recognition of its new international status derived from its recently discovered oil wealth: "Once an introspective and reluctant satellite of its neighbor to the north, Mexico has been transformed by oil into a burgeoning regional power, anxious to raise its voice on international affairs, quick to cross swords with Washington."[5]

The third group think that Mexico is not only a major political actor in the region, but in the future will be the principal competitor of the United States for hegemony in the area. A representative exponent of this line of thinking is Charles Maynes, formerly an official in the State Department, who wrote: "The United States thinks that its main competitor in Central America is Cuba or the Soviet Union. In the immediate crisis this might be the case, but in the long-run perspective the competitor is clearly Mexico."[6] Maynes bases his claim on the fact that Central America was a Mexican territory from 1821 to 1823 and on the argument that, for decades before the construction of the Panama Canal, Mexico was the dominant power in Central America.

Most of these interpretations constitute gross exaggerations; others are based on simplifying generalizations. Some of the latter, however, are not entirely incorrect, but they miss the fact that the problem is much more complicated because it is deep-rooted in the history of the country and in the traditions of Mexican foreign policy. The problem is also intertwined with the issue of the new oil wealth, although not for the reasons put forth in these interpretations. Rather, the issue is how oil revenues will be used in relation to Mexico's national project.

The Mexican Perception of the Crisis

For a second time in Mexico's history, the oil question has arisen as a focal point for the development of important changes in national life. During the first experience, the oil question—embodied in the nationalization of foreign companies—signified national control over one of the key resources needed for the industrialization and modernization of Mexican society. The second time signals the possibility of correcting the imbalances resulting from this policy and of establishing a more stable and egalitarian society internally and a more independent nation externally. The new oil wealth, however, constitutes a hope that can vanish amidst external pressures and conflicts that could distort the domestic use of petroleum resources.

As is the case with most developing countries, Mexico's decision-making process is severely influenced by prevailing international relations. The formulation of a foreign policy that stresses the transcendent values of national interest is utilized by some countries in the conduct of their international relations. To the degree that this interest takes on special significance for the correlation of the dominant international forces, foreign policy becomes more important for national development.

In the case of Mexico, the possession and control of a resource with worldwide strategic importance has clearly forced the revitalization of foreign policy as an instrument of domestic policy.

The possibilities that Mexico has for developing an independent foreign policy[7] in a consistent and stable manner actually depend on the real impact of its oil wealth over the economic and social well-being and internal political stability of the country. An economy that is strong in terms of its ability to bring about a more equitable society is an essential prerequisite of an active, independent foreign policy. As long as this prerequisite is not met, foreign policy must be fundamentally defensive and cautious, though it may at times, in its formal rhetoric, appear aggressive and radical.

The historic coincidence of the Central American crisis with the appearance of the new petroleum wealth in Mexico has supplied the conditions for a new Mexican international policy in the region. Furthermore, both the deepening of the crisis as well as the role that Mexico will have to plan with regard to it have been the object of increasing concern in international circles. The very evaluation of events by Mexican officials and by some media groups in the country has itself provoked numerous commentaries both on the international level and among domestic political forces. Generally, some of these commentaries (as we have seen) consider the Mexican attitude as an expression of international activism sustained by the petroleum wealth and aimed at gaining a position of power in a region historically considered part of the U.S. domain. At the extreme, this view holds that the ultimate objective of this policy is to replace U.S. hegemony in Central America and the Caribbean: to change the *Pax Americana* for the *Pax Mexicana*. It is evident that this view attempts to ignore the content and the nature of the Central American crisis in its direct relation to the hegemonic position of the United States; furthermore, it attempts to confuse Mexican efforts to guarantee democratizing processes in Central America through her political support, representing this support as a usurping of American interests. In any case these commentaries leave aside the logical convergence of the interests of some political sectors of the Central American countries with the Mexican national interest. This reality, characterized by the necessity of change in Central America and the possibility of consolidating a nationalist project in Mexico, is what governs the position of Mexico most favorable to peace and stability in the region.

There is sufficient basis to think that Mexican policy toward Central America is fundamentally cautious and defensive, designed to guarantee the conservation of her national project as it emerged from the revolution of 1910, but at the same time adjustable to the need for social and political change in Central America. It is thus to defend the national project that Mexico responds to the crisis by increasing her presence in Central America.

The interest of the Mexican government appears to lie in its ability to implement national development without having a generalized focus of tension next door. Such tension, if it were to develop into a subregional war, would only serve to legitimate the position of those trying to take a harder line in the general policy of the current Mexican regime. In that event, there would be advocacy of growing militarization with the pretext of protecting the oil fields, which would entail increased public expenditure and the alteration of political objectives leading, consequently, to a distortion of priorities in the assignment of resources derived from petroleum. As a result, a growing regional instability, far from aiding the objective of consolidation of economic development and ultimately the expansion of autonomy in foreign policy, would lead to a strengthening of that political view favoring Mexican militarization and affiliation with the most traditional interests of American security.

It is clear that Mexico does not now have the capacity in real power to generate by its own actions a balance of power exclusive of and competitive with the United States in Central America and the Caribbean. It is also clear that the United States has not abandoned its position of power in the region. Consequently, Mexico's position in the Central American crisis may not hold great importance in power terms for the United States. Rather, the critical objective for the United States is to prevent Mexico from breaking a united front of regional countries through its own noninterventionist stand and the encouragement of other governments to follow suit. The best way for the United States to achieve this is to bring pressures to bear on Mexico to invert the order of priorities in its relations with Central America: that is, that Mexico not look for nor promote a political solution in Central America, but rather that it isolate itself and prepare internally to avoid the contagion of the crisis. It would be a matter, then, of promoting in Mexico a development strategy based on the requirements of national security, consistent with the American definition, which some political and military sectors in Mexico seem eager to assimilate. While the United States understands national security as a lack of Soviet and Cuban expansion in the region, Mexico interprets it as an atmosphere favorable to the expression of those forces that promote social change in the area as an independent process from international ideological confrontations. As a consequence, the United States, in order to guarantee her security, finds the solution to the Central American crisis in military confrontation. Mexico, for its part, finds the solution in political negotiation in order to guarantee its own stability.

The unleashing of a generalized armed struggle in the region could force a new Mexican vision of the problem; that is, the need to resort to an armaments policy with all that implies for the objectives of her own development. In economic terms it would signify a diversion of resources from productive areas that are urgent for the consolidation of the economy; in political terms it would signify the weakening of the traditional political class, which would be increasingly forced to share the strategies of development with the military sector. Furthermore, a development policy openly joined to U.S. notions of security would lead to the failure of the present government's efforts to incorporate political pluralism into the political system. The efforts carried out in recent years to incorporate greater political openness by institutionalizing the participation of diverse ideological forces in the electoral process would become useless. Security considerations would wind up dominating those of domestic political modernization. The social crisis predicted for Mexico by supporters of the domino theory, among others, would shortly become reality, but for different reasons. A policy of political strife would spoil the efforts of democratization and could bring on critical confrontations in Mexican society.

A growing role of the army has been observed recently at the ideological level as well as the operational level (improved quality of the domestic military industry, acquisition of armaments, and so forth), suggesting that Mexico may have already embarked on a policy of development with military security. This may, nonetheless, be a preventive action and entail limited modernization, not yet reaching the level of a truly new policy approaching the undertaking of other Latin American governments. But it may be as well an indicator of such an undertaking. The Mexican political class realizes this and, therefore, insists on promoting a negotiated solution in the Central American crisis.

This negotiation seems to be carried out on two levels: on the one hand, using direct channels of communication with Washington and, on the other hand, using political channels of communication with the local organizations that promote change in Central America (revolutionary organizations, political parties, local interest groups).

On the first level, United States-Mexican negotiations focus on a settlement of the different perceptions of the crisis as a result of the respective notions of national security; on the second level, they focus on Mexico's role as guarantor of U.S. nonintervention in exchange for the acceptance, by the revolutionary forces, of the role of Mexico as a moderating actor.

The Mexican government, contrary to what is claimed by Washington, seems to realize that in Central America there is in the long run no alternative to revolutionary change; that the crisis arises from the unraveling of political models imposed by force—on more than one occasion with United States support—and not so much from expansionist plans arbitrarily embarked on by Havana and Moscow. It thus seems that, according to the Mexican view, direct or indirect intervention by the United States or other powers will not, in the long run, be sufficient to suppress this option. Furthermore, Mexico is fearful that a Vietnam could arise in her own backyard, especially if it is artificially created by the necessity of reasserting U.S. hegemonic power in the world. Such a turn of events would be equivalent to laying the basis for a profound instability in the relations of the United States with a good part of Latin America and particularly with Mexico. This instability would ruin the possibilities of an economically strong Mexico with political stability and on good terms with the United States. In that event, Mexico would perhaps reaffirm national unity, but as an emotional reaction, not as the result of a more developed and mature society graced by regional peace.

In this way, the Mexican position in Central America, in accord with her national interests, is to obtain a negotiated solution to the regional crisis. This position necessarily leads to negotiation with the parties involved in one way or another in the conflict. It is obvious that principal among these is the United States, a nation that historically has exercised hegemony over the Central American nations, a fact that itself accounts for a good part of the reasons for the conflict. If the route of negotiation centers around the U.S. position, it is evident that there are other nations to take into account, particularly those that have become sources of subregional power, whether for political reasons like Cuba, for economic factors like Venezuela, or even because of democratic prestige, like Costa Rica.

Among these latter nations, Mexico is the one that in recent years has succeeded in combining both political and economic capacities at the same time that her strategic position, based on her petroleum wealth, gives her the potential power to exercise greater regional influence. The borders within which this power may be exercised are, however, limited.

Mexico is tied to U.S. pressures to influence the Central American crisis, not only because of the limits of its real power, but because of the high degree of penetration of U.S. interests in the national economy. These interests must not be overlooked in an analysis of the Mexican position with respect to the Central American crisis. Furthermore, given the importance of Mexico's bilateral relations with the United States, both the government itself as well as private nationalist forces have limited room for imposing their point of view.

As a result, Mexico's great difficulty consists in reconciling the defense of her national interests vis-à-vis Central America with the need to not adversely affect its bilateral relations with the United States. This is not a new story for Mexico. Further, one could characterize the constant dilemma of Mexican foreign policy as the choice between—or the conciliation of—two principal objectives: maintaining her noninterventionist line and not overly contradicting the United States, given Mexico's high degree of economic dependence.

The Mexican position with respect to Central America, therefore, seems to be to avoid insofar as possible the generalization of the crisis by proposing a political solution that would include the most important political forces of the Central American societies. A case in point is the Mexican communique issued jointly with the French government of Francois Mitterrand on August 28, 1981. The communique recognizes the revolutionary organizations of El Salvador as a "representative force" qualified, therefore, to participate in negotiations with the governing junta. This initiative was strongly criticized by some Latin American governments, most of them of a military nature, on grounds that it represented Mexican intervention in the internal affairs of El Salvador. The association of Mexico with an extra-continental power was also criticized as a violation of the long-established practice of keeping outsiders out of regional affairs. President Lopez Portillo responded by declaring that Mexico did not consider this action as interventionist, but as a simple recognition of a fact. In a clear reference to Washington, Mexico noted that to give military assistance to any of the parties involved truly represented intervention in the internal affairs of the country.

This Mexican initiative can thus be distinguished from the breaking off of relations with Somoza. The Franco-Mexican communique is designed to protect the possibility of a self-determination process in El Salvador by recognizing the legitimacy of both parties. Although the practice of international law might consider it otherwise, the Mexican government was taking a preventive political measure; Mexico was hoping to moderate any possible action by the United States and to avoid internationalization of the conflict.

A similar initiative was undertaken by Mexico later in the United Nations, with the backing of some European countries. This second initiative extended a plea to the rival forces in El Salvador to reach a negotiated political solution. At the same time, during the visit of Secretary Haig to Mexico City on November 25, Mexico invited the United States and all parties involved or concerned with the Central American crisis (including Nicaragua and Cuba) to de-escalate the verbal war of mutual accusations. Mexico took such action in the hope that this would help to create a propitious climate for conversations that might lead to political solutions in the region.

In conclusion, it is obvious that the Mexican attempt to convince all sides to come to the negotiating table in order to reach a political solution may encounter the opposition of an administration in the United States that appears inclined toward a military solution in El Salvador and hostile to the Nicaraguan revolutionary government.

The Mexican Presence in Central America

In spite of geographic proximity, common historical background, and cultural similarities, relations between Mexico and Central

Table 7.1 MEXICO: EXPORTS FROM CENTRAL AMERICA BY COUNTRY AND TYPE OF GOODS
(In Thousands of Dollars and Percent)

	1979*				1980*			
	Total	Consumer goods	Intermediate goods	Capital goods	Total	Consumer goods	Intermediate goods	Capital goods
TOTAL EXPORTS	8,798,245	1,573,987	7,029,526	194,732	15,307,480	1,635,435	13,428,112	243,933
Central American Comon Market	136,724	31,517	83,720	21,487	228,665	34,092	168,427	26,146
Costa Rica	35,501	6,985	24,357	4,159	95,581	8,107	82,238	5,236
El Salvador	25,340	5,983	14,400	4,957	11,610	3,881	6,793	936
Guatemala	52,843	11,869	35,156	5,818	59,201	12,651	41,795	4,755
Honduras	19,101	5,419	7,207	6,475	18,987	4,982	9,501	5,504
Nicaragua	3,939	1,261	2,600	78	43,286	4,471	28,100	10,715
Central American Common Market	100.0	23.1	61.2	15.7	100.0	14.9	73.7	11.4
Costa Rica	100.0	19.6	68.6	11.8	100.0	8.5	86.0	5.5
El Salvador	100.0	23.6	56.8	19.6	100.0	33.4	58.5	8.1
Guatemala	100.0	22.5	66.5	11.0	100.0	21.4	70.6	8.0
Honduras	100.0	28.4	37.7	33.9	100.0	26.2	50.0	23.8
Nicaragua	100.0	32.0	66.0	2.0	100.0	10.3	64.9	24.8

SOURCE: "Comercio Exterior de México," vol. 4, núm. 1 (Internal Document) Secretaría de Programación y Presupuesto, 1981.
*January to December.

Table 7.2 MEXICO: IMPORTS FROM CENTRAL AMERICA BY COUNTRY AND TYPE OF GOODS

(In Thousands of Dollars and Percent)

	1979*				1980*			
	Total	Consumer goods	Intermediate goods	Capital goods	Total	Consumer goods	Intermediate goods	Capital goods
TOTAL	12,502,626				19,516,959			
Transportation and Insurance	517,049				944,754			
Commercial Value	11,985,577	1,001,916	7,406,358	3,577,303	18,572,205	2,425,937	11,027,713	5,118,555
Central American Common Market	13,017	1,599	10,716	702	32,047	3,866	22,306	5,875
Costa Rica	685	241	350	94	854	468	137	249
El Salvador	581	443	94	44	1,260	483	552	225
Guatemala	9,969	433	9,108	428	25,876	2,802	21,244	1,830
Honduras	807	157	638	12	3,871	86	269	3,516
Nicaragua	975	325	526	124	186	27	104	55
Central American Common Market	100.0	12.3	82.3	5.4	100.0	12.1	69.6	18.3
Costa Rica	100.0	35.2	51.1	13.7	100.0	54.8	16.0	29.2
El Salvador	100.0	76.2	16.2	7.6	100.0	38.3	43.8	17.9
Guatemala	100.0	4.3	91.4	4.3	100.0	10.8	82.1	7.1
Honduras	100.0	19.4	79.1	1.5	100.0	2.2	6.9	90.9
Nicaragua	100.0	33.3	53.9	12.8	100.0	14.5	55.9	29.6

SOURCE: "Comercio Exterior de México," vol. 4, núm. 1 (Internal Document) Secretaría de Programación y Presupuesto, 1981.
*January to December

America have not been as close as one might expect. Trade has been traditionally poor even with respect to Guatemala, with which Mexico shares a common border. On the other hand, traditional Mexican distate for military governments and continuous changes of government in Central America have accounted for a lack of political cooperation between them, with the exception of Costa Rica and more recently Nicaragua.

Trade between Mexico and Central America has been poor both in absolute terms and in relation to total exports and imports with the rest of the world. Mexican exports to the area accounted for only $52 million in 1973; $73 million in 1976; and then grew significantly to $111 million in 1977 because of the devaluation on the Mexican peso. A spectacular jump came in 1980, when exports grew with respect to 1979 from $136 to $228 million because of Mexican oil exports to the region. However, the general levels of trade are so low that not even this spectacular jump created by oil could really affect the importance of commerce in relative terms. For example, in relative terms $228 million constituted only 1.5 percent of total Mexican exports. (See table 7.3.)

On the import side, the picture is even poorer. In a very erratic manner Mexican imports from the Central American Common Market rose from $6.8 million in 1973 (representing 0.18 percent of total imports) to $32 million in 1980. (Given the increase in total Mexican imports, however, this figure represented only 0.16 percent of that total.)

The Mexican share of total foreign trade of the Central American Common Market has also been, historically, very small. Even with respect to Guatemala and Costa Rica, traditionally the leading partners, the share has never reached the figure of 5 percent, either for exports or imports. However, it is worth noting that Mexico has enjoyed a permanently favorable balance, which in 1980 reached $196 million.

Mexican direct investment in the area gained a certain dynamism during a short-lived honeymoon between Mexico and its neighbors to the south at the initiative of Mexican President Díaz Ordaz (1964–1970).[8] However, most of that investment has been sold back to those countries. Tourism has been relatively important in the past, accounting for 8 to 10 percent of total foreign travelers entering Mexico in the years before the Salvadoran and Nicaraguan revolutions. Since 1980 an increasing stream of migrants and political refugees, whose real number nobody knows exactly, have entered Mexico. It has been estimated, however, that most of these migrants have the United States as a final destination.

Table 7.3 MEXICAN TRADE WITH THE CENTRAL AMERICAN
COMMON MARKET 1973–1980

	EXPORTS		IMPORTS		
	Thousands of Dollars	*% of Total*	*Thousands of Dollars*	*% of Total*	*Balance (Thousands of Dollars)*
1973	51,952	2.51	6,886	0.18	45,066
1974	78,468	2.75	8,543	0.14	69,925
1975	81,204	2.84	16,191	0.25	65,013
1976	73,290	2.21	23,515	0.39	49,775
1977	111,635	2.67	16,763	0.30	94,872
1978	131,301	2.32	9,380	0.12	121,921
1979	136,724	1.55	13,017	0.10	123,707
1980	228,665	1.49	32,047	0.16	196,618

SOURCE: 1973 to 1977: "Anuario Estadístico de Comercio Exterior de los Estados Unidos Mexicanos," Secretarí de Programación y Presupuesto, respectively.

1978: Secretaría de Hacienda.

1979–1980: "Comercio Exterior de México," vol. 4, núm. 1 (Internal Document), Secretaría de Programación y Presupuesto.

The only important aspect of the relationship has been in the cultural field. Thousands of Central Americans have traditionally preferred to continue their education in Mexican institutions of higher education. There has also been, historically, a permanent flow of Mexican artists to Central America, and Mexican television programs are a common feature there. There is no doubt that Mexico exercises an important cultural influence over the area. This explains why many talented Central Americans have come to Mexico for intellectual and artistic recognition. Finally, and more importantly, Mexico traditionally has been the place of shelter for many Central American exiles.

This general picture of mutual commercial neglect, however, has begun to change, mainly because of oil exports. It is only with respect to Nicaragua, whose revolution Mexico is warmly supporting, that it is possible to speak about an ample presence of Mexico in the region. And even there, the support has been mainly political, with only a tiny flow of trade taking place apart from oil. The fact that the Mexican and Central American economies present few opportunities for complementarity constitutes the key explanatory variable.

The six Central American countries, including Panama, plus the Caribbean countries of Barbados, Haiti, Jamaica, and the Dominican Republic, together imported a total of 236,000 barrels daily (b/d) of crude oil and refined products in 1977. This figure fell to 222,000 b/d in 1979. Most of this imported oil came from Venezuela under special

Table 7.4 IMPORTANCE OF COMMERCE WITH MEXICO FOR CENTRAL AMERICA

Country	1973 Thousands of Dollars	1973 % with Mexico	1974 Thousands of Dollars	1974 % with Mexico	1975 Thousands of Dollars	1975 % with Mexico	1976 Thousands of Dollars	1976 % with Mexico	1977 Thousands of Dollars	1977 % with Mexico
Costa Rica										
Exports	344,800	0.3	440,200	0.6	493,100	1.5	592,400	1.2	814,800	0.1
Imports	412,100	2.9	648,400	3.0	627,200	4.2	695,400	3.0	909,100	2.7
El Salvador										
Exports	358,400	0.2	463,900	0.0	531,600	0.3	743,300	0.6	972,300	0.3
Imports	339,800	3.0	522,200	2.8	550,500	2.5	683,600	1.5	858,500	1.9
Guatemala										
Exports	422,000	0.6	582,300	0.7	640,900	0.8	784,400	0.6	1,191,600	0.5
Imports	391,400	4.2	631,500	3.8	672,400	3.6	959,200	2.8	1,140,900	3.8
Honduras										
Exports	266,600	0.0	298,700	0.0	307,800	0.6	403,400	0.6	522,100	0.0
Imports	243,400	1.9	387,900	2.1	377,600	2.2	427,100	1.5	549,800	2.5
Nicaragua										
Exports	275,100	0.8	377,000	0.3	371,300	0.0	538,500	0.9	625,900	1.1
Imports	326,900	2.6	540,300	2.4	482,100	1.7	485,000	1.8	704,000	2.0

SOURCE: "Banco Interamericano de Desarrollo, Informe Anual 1978" and *Anuarios Estadísticos de Comercio Exterior de los Estados Unidox Mexicanos*, various years.

Table 7.5 MEXICAN PETROLEUM EXPORTS BY COUNTRY
JANUARY 1981
(Barrels daily)

United States	733,000
Spain	220,000
Japan	100,000
France	100,000
Canada	50,000
Israel	45,000
Brazil	40,000
India	30,000
Costa Rica	7,500
El Salvador	7,500
Nicaragua	7,500
Yugoslavia	3,000

SOURCE: Statements of the director of PEMEX, Jorge Diaz Serrano, to the press. *Excélsior,* Jan. 28, 1981, pp. 1 and 8.

conditions granted by that country unilaterally. To a lesser degree, the area imported oil from Curaçao, Trinidad-Tobago, and Ecuador, as well as from extraregional countries such as Saudi Arabia, Nigeria, Indonesia, and Libya.

In August 1980, the presidents of Mexico and Venezuela, López Portillo and Herrera Campins, met at San José, Costa Rica, and agreed to develop a program for the supply of oil to the region on the basis of special treatment. The San José agreement established a supply of oil up to a quantity of 160,000 b/d, to be distributed in equal parts by Mexico and Venezuela at prices similar to those that each country charges its other customers. There is, thus, no direct special price concession. However, both governments agreed to grant a credit of 30 percent of total sales to each country on very liberal terms: a five-year amortization period with an interest rate of 5 percent. Moreover, the agreement established that, if the recipient countries agree to use the energy resources acquired under the credit system for priority de-

Table 7.6 NEW MEXICAN EXPORT AGREEMENTS
FOR 1981
(Barrels Daily)

Sweden	70,000
Jamaica	13,000
Phillipines	10,000
Panama	12,000
Guatemala	7,500
Honduras	6,000
Haiti	3,500

SOURCE: See Table 7.5.

velopment projects, particularly those related to the energy sector, credits may be granted up to a twenty-year period with an interest rate of 2 percent.

It is logical to assume then that through this agreement Mexico and Venezuela have gained a certain degree of political influence in the region. The least that could be said is that through this mechanism both countries wish to help to alleviate social tensions and economic difficulties deriving from rising oil prices. Thus, Mexico and Venezuela should be seen as trying to contribute to the stabilization of the region. In this sense, the Mexican role in the region seems to be in supporting moderate change rather than in patronizing revolutions. After all, countries such as Guatemala and El Salvador are also beneficiaries of the San José agreement.

But the San José agreement should also be seen, at least in the case of Mexico, as a way to compensate vis-à-vis its domestic public opinion for what from a Mexican perspective appear as huge sales of oil to industrial countries such as France, Japan, and the United States, which together accounted for nearly 70 percent of total Mexican oil exports in 1980. In addition it should be noted that in this manner Mexico is implementing its own project submitted at the United Nations, which called for an international plan to rationalize oil production and consumption.

In the particular case of Nicaragua, Mexico has extended its energy assistance to the field of exploration. PEMEX, the national petroleum company, has initiated some projects in hopes of discovering fields that might rescue Nicaragua from its present heavy dependence on foreign oil. Simultaneously, Mexico has been supporting the reconstruction efforts of the Nicaraguan revolutionary government in other various ways.

A good example of this is the creation of a binational state enterprise for the exploitation and industrialization of forest products. Other important areas such as mining, geothermal energy, fishing, communications and transportation have received increasing attention from Mexican programs of economic and technical aid. Technical assistance has also been extended to public entities in charge of programs of social welfare, such as food distribution, health, housing, and urban public transportation.

It is difficult to assess the general amount of Mexican assistance to Nicaragua since there is no central office for the coordination of the various programs.[9] However, independent sources considered Mexico as the "chief external patron" of the Nicaraguan Revolution in 1980.[10] In the early months of 1981, however, this picture must have changed, since Libya entered the scene with a general credit of $100 million to offset the United States decision to suspend aid to Nicaragua on charges that Nicaragua was supplying arms to the Salvadoran guerrillas. Nevertheless, it is worth noting that Mexico's aid was considered higher than that granted by the United States and other Western industrial countries such as the Federal Republic of Germany. An undisputed fact is that Mexico has been the chief source of Latin American aid to Nicaragua. Another independent and more recent estimate considered that "Of all of the financial aid received by the Sandinista government through early 1981, Mexico supplied fully 16 percent, more than twice the amount coming from any other Latin American nation."[11]

However, the main support that Mexico has given to the Nicaraguan Revolution has been of a political nature. Mexico broke off relations with the Somoza government in an effort to accelerate its downfall and to enlist other governments behind the cause of the Nicaraguan Revolution. Equally important, the Mexican government committed itself officially as guarantor of the Nicaraguan external debt some days before Nicaragua entered into negotiations with its creditors. Mexico thus was putting her solvency, derived from the oil reserves, at the service of the Nicaraguan Revolution. Moreover, Mexico was demonstrating to the world at large its public commitment for the cause of the Nicaraguan Revolution.

Another illustrative case is the Mexican mediation between Nicaragua and Honduras. In May 1981, Daniel Ortega, coordinator of the Nicaraguan Junta of National Reconstruction, made an official visit to President López Portillo in Mexico City. Ortega visited Mexico at a time when there was strong speculation regarding open hostilities between Nicaragua and Honduras. The speculation had a certain basis in reality given the series of incidents on their border. On the occasion of the visit, President López Portillo made public an offer to mediate between the two countries. This action had an almost automatic and immediate effect. Upon his return to Nicaragua, Ortega met with Honduran President Policarpo Paz at the border between the two countries and both agreed to a joint declaration stating that their governments were committed to keeping peace between their countries. They also decided to immediately set up joint commissions that would study realistic measures to stop the continuation of border incidents.[12] This was a very important achievement for the Nicaraguan government, since the basic concern over national security has centered around the border with Honduras, a country in which the major concentration of Somoza's National Guard took shelter.

But the most important way in which the Mexican government of

López Portillo has given political support to the Nicaraguan revolution is as guarantor of U.S. nonintervention. Mexico has taken great efforts to convince Washington neither to intervene directly nor to support the counterrevolutionary groups in an action against Nicaragua. This role became definitively important after the arrival to power of the Reagan administration. It is always difficult to speculate about what could have happened in the absence of such Mexican action. However, there are grounds to believe that, without the mediating role of Mexico, Washington would have undertaken, perhaps not definitive action against the Nicaraguan government, but at least a destabilization effort through a de facto economic blockade and convincing other countries of the region to enter into a campaign of diplomatic isolation and political condemnation of Nicaragua.

The Past Experience of Mexican Foreign Policy

We can expect that Mexico will continue to pursue a policy of nonintervention with respect to the crisis of El Salvador and similar ones that may arise in the region in the future. But it is important to underline that this policy will concern Washington as much as Moscow, Havana, and other potential actors. If history is a solid basis for explaining the present, we must look to past experience if we want to understand the current position of Mexico and predict its behavior in the immediate future. To do this, we could turn to the decade of the 1960s, when the emergence of a Socialist regime in Cuba and its subsequent alliance with the Soviet Union abruptly placed Latin America on the cold war map.

During the conflicts of the 1960s, Mexico always opposed intervention in Cuba, most notably at the meeting of foreign ministers at the OAS. In 1962, at Punta del Este, Mexico opposed the exclusion of Cuba from the inter-American system and in 1964, in Washington, Mexico voted against the resolution calling upon all members of the OAS to break off relations with Cuba. Not only did Mexico oppose a legally binding resolution, it decided not to honor it; other countries, such as Chile, Bolivia, and Uruguay, which by that time were the only countries, along with Mexico, that still maintained relations, broke their ties with the Cuban government in response to the mandatory resolution.[13] One year later, in 1965, again in Washington, this time with respect to the political crisis in the Dominican Republic, Mexico voted against the creation of an inter-American peace force and introduced a resolution that the U.S. expeditionary force leave the Dominican Republic. Mexico simultaneously introduced a similar resolution at the United Nations.

However, there is another case that it is important to consider. At the time of the so-called missile crisis in October of 1962, the council of the OAS unanimously approved a resolution supporting measures that assured the withdrawal of the Soviet missiles from Cuba, "including the use of armed force." The Mexican delegation, together with those of Brazil and Bolivia, introduced a reservation to the effect that this resolution should not be taken as a justification for an armed attack on Cuba. In other words, while it is true that Mexico, Brazil, and Bolivia voted to approve a naval blockade of the island, including perhaps a "surgical" bombing of the bases, on the other hand they opposed the use of this approval as an excuse to invade Cuba and overthrow the revolutionary government. Approval of the resolution, but with this reservation, suggests that these three countries opposed the conversion of Cuba into a military base of an extracontinental power, but at the same time opposed intervention in the internal affairs of an American republic; that is, they opposed use of the crisis as an excuse for a "definitive" action against the Cuban Revolution. Thus the distinction between a regional and a global confrontation remained explicit.

Another relevant past experience was the resolutions approved in 1967 by the Organización Latinoamericana de Solidaridad (OLAS), an organization created in that year under the auspices of the Castro government to foment revolution in Latin America. On that occasion, Mexico also came out in defense of the principle of nonintervention, this time confronting Cuba itself. It is interesting to examine the statement of the Mexican foreign ministry:

> There can be no doubt that the Mexican government disapproves the resolutions voted in Havana in July and August of this year by an organization called Latinoamericana de Solidaridad; just as in a previous occasion the Mexican Delegate in the Council of the OAS expressed it with respect to some of the conclusions of the Conferencia de Solidaridad de los Pueblos de África, Asia y América Latina, which was also celebrated in Cuba during the first half of January 1968.
>
> As all of you can confirm, Mexico has tried very hard to understand Cuba and to defend the principles of Non-Intervention and Self-Determination which protect its people to allow it to freely modify its institutions and its form of government; but if in violation of these principles there is an attempt to disregard our free self-determination, intervening in matters which only Mexico has a right to decide, there will be no other recourse but to take the measures which our own defense counsels.[14]

In 1967 Pat Holt, then influential advisor to the Committee on

Foreign Affairs of the U.S. Senate, made a statement that is most important and revealing for our analysis:

> It is worth the trouble to note the apparent paradox that Mexico is the Latin American country with which the United States has maintained the best relations and also the one which most inflexibly resists all types of collective action against Cuba. Even more, Mexico is the only country in Latin America which has for principle refused to sign an agreement guaranteeing United States investment and is one of the most attractive places for United States investment. It is the only Latin American country which does not have an agreement for military assistance with the United States (again for principle) and is one of the few Latin American countries where there is unquestionably civil control of the armed forces.[15]

One year after posing this paradox, Holt himself undertook to explain it:

> It is somewhat strange in the United States, but it appears that Mexico has a special dispensation to [dissent]. If the Mexicans oppose in the OAS something which the Department of State strongly desires, every one takes it in stride, no one is upset, and we remain friends with the Mexicans.[16]

In effect, there seemed to exist a sort of tacit understanding between Mexico and the United States by means of which Washington recognized and accepted Mexico's need to dissent from U.S. policy in everything that was fundamental for Mexico, even though it was important, but not fundamental, for the United States. In exchange, Mexico offered its cooperation in everything that was truly fundamental for the United States. It seems clear that this is what happened in the case of the missile crisis in 1962: Mexico supported the resolution that approved the measures that assured the dismantling of the Soviet missile bases in Cuba, "including the use of armed force," but at the same time introduced a reservation to the effect that this should not be taken as a justification for a "definitive" action against the Cuban revolutionary government.

However, history has also taught us that events do not repeat themselves in exactly the same way and, while these situations are very similar, each has its own peculiarities. While it is true that the 1980s tend to point to the resurgence of the cold war, there have been important changes in the international and regional structures since the 1960s. In the first place, as Abraham Lowenthal has well stated, U.S.

power in the world has diminished appreciably in relative terms.[17] That is to say, not that the United States is less strong today than in the 1970s, but a number of countries are less weak than they were twenty years ago. In the second place, Mexico today possesses a concrete instrument of economic power and political influence in its petroleum; even though we do not yet know to what degree of political use it will be put, there can be no doubt that it is an important element for negotiation and international influence. Third and last, there appears to exist today a regional atmosphere more conducive to solidarity and cooperation among the countries in the area. Perhaps this new atmosphere is also conducive to a complementary energy trade between Venezuela and Mexico and the rest of the countries in the region. There is no doubt that there has been a heightened consciousness—at least among countries with civil governments such as Colombia, Costa Rica, Jamaica, Venezuela, and Mexico—of the necessity of strengthening ties through economic cooperation and political solidarity in the face of an increasingly shaky world economy.

Regional Politics vs. Bilateral Relations

The constant dilemma of Mexican foreign policy has been the choice between—or the conciliation of—two principal objectives: maintaining her noninterventionist line and keeping good relations with the United States. The first objective is important in order to keep continuity and consistency in foreign policy matters for both internal as well as external considerations. The second reflects the importance and the complexity of the bilateral relationship and Mexico's high degree of economic dependence upon the United States.

The cases of Cuba and the Dominican Republic again illustrate this dilemma. By opposing the breaking of relations with Cuba and U.S. intervention in the Dominican Republic in 1965, Mexico became subject to U.S. economic sanctions.[18] It seems clear that in the cost-benefit analysis that preceded these decisions, the economic losses resulting from possible sanctions were considered less important than the weakening of the continuity of Mexico's nonintervention policy, which forms the basis of the country's defense in the long term. Furthermore, the Mexican government was concerned that a break with Cuba could generate internal instability. In other words, the fear of approving measures that would break from its policy of nonintervention and that in the future could work against Mexico, making it a victim of intervention from one side or another, explain in great part Mexican policy within the inter-American regional system.

The United States has also sought to maintain a clear-cut line between regional politics and bilateral relations in her relationship with Mexico, if only in recognition of Mexico's need to adhere to tradition. The international behavior of Mexico during the last three or four decades suggests a consistent pattern and the acceptance or tolerance of this pattern by the United States. This tends to suggest, in turn, a second type of tacit agreement by which Mexico's dissent is tolerated on matters of economic and symbolic global issues, as well as in regional political issues, in exchange for cooperation on important global political issues. Since the limits are not of course perfectly defined, at times there emerges a confrontation between the two governments, as was the case with Cuba in 1964 and as is the case today with respect to El Salvador.

There are various recent cases that substantiate this assertion. Mexico has dissented from U.S. actions on matters mainly of a regional character. Among decisions that otherwise could have had an important impact on domestic politics are the following: Mexico did not join the boycott to the Moscow Olympic Games; it refused to grant a second visa to the shah, once the Iranian students had taken the U.S. Embassy and kept the personnel as hostages; it broke off relations with Somoza and today gives support, political as well as economic and technical, to the revolutionary government in Nicaragua; it dissents from U.S. policy to El Salvador and keeps very good relations with Cuba; and finally, Mexico did not join the General Agreement on Tariffs and Trade (GATT).

On the other hand, Mexico directed its first oil exports to Israel and the United States at a time when there were many potential customers and some Latin American countries were facing great difficulties; it has not joined OPEC, thereby helping to brake the force of the organization; it revised the ceiling of oil production in 1980 for a second time, to be able to meet demands from Western industrial customers, as well as from some developing nations such as India; it condemned the occupation of the U.S. Embassy in Teheran and the holding of its personnel as hostages; it also condemned the intervention of Soviet troops in Afghanistan; and finally, it submitted at the United Nations, with the obvious discomfort of the OPEC countries, a project for a global plan of rationalization of production and consumption of energy.

The case of Nicaragua—the breaking off of relations with Somoza—is a special one. Mexico was pushed by circumstances to adopt the Sandinista revolutionary movement. The first government to support the Nicaragua Revolution was that of Carlos Andrés Pérez of Venezuela with the assistance of Panama and Costa Rica. But by March 1979 Pérez had ended his presidential term, and the opposition Christian Democrats had been elected. The new Venezuelan government discontinued its assistance to the Nicaraguan revolutionaries, leaving a vacuum that could well have tempted either the United States or Cuba to enter the scene. In that event, the danger of an internationalization of the civil war could have been very real. At that moment Mexico entered the field, breaking off relations with Somoza and adopting the revolutionaries.

On the other hand, there are historical ties between Mexico and the Sandinistas. In the 1920s the Mexican government supported Augusto Sandino (from whom the present-day Sandinistas take their name) in his struggle against U.S. occupation. Moreover, the 1978–1979 revolution in Nicaragua was a clear-cut struggle between a pluriclass, nationwide alliance, against an old, hereditary military dictatorship that originated through an imposition by a foreign power. This facilitated the continuing identification of Mexico with the anti-Somocista struggle.

In this discussion of Mexican foreign policy, also worth noting is a dramatic example of the pragmatic formula by which the Mexican government faces the ever-present dilemma of its foreign policy: maintaining an independent, nationalist posture without affecting its bilateral relations with the United States. The very same day in which President López Portillo announced the decision to increase the ceiling of oil production—a decision that obviously pleased Washington but that displeased the nationalists in Mexico—he also announced the decision not to join the GATT—a decision that obviously displeased Washington but pleased Mexican nationalists.

Finally, although it is impossible to predict events in the immediate future with complete certainty, we would like to end this chapter with a quotation from a statement of President López Portillo that confirms and summarizes the principal thesis put forth here: that with respect to Central America, the Mexican government will adhere to the principles of self-determination and of nonintervention, simultaneously encouraging political solutions and striving to ensure that this position does not adversely affect the bilateral relations of Mexico and the United States. In an obvious effort to attempt to explain this position to the American people in order to lessen tensions and avoid prejudicing bilateral relations, the Mexican president, taking advantage of a nationwide interview broadcast by CBS television in the United States, stated the following:

I would like, if I may take the opportunity, to let the people of the United States know that Mexico is not a troublesome country nor does it arrogantly oppose the actions of the authorities of your country; our position is a question of principles and we believe in principles; we do not believe in the principle of force, but in the force of principles, and in that belief we are firm and constant; we are not hostile. Naturally we do not want to have problems with our very powerful neighbor; but I believe that our principles must be defended if we believe in them.[19]

NOTES

1. On this subject, see the article by Roman Mayorga in *Foro Internacional,* forthcoming.

2. *Hanson's Latin American Letter,* no. 1826, Washington, D.C., Mar. 15, 1980.

3. Ronald Yates, "Appeasement: López Portillo Following Course Set by Neville Chamberlain." *Houston Post,* Apr. 1, 1981.

4. Constantine Christopher Menges, "Current Mexican Foreign Policy, Revolution in Central America and the United States," mimeographed, The Hudson Institute, Arlington, Va., June 1980, p. 3.

5. Alan Riding, *New York Times Magazine,* Jan. 11, 1981, p. 22.

6. Charles Maynes, *Los Angeles Times,* Mar. 1, 1981. Cited by Jorge Bustamante, *Uno Mas Uno,* Mexico, D.F., Mar. 2, 1981, p. 2.

7. Given the profound dependence of Mexico on the United States, "independent" here signifies a policy that allows a greater capacity to negotiate Mexican positions with the United States (bilateral affairs); second, a greater autonomy to evaluate and decide actions in the multilateral arena with other industrialized powers; and third, to understand relations with countries with which Mexico shares geographical ties, in accord with a framework of priorities consistent with its national interest, independently of the hegemonic interests of other nations.

8. See in this respect the chapter by Ramon Medina Luna in Mario Ojeda et al., *Mexico y America Latina* (Mexico: El Colegio de México, 1974).

9. For the joint industrial development projects, see the December 1, 1980, issue of *El Mercado de Valores* (Mexico, Nacional Financiera, S.A.).

10. See in this respect, "Aiding Democracy," *Latin America Regional Report,* Feb. 15, 1980, p. 4.

11. Edward J. Williams, "Mexico's Central American Policy: Revolutionary and Prudential Dimensions," paper presented at the annual meeting of the Caribbean Studies Association, Saint Thomas, U.S. Virgin Islands, May 1981, p. 9.

12. *Excélsior,* Mexico, May 8, 9, and 14, 1981.

13. In the OAS in the 1960s, a resolution approved by two-thirds of the members obligated all members, even those who voted against the resolution.

14. Speech of Mexican Foreign Minister Antonio Carillo Flores before the Twelfth Consultive Meeting of the OAS held in Washington in 1967. *Memoria de la Secretaría de Relaciones Exteriores* (México, 1968), pp. 390–394.

15. Pat Holt, *Survey of the Alliance for Progress: The Political Aspects,* study prepared for the Subcommittee of American Republics Affairs, Committee of Foreign Relations, U.S. Senate, Washington, 1967, p. 14.

16. U.S. Senate, "Survey of the Alliance for Progress," *Hearings before the Subcommittee of American Republics Affairs,* Washington, 1968, p. 218.

17. "United States-Latin American Relations in the 1980s," in Prosper Gifford (ed.) *The National Interests of the United States* (Woodrow Wilson International Center for Scholars, Smithsonian Institution, Washington, D.C.: University Press of America, 1981).

18. In 1965 the U.S. Congress decided to reduce the Mexican sugar import quota by 50,000 tons. Asked why, the president of the Agriculture Committee of the Senate replied that Mexico did not depend primarily on her sugar exports and that "her foreign policy is not very close to that of the United States, especially in the OAS." Earlier, Charles Teague, a member of the House of Representatives, had stated: "It would please me if we note in the record that we would have had a more favorable reaction to Mexican interests if Mexico had given us her support in Cuba and the Dominican Republic." See notes in *El Día,* Aug. 21 and Sept. 29, 1965. The application of these sanctions was publicly confirmed a year later by Ambassador of Mexico to the United States Hugo Margain, who stated that the sanctions had been granted "based on inappropriate criticism in our international policy, with reference to the attitude adopted by our country with respect to Cuba, with respect to the armed intervention in the Dominican Republic, and for our supposed lack of support for the Alliance for Progress." He added that this could be confirmed in the Daily Record of Debates in the United States Congress for Oct. 22, 1965, pp. 27, 339. See *El Día,* Oct. 8, 1966.

19. CBS interview broadcast in the United States on Mar. 17, 1981. Text reproduced in *Uno Más Uno,* México, Mar. 18, 1981.

8. Venezuelan Policy in the Caribbean Basin

Robert D. Bond

We reject any attempt to transfer to the Caribbean the frictions and confrontation between the big powers or to convert it into an area of ideological and political influence. We hope regimes that are the legitimate expressions of the people's desires will be established in the area. We hope those regimes will promote the growing process of social, economic, political, and cultural development.
—*Luis Herrera Campins, State of the Nation Address, March 14, 1980, Caracas.*

Venezuela has always been a part of the Caribbean basin. The country possesses a six-hundred-mile coastline that is washed by the Caribbean Sea, and there exists a long history of political and economic interaction with the peoples of the islands and Central America. Simón Bolívar and others in the liberation struggle sought refuge there, as did political exiles down to the present century.[1] And there have always been substantial trade and interchange of peoples between Venezuela and its Caribbean neighbors.

It is only in recent times, however, that Venezuela has assumed an active leadership role in the subregion. Indeed, it is fair to say that prior to 1969 successive Venezuelan governments paid only marginal attention to the Caribbean basin (except for Cuba), tacitly acknowledging Spanish, British, and North American dominance of the area. However, during the Social Christian government of President Rafael Caldera (1969–1973), Venezuela initiated a policy of a heightened Venezuelan presence in the Caribbean.[2] For example, by the end of Caldera's term in office, the head of government of every political unit in the English- and Dutch-speaking Caribbean except Barbados had visited Venezuela at least once, and Foreign Minister Aristides Calvani had made five major trips into the Caribbean. Subsequent administrations expanded Venezuela's influence in the Caribbean through the

187

judicious use of petrodollars following the quadrupling of oil prices in 1973–1974. President Carlos Andrés Pérez (1974–1978) of the Acción Democrática party (AD) championed Panama's right to control the Canal, inaugurated a series of bilateral concessional loans to offset the higher cost of petroleum, and promoted the reintegration of Cuba into the Latin American community. President Luis Herrera Campins of the Social Christian party Copei (1979–1983) expanded the program of concessional loans to finance oil purchases, contributed over $100 million in financial assistance to Nicaragua following the revolution, assisted Jamaica with its balance of payment difficulties, and has been a staunch supporter of the government of José Napoleón Duarte in El Salvador. In recent years, Venezuelan foreign assistance has amounted to approximately 2 percent of its gross domestic product, most of which is earmarked for the countries of the Caribbean basin.

While the thrust of Venezuelan initiatives in the Caribbean basin is clear, the overarching goals of policy toward the subregion remain elusive. Until the revolution in Nicaragua and the current crisis in El Salvador, Venezuela enjoyed the luxury of confronting the geopolitical and development issues of Central America and the Caribbean in relative isolation one from the other. The plethora of newly emerging nation-states in the area, most of them bitterly poor, made the region ideal for the disbursement of limited amounts of financial assistance, thereby deflecting charges that Venezuela was benefiting from high petroleum prices at the expense of its neighbors. In addition, the absence of any immediate security interests in Central America and the Caribbean permitted Venezuelan policymakers to pursue a long-term policy of gradually expanding Venezuelan influence in the region.

Today Venezuelan policymakers confront a radically different situation in the Caribbean basin—especially in Central America—than the one prevailing in the early 1970s when Venezuela's active involvement in the region began. The political climate in several Central American countries has become increasingly polarized and militarized, raising questions about Venezuela's strategy of promoting long-term stability through economic assistance. Cuba has returned to an active role in support of revolution in Latin America, supporting the Sandinistas in Nicaragua and channeling arms to the guerrillas in El Salvador. The United States, reacting to deteriorating political and economic conditions in the area and to evidence of Cuban-Soviet involvement, is attempting to reassert its traditional dominance over the Caribbean. And finally, Venezuelan policy toward the Caribbean basin has become a hotly contested partisan issue, with the government of Luis Herrera Campins attempting to promote Christian Democracy in the region while a majority of the leaders of AD are aligned with the policy of the Socialist International in support of revolutionary change.

The internationalization of conflict in the Caribbean poses a number of problems for Venezuelan foreign policy. In the analysis that follows, I develop three main themes. First, for the last decade Venezuela has been playing a major role in the Caribbean. Second, the Herrera administration strongly supports the Salvadoran junta headed by their Christian Democrat colleague, Napoleón Duarte, but the Venezuelan government is likely to press increasingly for a political solution to the Salvadoran conflict. Finally, although Venezuela can be expected to continue its active role in the region over the long term, it is at least possible that it will decrease its involvement in the near term for essentially domestic political reasons.

The Origins and Conduct of Venezuelan Foreign Policy

Before turning to a detailed examination of Venezuelan policy toward the Caribbean basin, it is helpful to begin with a few more general observations. First, Venezuela's role in international affairs is inextricably tied to oil. Venezuela has been a major oil producer for over fifty years, and it was a cofounder of the Organization of Petroleum Exporting Countries (OPEC).[3] Today Venezuela continues to export more petroleum than any other nation in the Western Hemisphere—an average of about 2 million barrels per day (mbd) over the last six years. Although recent discoveries in Mexico have attracted considerable attention, Venezuela's importance to the hemispheric oil trade remains undiminished. Mexico's oil exports will probably trail Venezuela's until late in the 1980s, although total Mexican production will be greater. Venezuela has proven reserves of 18 billion barrels of conventional oil, and Venezuelan authorities claim that it is highly probable that they will discover additional deposits of conventional oil that will increase proven reserves to 30 billion barrels. There also exist an additional 700 billion to 1.5 trillion barrels of heavy crude in the Orinoco oil belt, which Venezuela is now beginning to develop with a target of 1 million barrels per day by the year 2000.

Second, the priority foreign policy issues for Venezuela are those that have a direct bearing upon the nation's political and economic development program.[4] Since 1958, Venezuela's democratic leaders have pursued a cluster of development goals: consolidation of a democratic political system; nationalization of the petroleum industry (accomplished in 1976); diversified economic growth; and greater equity in the distribution of the benefits of economic progress. This means that Venezuelan policymakers *must* focus on oil matters generally—OPEC, the legitimization of cartels, and bilateral trade relations with the United States. Relations with Latin America are important insofar as Venezuela does not want to be isolated on a continent of authoritarian regimes; nor does it want to be accused of benefiting from high petroleum prices at the expense of its neighbors.

Third, personal leadership plays an important role in determining Venezuelan foreign policy, especially in nonoil matters. Both tradition and the Venezuelan constitution grant the president a preponderant role in the conduct of international relations. In recent years Venezuelan presidents have tended to be their own secretaries of state, trusting in a small cadre of foreign policy advisors. This was particularly true of the presidency of Carlos Andrés Pérez, who seemed to be guided in hemispheric policy by a Bolivarian vision of a unified Latin America. The current Venezuelan president, Luis Herrera Campins, is more reserved and less energetic in policymaking than was Pérez, but he remains the key actor in determining foreign policy. It should also be noted that the quality of the Venezuelan foreign service is decidedly uneven, although the level of professionalization is being slowly upgraded.

Finally, over the years Venezuelan foreign policy has developed a distinctive style, perhaps as a result of ongoing attempts by Venezuela's leaders to institutionalize democracy at home. Franklin Tugwell has characterized the foreign policy style of Venezuela as "consociational." By this he means:

> This refers not just to willingness to work together with others to resolve problems, but more important, to a strong inclination wherever possible to build institutional and associational frameworks to handle problems on a more organized, long-term basis. It also refers to a willingness to disaggregate conflicts, i.e., to prevent one issue in conflict from overlapping with others and to prevent adversarial aspects of a relationship from overriding and obscuring opportunities for cooperation in other areas.[5]

Examples of the preference of Venezuela's foreign policy decisionmakers for institutional mechanisms for dealing with problems include OPEC, the Andean Pact, the Latin American Economic System (SELA), and the Latin American Energy Organization (OLADE). In essence, under all its democratic presidents, Venezuela has projected its democratic values into its foreign policy.

Venezuela and the Caribbean Basin from Betancourt to Herrera

During the presidencies of Rómulo Betancourt (1959–1963) and Raul Leoni (1964–1968), conflict was the theme of Venezuela's relations with the Caribbean basin. Specifically, Betancourt and Leoni battled to prevent armed intervention in Venezuelan affairs from the Dominican Republic and Cuba.

The central tenet of Venezuelan foreign policy in the 1959–1968 period was the "Betancourt Doctrine," which demanded the withholding of diplomatic recognition from illegitimate regimes. This doctrine was applied most importantly to two Caribbean regimes, those of Rafael Trujillo in the Dominican Republic and Fidel Castro in Cuba. Trujillo, dictator of the Dominican Republic from 1930 to 1961, enjoyed close relations with Venezuelan dictator Marcos Pérez Jiménez (1952–1958), and correspondingly vituperative ones with Venezuelan democratic leaders. After initial attempts to establish normal relations with Trujillo, by June 1959 Venezuela had joined with other Latin American states in seeking his overthrow. For example, Venezuela openly assisted the armed invasion on June 14, 1959, of the Dominican Republic originating in Cuba. In retaliation, Trujillo aided three attempts by right-wing military officers to overthrow Betancourt, including an assasination attempt on June 24, 1960. Ultimately Trujillo himself was assasinated on May 30, 1961, and Betancourt claimed that the policy of Venezuela had stimulated the act.[6]

Hostility also characterized relations with Cuba beginning early in 1960. During the Betancourt administration, ideological rivalry between Cuban socialism and Venezuelan democratic reformism as developmental models for Latin America was acute with Venezuela becoming a strong advocate of civilian rule in opposition to authoritarianism of the left and right. Throughout 1960 and 1961 Venezuelan spokesman denounced Cuban interference in Venezuelan politics.[7] On November 11, 1961, Venezuela broke diplomatic relations with Cuba, and in January 1962 it voted to exclude Cuba from the inter-American system. Throughout 1962 and 1963 Venezuelan government officials repeatedly charged that Cuba was training and arming Venezuelan guerrillas, and in November of 1963 Venezuelan troops discovered a cache of arms that subsequent investigation proved to have come from Cuba. In July 1964 the OAS voted to sever diplomatic and consular relations with Cuba and to suspend trade, based on Venezuela's charges. In 1966 and 1967 Venezuela renewed its charges of Cuban subversion, and in May 1967 Venezuelan troops captured a small landing party of guerrillas led by a lieutenant of the Cuban army.

By 1969 guerrilla activities in Venezuela had become a sporadic phenomenon. Accordingly, in his inaugural address Rafael Caldera of the Copei party announced his intention to abandon the Betancourt Doctrine, replacing it with the concepts of international social justice and ideological pluralism. In his inaugural address of March 1969, Caldera explicitly stated that "public opinion favors the establishment of relations with countries of political organization and ideology different from ours, for their presence can not be ignored."[8]

Under President Caldera, a new era opened in Venezuelan relations with the states of the Caribbean basin. The architect of this new Caribbean policy was Caldera's foreign minister, Aristides Calvani. Born in Trinidad and well-acquainted with the entire area, Calvani viewed the Caribbean as important to Venezuela in geopolitical terms for several reasons. First, Calvani viewed the islands lying off Venezuela's coast as crucial in guaranteeing the safe passage of Venezuelan oil to its chief market—the east coast of the United States. Second, Calvani was suspicious of Brazilian expansionism, and apparently believed Brazil wanted to extend its influence through Guyana to the Caribbean.[9] Third, Calvani saw the poor and backward island states as inherently unstable politically and, therefore, a security threat to Venezuela. Finally, Calvani saw in the Caribbean a potential market for Venezuelan products, particularly in such areas as textiles, food processing, light industry, and petrochemicals.

Accordingly, Calvani initiated a flurry of diplomatic activity with regard to the Caribbean. Most importantly, Venezuela sought to institutionalize contacts with its Caribbean neighbors, such as the informal consultative meeting of foreign ministers of Caribbean countries called by Venezuela and held in Caracas on November 24–26, 1971. The foreign ministers of Barbados, Colombia, Costa Rica, El Salvador, Guatemala, Haiti, Jamaica, Mexico, Nicaragua, Panama, the Dominican Republic, and Trinidad-Tobago attended and authorized Venezuela to call two more meetings to deal with regional transportation problems. In addition, in April of 1973 Venezuela became the first non–English-speaking member of the Caribbean Development Bank.

The administration of Carlos Andrés Pérez (1974–1978) pursued essentially the same foreign policy goals of President Caldera with regard to the Caribbean basin. For example, Pérez resumed diplomatic and trade relations with Cuba, a step that Caldera and Calvani had contemplated but decided to postpone because of the 1973 elections. Moreover, the belief that the stability of the Caribbean states was important to the long-term security of Venezuela remained. What was new about Pérez's policy was the scale: the sudden rise in oil prices provided Venezuela with the financial resources to play a much larger role in the subregion, extending Venezuelan influence to the Central American isthmus.

Pérez moved quickly to intensify Venezuela's ties with Central America.[10] In December 1974 at Puerto Ordaz, Venezuela agreed to a cash–loan-plan program to offset the increase in the oil costs of Central American countries because of OPEC price increases since 1971. The scheme called for the Central American promoters to pay roughly 50 percent of the market price. The remainder was placed as a loan in the respective countries' banks. Interest was set at 8 percent, and repayment could stretch over twenty-five years; the estimated value of the program was $460 million. Also at the Puerto Ordaz meeting, Venezuela announced a $40 million loan to the Central American Bank for Economic Integration and pledged $80 million to support a Central American coffee producers' scheme to withhold their 1973–1974 and 1974–1975 crops from the market in an attempt to raise prices.

In addition to economic assistance programs, the Pérez administration took strong stands on two political issues: the Panama Canal and the controversy over Belize. Pérez was instrumental in rounding up Latin American support for Panama's claims against the United States, and he also clandestinely financed publicity campaigns in the United States designed to swing public opinion behind the two treaties eventually negotiated.[11] In Belize, Pérez was mindful of the concerns of his Caribbean neighbors, announcing in November 1975 that Venezuela would not support Guatemala in the boundary controversy.

Perhaps the most controversial policy toward Central America adopted by Venezuela during the Pérez administration was support of the Sandinista Liberation Front in the revolution against Somoza in Nicaragua. In 1977 and 1978, Venezuela gave strong public and clandestine military support to groups in opposition to Somoza, and successfully opposed U.S. proposals in the Organization of American States for an inter-American peacekeeping force to separate the two sides in the Nicaraguan civil war. The Pérez administration adopted its stance of active opposition to Somoza for several reasons: (1) Several leaders of AD had a long-standing antipathy for the Somoza dynasty dating from their period in exile (1948–1958) when the Somozas cooperated with Pérez Jiménez; (2) AD leaders believed that economic and social inequalities, not Communist influence, were the root causes of the civil war; (3) AD leaders were opposed to U.S. intervention in the region; and (4) AD leaders believed the prospects for the emergence of a social democratic regime in Nicaragua would be increased if Somoza were overthrown sooner rather than later.[12]

President Luis Herrera Campins assumed office in March 1979 at a difficult juncture in Venezuelan policy toward the Caribbean basin. The Somoza regime in Nicaragua was about to be replaced by a revolutionary government; the escalating violence in El Salvador would soon result in a military coup and the formation of a civil-military "reformist" junta; and Venezuela's relations with Cuba would worsen significantly. In response to these developments, Herrera soon fashioned a new policy toward the subregion that combined the traditional support for democratic values and the use of oil as a political tool with a dramatically new orientation—the promotion of Christian Democratic interests.

The Herrera administration, like its two predecessors, viewed a politically stable and economically prosperous Caribbean basin as enhancing the long-term security interests of Venezuela. Herrera and his advisors believed that Venezuela should continue to assist its more disadvantaged neighbors in meeting their oil requirements and development aspirations. As a result, the Herrera government decided to extend the program of financial and technical assistance to the Caribbean begun six years earlier by President Pérez. More specifically, Venezuela and Mexico agreed to supply equal shares of the oil needs of nine Caribbean countries (Barbados, Costa Rica, El Salvador, Guatemala, Honduras, Jamaica, Nicaragua, Panama, and the Dominican Republic), and to extend loans for 30 percent of the oil bills for a five-year period at 4 percent interest, which could be converted to twenty-year loans at 2 percent if invested in high priority economic and energy development projects. The cost of this program is estimated at $700 million per year. Venezuela initiated the proposal, with Minister of Mines and Hydrocarbons Calderon Berti playing the leading role, as a way of promoting stability in a region where several countries are facing serious economic problems because of oil imports. However, it should be noted that the Venezuelan Foreign Ministry has failed to develop a program of economic assistance for the Caribbean basin, and there is little likelihood that it will do so. The Venezuelan Foreign Ministry, particularly in comparison to the Mines Ministry, is seriously understaffed and lacks trained technicians knowledgeable about the region who are capable of implementing a sustained aid program.

The new Christian Democratic orientation of Venezuelan foreign policy toward the Caribbean basin was most evident in the cases of Nicaragua, Cuba, and El Salvador. In Nicaragua, where the Sandinistas enjoyed the strong support of the Pérez administration and the Socialist International generally, President Herrera has added an ideological dimension to Venezuelan policy toward the Nicaraguan government. During his visit to Nicaragua in 1980, Herrera conspicuously sounded the praises of democratic government and cautioned the Sandinista leaders that continued Venezuelan aid would depend on the acceptance of democratic leaders, especially Christian Democrats, into the highest levels of government.

Venezuelan-Cuban relations are at their lowest point since the mid-1960s. Although relations with Havana began to cool toward the end of the Pérez administration, they have deteriorated significantly under President Herrera's government.

One cause of tension was the treatment, beginning in 1975, of Cubans who sought asylum by taking refuge in the Venezuelan embassy in Havana. Cuba argued that such persons were common criminals, lacking the right to seek asylum, while Venezuela maintained that they were political dissidents and, therefore, eligible for guarantees of safe conduct off the island. By April of 1980, the controversy had escalated to the point that both countries recalled their ambassadors. For all practical purposes, the controversy over the right of asylum amounted to the end of constructive ties between Venezuela and Cuba. A second source of tension was the decision by a Venezuelan military tribunal in September 1980 to acquit four anti-Castro Cuban terrorists believed to have been responsible for the sabotage in October 1976 of a Cuban airliner that crashed off Barbados at the cost of seventy-three lives. While the Herrera administration claimed to be powerless to reverse the decision, this assertion was greeted by skepticism in Havana, and Cuban diplomatic personnel were withdrawn from Caracas. Although the two governments have not formally broken diplomatic ties, relations can be accurately characterized as "very cold"—the phrase used by President Herrera in response to a question during his visit to Mexico in April 1981.

The clearest indication of the Christian Democratic orientation of the Caribbean policy of the Herrera administration is in El Salvador, where Venezuela is staunchly supporting the junta. Following the reorganization of the junta in December 1980, when José Napoleón Duarte was named president, the Herrera administration issued a statement of approval and indicated its economic support would continue. In contrast, AD's leaders have called for the suspension of economic aid until the Salvadoran junta begins negotiations with the Revolutionary Democratic Front (FDR) coalition.

The reasons for the Herrera administration's support of the Salvadoran government are varied, reflecting the pragmatic, personal, and ideological dimensions of Venezuelan foreign policy. From a pragmatic standpoint, Copei's leaders argue that the current civil-military junta represents the political center in El Salvador and is, therefore, the only hope for a moderate solution to the ongoing civil war. Copei leaders state that they too favor an end to the oligarchical domination of El Salvador's political and economic life, but express concern that totalitarianism of the left may replace that of the right, induced by outside agents. According to government spokesmen, the only option open to Venezuela is to continue to strengthen Duarte, for he is the key to controlling the Salvadoran security forces.

A second reason for the Herrera government's support of the Salvadoran junta concerns the personal friendships that exist between

Napoleón Duarte and leading Copei politicians. Following his exile in 1972, Duarte lived for seven years in Venezuela. During that time he formed a number of enduring friendships with his Social Christian colleagues, including former president Rafael Caldera and former foreign minister Aristides Calvani. Not surprisingly, Calvani, who is deputy secretary general of Copei, is a leading advisor to President Herrera on Central American policy.

The final reason for the Herrera administration's support of the Salvadoran junta is ideological. The party Napoleón Duarte heads is regarded by Copei leaders as a sister member of the international Christian Democratic movement. Importantly, President Herrera once served as secretary-general of the Latin American Christian Democratic Organization (ODCA), and Aristides Calvani is the current secretary-general. They and other Copei leaders believe strongly in the necessity of confronting Marxism in Central America with an ideology of social justice, as defined in papal encyclicals.[13]

For the past decade, Venezuela has been pursuing an active and vigorous role in the Caribbean. Its role evolved at a time of detente between the superpowers, a more open and flexible subsystem of international relations for "middle powers" such as Venezuela, and the vast influx of petrodollars after the oil price hikes of 1973–1974. Accordingly, Venezuela sought to further its geopolitical and ideological interests in the Caribbean basin through the use of petrodollars to promote socioeconomic change and political stability. Now that the international environment has changed considerably, it is necessary to examine possible future directions of Venezuelan policy toward Central America.

Venezuela and Central America: Future Directions

As in the United States, governmental policy toward recent events in Central America is a hotly debated topic in Venezuela. Currently, the posture of the Herrera government toward this subregion converges remarkably with that of Ronald Reagan: very cool relations with Cuba; bilateral aid for selected countries; encouragement of democratic forces in Nicaragua; and support for the government headed by Napoleón Duarte in El Salvador. There are, of course, major differences. Venezuelan authorities clearly favor an end to the oligarchical and military regimes in Central America, they would prefer that the United States not intervene in the region nor make the Caribbean an area of ideological confrontation with the Soviet Union and they would like to see the democratic states in the subregion work together to prevent situations like the one in El Salvador from becoming polarized.

The Herrera government is not very comfortable with its role as a leading supporter of the Salvadoran government. Nor are government officials pleased at what they term a "coincidence of interests" with the United States with regard to the crisis in El Salvador.[14] The ongoing civil war in El Salvador confronts Venezuelan policymakers with a number of apparent contradictions:

1. Under its democratic presidents, Venezuela's foreign policy has exhibited a pronounced democratic bias. From the Betancourt Doctrine of the early 1960s to the strong support of Presidents Pérez and Herrera for the return to democracy in the Andean countries, Venezuelan foreign policy has firmly opposed authoritarian regimes of the right and left. Yet Venezuelan leaders now find themselves supporting a government whose security forces are believed to be responsible for 80 percent of the deaths in El Salvador.

2. Venezuela has taken the position that the Caribbean basin should not be the arena for an ideological confrontation between the superpowers. Yet Venezuelan policymakers increasingly find a coincidence of aims between their country and the United States in supporting the Salvadoran junta at a time when the Reagan administration is clearly drawing the line in Central America against Soviet expansionism.

3. Venezuela's consociational foreign policy style, and its belief that actions in the Caribbean should be taken only by democratic states in the region, naturally inclines it to work with Mexico to resolve the Salvadoran crisis. Yet while relations between Mexico and Venezuela are good, the Salvadoran issue is a source of tension because they have chosen to support opposite sides in the civil war.

4. For the past decade Venezuelan policy toward the Caribbean basin has enjoyed considerable bipartisan political support. Yet efforts by the Herrera administration to use oil diplomacy on behalf of the Christian Democratic ideological movement has eroded the consensus undergirding Venezuelan foreign policy generally.

The Herrera administration has attempted to mix oil and ideology in its relations with the countries of the Caribbean basin. The main elements of this diplomacy, as well as the dilemmas it poses for Venezuela, are well-conveyed by John Martz:

> What seems implicit is a Venezuelan approach whereby oil-related assistance would be conditional for governments of an ideological outlook congenial with Christian Democracy. Contracts and commitments may be negotiated only for a short term, subject to periodic review and reassessment in Caracas. Such an outlook has not only stirred animos-

ity in some recipient countries, but has fanned the flames of opposition within Venezuela. While foreign affairs are often regarded in a nonpartisan fashion, the injection of Christian Democratic objectives has precipitated predictable criticism from the AD as well as the Marxist organizations. An important element has been the concomitant charge that current Venezuelan policy toward El Salvador, Nicaragua, Jamaica, the Dominican Republic, and Cuba is perilously similar to that of the United States, stirring allegations that Herrera is serving as a virtual sword carrier for Washington in the region.[15]

Such charges are clearly exaggerated. Venezuela has no interest in serving as a U.S. proxy in the region, nor does the country possess the financial resources, military power, or bureaucratic capacity to play such a role. For example, Venezuela's armed forces are adequate for purposes of self-defense, but they are not capable of exercising authority in the Caribbean basin. Nevertheless, the charges will mount, particularly as Venezuela moves toward elections in December 1983.

There are some recent indications that the Herrera administration would like to lessen its involvement in Central America, perhaps through the medium of a negotiated political settlement on the Salvadoran crisis. Mounting domestic criticism in Venezuela, the increasing military involvement of the United States in El Salvador, and the continued inability of the Duarte regime to control the violence perpetrated by the security forces all serve to push the Herrera administration toward this position. During his state visit to Mexico, President Herrera discussed the possibility of a negotiated political solution to the Salvadoran conflict, but it is unclear how far he is prepared to go in pressuring Duarte to negotiate with Guillermo Ungo, spokesman for the FDR. In addition, in March 1981 the Venezuelan foreign minister made a much-publicized trip to the Southern Cone countries that some observers interpreted as heralding an attempt by Venezuela to involve Brazil and Argentina in a Latin American effort to mediate the Salvadoran conflict.

As long as Napoleón Duarte remains in the government, the Herrera administration will staunchly support him. While the Venezuelan government might prefer a political solution to the crisis, it is unlikely to adopt any policy that would weaken Duarte's tenuous control of the military-civilian junta. However, a number of events could trigger a withdrawal by Venezuela: a sharp escalation of U.S. military involvement in El Salvador, the overthrow of Napoleón Duarte by rightist factions in the military, U.S. efforts to destabilize Nicaragua economically or through covert means. Moreover, Venezuela's geopolitical and economic interests in the region are more potential than real.

Venezuelan trade and investment in the Caribbean is slight, and Venezuela's conservative private sector has been very slow to follow the government's lead into the region. Militarily, there is little likelihood that Venezuela would be invaded by any country in the area, or that the United States would permit a disruption of the flow of Venezuelan oil through the Caribbean to the United States.

Conclusions

There is little question that Venezuela will continue to expand its influence in the Caribbean basin in the 1980s. Geography, natural resources, ideology, and the constellation of domestic forces all suggest an active Venezuelan presence. The challenge confronting the Venezuelan government is how best to contribute to what it sees as desirable outcomes in the region: the fostering of democratic governments, the promotion of social and economic change, and the prevention of great-power rivalry for ideological and political influence.

Until the crisis in El Salvador, bipartisan political support for an active Venezuelan role in the Caribbean basin existed. The consensus between AD and Copei was based on the belief that it was in Venezuela's national interest to encourage the establishment in the region of stable democratic regimes capable of promoting economic change. That consensus has evaporated because of serious domestic disagreements between the two parties that have spilled over into foreign policy, because of the personal and ideological dimension of Copei support for the Napoleón Duarte regime, and because of the decision by the Reagan administration to make Central America the focus of ideological confrontation with the Soviet Union. Thus, Venezuela's role in the Caribbean has become a hotly contested political issue, with opponents of the Herrera government contending that Venezuela has become a proxy for the United States in El Salvador out of narrow partisan concerns for the survival of Napoleón Duarte.

Venezuelan policymakers are confronted by a dilemma in El Salvador. On the one hand, they do not want to be drawn into the East-West confrontation being promoted by the Reagan administration, nor do they want Venezuela to be viewed as a "subimperialist power" in the Caribbean doing Washington's bidding. On the other hand, Venezuelan authorities do not want to abandon their support of the Duarte-led junta, nor to retreat strategically from the area. The only policy that would reconcile these conflicting desires—i.e., a negotiated solution to the Salvadoran conflict—seems beyond reach. Consequently, the Venezuelan government will probably continue to support the Salvadoran government, the AD-led opposition will become increasingly vocal, and the democratic consensus supporting Venezuelan foreign policy will continue to erode.

NOTES

1. For a historical treatment of Venezuela's role in the Caribbean, see Demetrio Boernser, *Venezuela y El Caribe: Presencia Cambiante* (Caracas: Monte Avila Editores, 1978).

2. Luis Esteban Rey, "Dos Lustros de Politica Exterior," *Semana,* May 29, 1978, pp. 17–18.

3. See Kim Fuad, "Venezuela's Role in OPEC: Past, Present, and Future," in Robert D. Bond, ed., *Contemporary Venezuela and Its Role in International Affairs* (New York: New York Univ. Press, 1977) pp. 120–155.

4. See my essay, "Venezuela's Role in International Affairs," ibid., pp. 227–262.

5. Franklin Tugwell, "Venezuelan Foreign Policy," manuscript, 1976, p. 22. Prepared for the Bureau of External Research, U.S. State Department.

6. Rómulo Betancourt, *Tres Anos de Gobierno Democratico, 1959–61,* vol. 2 (Caracas: Imprenta Nacional, 1962), p. 327.

7. On Cuban involvement in Venezuela in the 1960s, see D. Bruce Jackson, *Castro, the Kremlin, and Communism in Latin America* (Baltimore: Johns Hopkins Univ. Press, 1969).

8. Quoted in John Martz, "Venezuelan Policy toward Latin America," in Bond, *Contemporary Venezuela,* p. 162.

9. Donald L. Herman, *Christian Democracy in Venezuela* (Chapel Hill: Univ. of North Carolina Press, 1980), p. 186.

10. John Martz, in Bond, *Contemporary Venezuela.*

11. Confidential interview, New York, N.Y., January, 1981.

12. Interview with Simon Consalvi, former foreign minister of Venezuela, March 1978.

13. Demetrio Boersner, "Fuerzas e intereses de las potencias medianas regionales: el caso Venezolano," paper presented by the Friedrich Ebert Stiftung, Bonn, Germany, March 9–11, 1981.

14. Personal interviews, Washington, D.C. and Caracas, Venezuela, May 1981.

15. John Martz, "Ideology and Oil: Venezuela in the Caribbean," paper presented at the Caribbean Studies Association Meetings, Saint Thomas, Virgin Islands, May 27–30, 1981.

9. Western European Perceptions of the Turmoil in Central America

Wolf Grabendorff

W est European newspapers featured many headlines about Central America in the spring of 1981—not so much about the political violence there as about the intentions of the new U.S. administration to use El Salvador to test the willingness of the West European allies to join in drawing a line against Communist interventions in the U.S. "front yard."[1]

West European countries were both uneasy and surprised about this "linkage" between Atlantic alliance problems and the revolutionary process in a small Central American country. They felt uneasy because recent events in Central America had been greeted with some understanding, if not satisfaction, by the rather large constituency for Third World problems in most West European countries. They felt surprise because even those who generally favored a containment policy against Soviet global expansion did not consider Central America the most urgent place to press such a policy. Obviously the West Europeans lacked adequate understanding of U.S. sensitivities—in the country at large and among the decisionmakers of the Reagan administration in particular—with regard to this region so close to home.

Other chapters have discussed the rationale for U.S. policy concerning events in Central America. This paper addresses some of the factors that have contributed to different perceptions among political groups and governments in Western Europe, on the one hand, and among policymakers and others in the United States, on the other. It should be emphasized, however, that some conservative political groups in Western Europe share the dominant views in the United

States about the causes of and remedies for the crisis in Central America.

There are many reasons why West European perceptions and reactions to Central American developments since the late 1970s have differed from U.S. perceptions and reactions. Geographical distance is not the least important among them, but a fear that the East-West conflict could be intensified by the emergence of new areas of great-power rivalry in the Third World also plays a role. It is, therefore, important to contrast the different views about the causes of the Central American crisis before analyzing the real or perceived political implications of the crisis on Western Europe.

Internal and External Origins: A North-South Problem or East-West Rivalry?

The origins of the Central American crisis have been fiercely debated not only in the United States but also in Western Europe. Advocates of a "regional" solution to the political violence blame the problems on the extreme social injustice, illegitimate political systems, and continuing repression of popular participation in countries like Guatemala, Honduras, and El Salvador, and Nicaragua prior to its revolution. This group maintains that change in Central America is inevitable and that any attempt by Western powers to preserve the status quo in that area will only lead to more radicalization and violence—and increase the tendency in the area to turn to the Socialist bloc for help.[2] According to this group, the long-time association of the United States and Western countries in general with the "old order" has spurred "anti-imperialism" among people who favor a change in government. Previous Western policies make it very difficult for outsiders to try to mediate these basically socioeconomic conflicts in Central America. Because the internal and regional political processes have gone beyond the moderate reformist stages, any efforts to "modernize" political systems in Central America are believed to be doomed.

The advocates of a global solution do not deny the internal problems but stress the importance of external, radical forces—Communist-inspired if not Communist-directed—in the breakdown of the old order.[3] This group finds the authoritarian regimes in the region rather stable and their socioeconomic systems not at all repellant because "such societies create no refugees."[4] Since the representatives of the old order were "friendly," non-Communist elites, their weakening has almost automatically led to a decline of U.S. influence in the region.

This group views the ability of Marxist influence to destabilize Central American societies in the context of the East-West power struggle. Containment of communism and the Soviet influence in the Western Hemisphere is of decisive importance for all Western countries; therefore, the dissolution of the old order in Central America has to be stopped. The "globalists" prefer authoritarian governments to possibly totalitarian societies (such as what they fear is developing in Nicaragua). From this group's perspective, it would be in the best interest of the Central American societies themselves as well as of the West in general if the breakdown of regimes could be stopped and the external influence ended. Once the left has been cut off from external support, reform could be initiated to lead these countries toward more democratic systems. In short, a return to the *status quo ante* is not only possible but even desirable; it can be achieved by concerted efforts to defeat Communist—that is, Soviet and Cuban—influence.

Both groups have influenced West European perceptions of the Central American crisis. Generally, the regionalist approach seems prominent among the Social Democratic parties and governments, while the globalist approach is more representative of their Christian Democratic counterparts.[5] But this generalization is simplistic. The German Christian Democrats, for example, are well aware of both the importance of the internal origins and of the North-South dimensions of the conflict. The Social and the Christian Democrats differ more over the direction and instruments of change in Central America than over the causes of recent upheaval.

Throughout Western Europe, the regional approach to the Central American crisis has definitely taken priority over the global approach. The general view in Western Europe is that internal socioeconomic and political conditions must be improved before any stabilization of the region will become feasible. A return to the old order in Nicaragua and El Salvador or a continuation of it in Guatemala and Honduras is viewed as neither possible nor desirable. In both cases such a return would very likely involve extremely high political costs, which would be a burden not only for the United States but also for Western Europe, specifically with regard to relations with the Third World.

Political Implications and Economic Interests: Atlantic Alliance Cohesion or Third World Accommodation?

The political implications of the Central American crisis for Western Europe have to be seen in three contexts: the East-West conflict, the Atlantic alliance, and West European relations with the Third World. There can be little doubt that in all three areas West European interests are highly vulnerable. Therefore, West European reaction to developments that touch on all three areas will necessarily be strong but by no means united.

Most West European parties and governments believe that any Third World conflict involving one of the superpowers is likely to become an East-West issue. Afghanistan is one such case, and Central America could become another if the United States should become convinced that only military intervention could preserve her national interest. Such a development would seriously strain the Atlantic alliance, since Western Europe is unlikely to view possible changes of political systems in Central America as a threat to the security of the United States.

Many West Europeans who have come to accept the ever-present missiles on the other side of the Iron Curtain as a fact of life find it hard to understand the "Cuba trauma" that has haunted U.S. policymakers since the Cuban missile crisis and that seems to be of special importance to the Reagan administration. Many West European analysts also question whether every Socialist system established in Central America will automatically become a Soviet ally and base for offensive sophisticated weapons. Many Europeans consider the security-related preoccupations of the United States with regard to Central America as inconsistent with the U.S. position as a superpower.[6]

The argument of the U.S. government that outside interference in Latin America in general and in the Caribbean basin in particular must be viewed as a threat to the U.S. global position is based on the geopolitical concept of zones of influence.[7] West European policymakers well understand this concept, but some do not share it. Some of them fear that once criteria based on zones of influence are accepted, the Soviet Union might use them to defend her own aggressive policies in what she considers her zone of influence. If the United States views a change of government from a friendly, oligarchic, free-enterprise system to an unfriendly, Socialist system with a centrally planned economy as incompatible with her role as superpower, Europeans wonder, will that U.S. view infringe the sovereign rights of Third World countries to determine their own forms of government?

Some West European countries find it hard to preserve political unity within the Atlantic alliance with respect to Central America.[8] Those who view the conflict in North-South terms are unwilling to back U.S. policies because they feel that their own economic cooperation with the Third World should not be jeopardized by unreasonable U.S. opposition to any political change. Even Europeans who view the Central American crisis as an evolving East-West issue doubt whether this region really is the most important one in which to "stand up against Soviet expansion." Many Europeans who generally support a policy of getting tough with the Soviets consider the stakes much lower in Central America than in the Persian Gulf or Africa.

Another reason for the mixed reaction to the Reagan administration's appeal for European support of its policies was that prior consultation was minimal.[9] Christian and Social Democratic parties have had close contacts in Central America for more than a decade, so some European politicians were stunned when the United States failed to use these channels but instead asked West Europeans to support a policy they find hardly convincing—and only after the policy had already been established.[10]

Policymakers on both sides of the Atlantic have deplored the lack of a unified Western policy toward Central America, but a unified policy was hardly possible because of the differing views about the origins of and possible remedies for the upheaval in the region. Nevertheless, the basic interests of all partners in the Atlantic alliance remain the same:

• To prevent the Central American countries from adhering to the Socialist bloc;
• To avoid regional and internal instability due to interstate or intrastate violence;
• To guarantee economic cooperation through the support of free-market economies; and
• To further economic development and social justice through bilateral and multilateral aid programs.

The differences among the West Europeans themselves as well as between them and the Reagan administration lie mainly in the choice of instruments and strategies to achieve these goals, and in the establishment of priorities. The U.S. government—influenced by domestic political factors—seems to favor short-term solutions, while the West Europeans tend to accept some short-term instability in the interests of reaching long-term stability in the region.

Instruments and Strategies: Party Diplomacy or National Security Diplomacy?

Most Third World societies are, by definition, societies in change; as the old order in these countries crumbles, dealing with their political representatives becomes increasingly difficult. This is especially true in Central America. Maintaining relations only with the ruling forces in these countries has proved inadequate, since such action excludes contacts with the forces who not only may be more responsive to the needs of the majority of the population but also are very likely to be the governments of tomorrow. As a result of the deficiencies in the pattern of bilateral relations and in response to the needs of various political and pressure groups in Central American countries, West European nonstate, transnational activities have dramatically increased during the past decade. The churches and the trade unions have been in the forefront of such activities, but the political parties and some professional groups have followed their lead. The Christian and Social Democratic parties of West Germany—largely because of the expertise and efficiency of their respective political foundations (Konrad Adenauer Stiftung and Friedrich Ebert Stiftung)[11]—have become the most active West European groups in Central America. This has been supplemented during the last few years by the close cooperation of other West European political leaders in the Christian Democratic World Union and the Socialist International.[12] During the late 1970s, both organizations used their long-term relationships with a number of Latin American parties to advance democracy in the region. Their presence in Latin America, however, dates back to the 1960s, when Chile's Eduardo Frei had a close relationship with West Europeans.

External political and financial support are not new to Latin American regimes. Some Central American regimes have had very close links with U.S. administrations and business interests. Christian and Social Democratic groups in Central America found it quite logical, and to a certain extent necessary, to seek outside support, given the adverse outlook for democratic development in their countries and the frequent exclusion of these groups from privilege and power. Many times the initiative for closer party relations was taken in Central America rather than in Rome, Bonn, or Brussels. Some of the West European party leaders who had suffered extended periods of persecution and exile during the 1930s and 1940s had a strong moral commitment to help Central American victims of authoritarian governments or military dictatorships.[13] This commitment helped unite people who held different views about the methods and goals of political development in their respective countries.

The existence of extreme social injustice in all Central American countries except Costa Rica and the blocking of all reform measures for generations by the ruling elites spurred a strong commitment in the ranks of Christian and Social Democratic parties in Europe to social and political change in Central America. The Social Democrats particularly understood the reasoning behind the radicalization of the democratic left in Nicaragua, El Salvador, and Guatemala. They feared that these political groups would be forced into closer cooperation with

Cuba and the Socialist bloc if the Western democracies did not support their aspirations for revolutionary change in their countries.

Through transnational party cooperation, therefore, internal political struggles have indeed become internationalized. The question is, however, given the intransigence of the ruling elites, did the antiregime elements in these countries have any other course? U.S. support for the regimes had been almost uninterrupted until the advent of the Carter administration. When the Carter administration finally tried to shift some U.S. support toward the more reformist elements in some countries, it found the domestic political costs to be high and the local political environment in Central America no longer receptive to such initiatives.

Some West European politicians believe this experience proves that unless democratic groups have been prepared to cope with the problems of change of power, a shift of official policy among states cannot effect social change in Central America. Elections alone also are no remedy for societies torn by violence, especially since, historically, in most Central American countries elections have been fraudulent or the results have been annulled by the military. All groups that have a stake in social change and political participation see defeat of the military as their only hope to achieve their goals.

Transnational party cooperation grows out of an assumption that the main causes of civil strife in Central America are internal. When outside military intervention threatens, "national security diplomacy"[14] comes into play. The U.S. preoccupation with national security considerations must be seen in the context of Caribbean basin geopolitics and superpower global credibility. For its part, a recipient country like El Salvador or Guatemala seeks not only sufficient arms and training to defeat insurgent forces[15] but also endorsement for its policies and help in achieving token reforms that might, internally, buy time and, externally, legitimize the government. Both sides aim to address a real or perceived security threat without investigating the reasons why such a threat evolved or is seen to have evolved.

A national–security-oriented policy toward Central America, which was evolving during the last year of the Carter administration and has become the centerpiece of the Reagan administration policy toward all of Latin America, can be successful on a short- to medium-term basis. The political costs, however, are high. The short-term stability that might be achieved can succeed only through continuing the alliance with the forces within Central America that are associated with repression and persecution of all popular forces, including moderate political leaders. In any country an alliance with a weak political system tends to strengthen the military as opposed to the civilian component of society.[16] The recent history in Latin America has demonstrated that there is no easy way to have security first and democracy later.

None of the structural problems of the Central American socioeconomic systems can be solved by strengthening the security apparatus. The willingness to accept a political compromise—not a typical characteristic for Latin American military establishments anyway—will be further eroded as a side effect of national security diplomacy. But the high political price to be paid for such a relationship is not confined to the effects on the Central American countries' development. If the United States becomes too closely identified with a certain Central American regime—be it El Salvador's or Guatemala's—the United States will become, to a certain extent, hostage to that regime's policies. Criticism within the United States and from its allies will increase as military cooperation increases.[17] The United States will pay the highest price in its future relationships with the Third World.[18] If the United States' evolving relationship with Central America can be viewed as a model of U.S. relations with Third World countries in general,[19] a national–security-oriented policy might turn out to be a major long-term failure. As mentioned previously, it is over this point that Western Europe and the United States have their sharpest policy differences.

To avoid further internal as well as international polarization in Central America, some West European parties have tried to help to find a political solution for problems in El Salvador and to avoid an international isolation of Nicaragua. Neither effort has been very successful so far, partly because of the unwillingness of the most powerful groups in El Salvador—the military establishment and the guerillas—to cooperate, and partly because the United States did not want to participate in such efforts.[20] The German Social and Christian Democrats have been especially active in El Salvador, since both have exceptionally good connections with the government or the opposition. After some initial quarreling, both parties now avoid domestic conflict with regard to mediation approaches.[21] There is little doubt in Western Europe that actual mediation will take a very long time, especially since the positive example of Zimbabwe can be only partially applied. But a negotiated settlement seems to be the only way out of a civil war that neither side now seems able to win.[22] Obviously, leftist groups must be included in the mediation process, but no political settlement is likely to accommodate both extremes of the political spectrum, for which exile may be the only way out.

Many political groups in Western Europe have viewed the Nicaraguan Revolution with great sympathy, but their willingness to aid the process of building a new society in Nicaragua will depend greatly on the extent to which political pluralism is able to survive there.[23] In general, Europeans have not endorsed the U.S. response to the Nicaraguan Revolution, especially since the advent of the Reagan administration. The Europeans fear that a policy of isolation of Nicaragua will hardly serve Western interests, and believe that only cooperation with Western countries will give Nicaragua a chance to fulfill the goals of the Sandinista revolution. Given the history of Nicaragua's relations with the United States, U.S. pressure on Nicaragua might prove counterproductive. For the time being, therefore, it looks as if some West European countries will try to ease the pressure on Nicaragua rather than to follow the example of the United States.

From a West European viewpoint, such differences between the United States and her European allies are not necessarily crucial. The United States has had little experience to equip her to compromise with alien political forces and concepts in Central America. Inside the United States no strong leftist movement has ever challenged the political system; outside the country no forceful neighbor has ever required the United States to get used to living alongside a political or economic system not to her liking. Both experiences abound for many West European states, and their willingness to accept such situations may have contributed to the general postwar political stability in Europe. By counseling political compromise, Western Europe may help ease the turmoil in Central America, where obviously neither the traditional hegemonic role nor the position of strength of the United States seems to be helping to reduce internal or international tensions.[24]

Outlook

The events in Central America and the varying responses from other states and international groups demonstrate the changing power relationships within the international system. Small, minor countries in other parts of the Third World have become catalysts for major crises, if one or both superpowers chose to use them as a test of their relations with each other, their allies, or the Third World in general. Not since the Cuban missile crisis twenty years ago have such developments affected Latin America.

No wonder that the countries concerned and their neighbors usually seek to avoid becoming the center of international attention. New regional powers, which are dealt with in other chapters of this book, might offer the only long-term answer to the regional crises that evolve from power changes in some countries. Many Third World countries view with increasing skepticism the keen interest of the superpowers to impose their own ideological preferences on Third World countries once the old order has been overcome. Political systems like Mexico's might indeed serve as better examples for postrevolutionary society in Central America than do either West or East European models. Furthermore, Central American countries are likely to gain more maneuverability from a nonaligned foreign policy than from close relations with any of the superpowers.

The United States may need to become accustomed to increasingly independent, but not necessarily hostile, countries in her immediate neighborhood. For the United States as well as for Western Europe, the crisis in Central America could turn out to be a test of the adaptability of Western policies to necessary changes in the Third World. The willingness of the United States and Western Europe not only to tolerate but to facilitate structural socioeconomic changes to benefit the underprivileged in Third World countries would help avoid future upheavals in Central America—and elsewhere.

NOTES

1. For example, "Getting Serious about Central America," *International Herald Tribune,* Feb. 27, 1981; "El Salvador als Test fuer Reagan und Europa," *Neue Zuericher Zeitung,* Feb. 22, 1981; "El Salvador als Testfall fuer Reagans Politik und die Atlantische Allianz," *Frankfurter Allgemeine Zeitung,* Feb. 16, 1981.

2. Addressing the Eleventh German-American Conference in Princeton on Mar. 21, 1981, the deputy chairman of the German Social Democratic party, Horst Ehmke, drew attention to that fact: "We have for such a long time helped to defend outmoded structures that we should not be surprised that the revolutionary movements seek help wherever they are able to get it—and that the Soviet Union and Cuba are taking advantage of that situation." (Translation by Wolf Grabendorff.)

3. U.S. Department of State Special Report no. 80, Feb. 23, 1981, "Communist Interference in El Salvador," (p. 1), mentions "another case of indirect armed aggression against a small Third World country by Communist powers acting through Cuba" and "the gravity of actions of Cuba, the Soviet Union, and other Communist states who are carrying out what is clearly shown to be a well-coordinated, covert effort to bring about the overthrow of El Salvador's established government and impose in its place a Communist regime with no popular support."

4. Jeane Kirkpatrick, "Dictatorships and Double Standards," *Commentary,* November 1979, p. 44.

5. "La posición demócrata-cristiana alemana coincide en gran parte con la política estadounidense en el área." *América Latina: Informe Semanal,* Aug. 22, 1980, "Alemania y EE.UU. en divergencia." See also the article by a

leading Latin American specialist of the Christian Democratic Konrad Adenauer Stiftung, Josef Thesing, "Krisenherd Mittelamerika," *Politische Meinung,* November 1979, p. 72: "It is also remarkable that the United States government today is willing to assign the Christian Democratic parties (especially in El Salvador and Guatemala where they are strong) an important role in resolving the conflicts in Central America." (Translation by Wolf Grabendorff.)

6. This view is shared by some of the most prominent Latin American specialists in the United States; see, for example: Jorge I. Dominguez. "The United States and Its Regional Security Interests: The Caribbean, Central, and South America," *Daedalus,* Fall 1980, p. 122: "The Soviet Union and Cuba, therefore, do not pose a conventional threat, and pose a declining unconventional threat to the United States or other countries of the region. To the extent that a conventional threat is potential, the United States has sufficient force to meet it."

7. Viron P. Vaky, "Hemispheric Relations: 'Everything Is Part of Everything Else,'" *Foreign Affairs: America and the World,* 1980, p. 639, describes this view: "The problem which most Americans have in thinking about Latin America, in fact, is that they have come to consider the dominant U.S. position in the world and the overwhelming hegemony the United States exercised in the Hemisphere in the 20 years following World War II as the normal state of affairs."

8. For a very critical commentary, see Robert Held, "Die SPD und El Salvador," *Frankfurter Allgemeine Zeitung,* Feb. 2, 1981.

9. Pierre Schori, the international secretary of the Swedish Social Democratic party, writes: "We find it curious and unfortunate that instead of querying and counteracting the involvement of European social democracy the U.S. does not make positive use of it. Our purposes are not extremist or even extreme. We believe, like Mexico for example, that it is unrealistic to try to exclude from a solution armed resistance against the regime." "Central American Dilemma," *Socialist Affairs,* no. 1, 1981, p. 37.

10. See "Europe and El Salvador," *New York Times,* Feb. 21, 1981.

11. For a critical review, see "Bonn's Tilt Leftward in Central America Worries U.S.," *Washington Post,* Sept. 1, 1980.

12. For the Central American activities of the Socialist International, see Pierre Schori, "Central American Dilemma"; Daniel Waksman Schinka, "La I.S. en América Latina," *El Día,* Apr. 8 through 11, 1980; Klaus Lindenberg, "Die Sozialistische internationale verstaerkt ihr Engagement in Lateinamerika und der Karibik," *Neue Gesellschaft,* February 1980.

13. This is even recognized by Jeane Kirkpatrick, "U.S. Security and Latin America," *Commentary,* January 1981, p. 34: "Both the Socialist International and the radical Catholics conceive themselves as specialists in political rectitude, and their participation in Central American politics has enhanced its moralistic content at the same time that Cuban/Soviet participation has enhanced its violence."

14. I have borrowed this term from Alexandre S. C. Barros, who uses it for a different purpose in "The Diplomacy of National Security: South American

International Relations in a Defrosting World," in Ronald G. Hellman and H. Jon Rosenbaum, eds., *Latin America: The Search for a New International Role* (Beverly Hills: Sage Publications, 1975).

15. "When aid and comfort from the U.S. in the form of money, arms, logistical support, and the services of counterinsurgency experts are no longer available, governments like those of Nicaragua, El Salvador and Guatemala are weakened." Jeane Kirkpatrick, "Dictatorships and Double Standards," p. 35.

16. "Everybody knows—though it is passed over in silence—that a concentrated rollback in El Salvador and Nicaragua would set back the development of democratic parties and structures by many years" (translation by Wolf Grabendorff), Horst Bieber, "Aufs Falsche Pferd gesetzt," *Die Zeit,* Feb. 13, 1981, p. 12.

17. "The Socialist International has repeatedly made clear its support for revolutionary change in El Salvador". . . . "The Socialist International calls on all foreign governments and outside forces to halt any support direct or indirect to the Duarte regime." *Socialist International Press Release* no. 1/81, Jan. 23, 1981.

18. "The consequences of military aid to such a government for the long-term interests of the United States must be weighed with the utmost care. Rejecting the strong opposition of democratic allies in the region to U.S. military involvement places us on a path toward self-imposed regional isolation." Statement by Senator Edward M. Kennedy in the hearings "U.S. Policy Toward El Salvador," Mar. 5 and 11, 1981, Senate Subcommittee on Inter-American Affairs, p. 98.

19. "Our actions via-à-vis Latin America may well hold the key to our future relationship with all the Third World." Ronald Reagan, "The Canal as Opportunity: A New Relationship with Latin America," *Orbis,* Fall 1977, p. 563.

20. See "Gespraeche ueber El Salvador in Bonn," *Neue Zuericher Zeitung,* Mar. 5, 1981, and "Die Amerikaner halten wenig von Europaeischer Vermittlung in El Salvador," *Frankfurter Allgemeine Zeitung,* Mar. 6, 1981.

21. See "Hopes of Mediation Fade but the CDU Recognises a Problem," July 3, 1981 *Latin America Weekly Report* (WR-81-26), p. 3.

22. "We believe that both sides in the conflict will have to compromise, that a new deal will have to be made. For as things now stand, both blocs are powerful. They appear capable of continuing the conflict for a long time to come. Neither side can be conclusively defeated." Pierre Schori, "Central American Dilemma," p. 38.

23. The last mission of the Socialist International has made that point very explicit in Nicaragua. See *Latin America Weekly Report* (WR-81-26), p. 5.

24. "Chances for major United States policy successes will be virtually non-existent, while the risks of failure, embarrassment and even humiliation will grow in direct proportion to the extent of American commitments to maintaining at least the image of regional hegemony." Richard Millet, "Can We Live with Revolution in Central America?" *Caribbean Review,* Winter 1981, p. 53.

10. International Aspects of the Role of the Catholic Church in Central America

Margaret E. Crahan

The internationalization of the role of the Catholic church in the present crisis in Central America has its roots in the structural, theological, and pastoral transformation of the church in the last twenty years,[1] as well as in the challenge posed by continuing widespread poverty and deprivation in an area undergoing substantial economic development.* Ferment was already apparent within the church at the time of the Second Vatican Council (1962–1965), and that gathering of Catholic bishops served to promote far-reaching organizational, doctrinal, and operational changes at all levels of the church. In Latin America the depth of these changes was reflected in the conclusions of the Latin American bishops' conferences (CELAM) at Medellín, Colombia, in 1968, and at Puebla, Mexico, in 1979.[2] It is also apparent in the development of new theological formulations, especially in the theology of liberation, and the creation of innovative grass-roots structures, such as the *communidades eclesiales de base* (CEBs) (grassroots church communities), which emphasize reinterpreting the gospel in the light of contemporary conditions.[3] This has resulted in an increased identification with the poor, limited decentralization of decisionmaking authority within the church, modification of the traditional role of the episcopacy and the clergy, and, to a degree, the politicization of the church.

Such developments were, in part, the result of the church's histor-

*The author would like to thank the Woodstock Theological Center, Washington, D.C., for assistance in the preparation of this chapter.

ical inclination to adapt to its existential situation, in order to preserve itself institutionally. The challenges presented by rapid socioeconomic change and increasing official repression in post-World War II Latin America required substantial modifications in the church's traditional pattern of behavior. Increased polarization of society resulted in the church's becoming much more directly involved in societal conflict on the side of the dispossessed than had previously been the case. As a consequence of this, churchpeople and ecclesiastical institutions became more frequent targets of rightist elements, who by the 1960s broke the taboo against physical attacks on priests and other religious. The torture and assassination of clerics, together with widespread violation of the human rights of the laity, affected even the most conservative sectors within the church. This caused the church to be more vocal and united in its condemnation of existing structures, thereby increasing the likelihood of attack.

As the traditional sanctity of the church began to dissipate in areas such as Central America, it increasingly called for assistance and solidarity from the international church. Divisions within the Central American churches over the proper response to repression and effective strategies to achieve fundamental change within society have caused such appeals, and the responses to them, to be somewhat varied.

This chapter will explore the structural, theological, and pastoral transformation of the Catholic church in recent years and how it contributed to the internationalization of the role of the Catholic church in Central America. In addition, the impact of contemporary socioeconomic and political conditions on the church in El Salvador, Nicaragua, Guatemala, Honduras, and Costa Rica will be examined in order to suggest how the church's analyses of those conditions have prompted it to take more progressive stances locally, and to urge them on the international church. Particular attention will be paid to this phenomenon with respect to the North American Catholic church and its attitude toward current U.S. involvement in Central America.

Recent Structural, Theological, and Pastoral Changes within the Catholic Church

The 1962 convening by Pope John XXIII of the Second Vatican Council in Rome[4] came at a time when the socioeconomic and political conditions described in chapter 1 of this book challenged the Catholic tradition of support for the status quo. Expansion and diversification of the agro-export economies of Central America, industrialization, urbanization, technological developments, reduction of rural isolation, increases in literacy and access to the mass media had considerable impact on Catholic clerical and lay leaders. As in secular society, there arose within the church a new class of professionals whose training inclined them to be more open to change and committed to the reduction of poverty and the political marginalization of substantial portions of society. This was, in part, the result of an increasing tendency of clerics to study abroad, especially in Europe where, in addition to theology and philosophy, some acquired degrees in the social and natural sciences. As a result they were inclined to take a more critical approach to the failure of capitalist economic development in Central America to improve adequately the condition of the poor. In addition, the calls of Latin American bishops for European and U.S. missionaries to compensate for the lack of indigenous vocations were increasingly heeded beginning in the 1960s. This introduced into relatively conservative churches individuals whose interpretation of the Central American situation was often more progressive than the local view. These circumstances combined to stimulate the previously lethargic Central American church. At the Second Vatican Council the emphasis on the church as a community of believers rather than as an institution reinforced the efforts of those churchpeople who had begun to experiment with alternative ecclesial forms. Many of these were based on broader lay participation and emphasized the responsibility of the Christian to struggle for social justice, peace, liberation, and human rights.[5] They also disseminated the theology of liberation and served, at times, in poor communities as the only institutional base for the poor to organize to fulfill their needs.

Vatican II stimulated change within the church by encouraging modification of traditional patterns of hierarchical authority in favor of local bishops organized in national bishops' conferences; religious who created their own representative groups; and lay leaders. The expansion in the number and activities of national bishops' conferences resulted in greater attention being paid to the church's response to local conditions and an increase in appeals to Rome and other bishops' conferences for assistance. In Latin America these national groupings first came together on a regional basis in Río de Janeiro in 1955. At this meeting the episcopacy still strongly reflected traditional church concerns designating Communism, Socialism, Protestantism, spiritism, and Masonry as its chief enemies. Vatican II modified such attitudes by eliminating some impediments to Christian unity and cooperation. This stimulated ecumenism in Latin America, while Rome's creation of a Secretariat for Non-Believers encouraged Marxist-Christian dialogue. The results of such initiatives were clear at the next meeting of the Latin American bishops' conferences, in 1968 at Medellín.

There the assembled prelates strongly condemned inequities resulting from capitalist development. Furthermore, they stated that in situations of acute socioeconomic injustice maintained by institutionalized violence, armed resistance was not immoral. This position gave rise to reports, particularly in the media, that the Latin American bishops were supporting violent revolution. Such statements were greeted with enthusiasm by a minority within the church and with consternation by conservative elements. The conclusions of the Medellín meeting encouraged greater social and political activism on behalf of the poor by some churchpeople, while at the same time it stimulated efforts by more traditional elements to rein them in. The election in 1972 of a Colombian bishop, Alfonso López Trujillo, as executive secretary of CELAM signaled the continued strength of the right.

A principal objective of López Trujillo was to diminish the impact of liberation theology. Using the journal *Tierra Nueva* as well as the CELAM secretariat, López Trujillo disseminated critiques of liberation theology and its proponents charging that it was based on a misreading of the gospels and provided too much of an opening for Marxist analysis. This position received some support at the 1979 CELAM meeting in Puebla, Mexico, where considerable care was taken to emphasize that the church's preferential option for the poor did not imply support for any particular political or economic system. The task of the church was to see to the salvation of individuals from all classes through an intensification of evangelization. Clerical involvement in partisan politics was specifically opposed. There was to be a reemphasis on pastoral activities, and the base communities were to be centers for the renewal of the faith rather than political action.

Following the lead of Pope John Paul II, who opened the conference by calling for socioeconomic change via an intensification of faith among Latin American Catholics, the bishops shied away from support of any specific strategies for change. While the church's preferential option for the poor was repeatedly alluded to, preoccupation with maintaining the universalist appeal of the church was also obvious. The bishops repeatedly affirmed that their goal was to work with all individuals of goodwill. They specifically rejected the idea that substantial socioeconomic change could only result from class warfare. The Puebla conference thereby clarified some ambiguities in the Medellín documents and served notice that, while the episcopacy was critical of inequities resulting from capitalist development, it was not supporting socialism.

The objective of the bishops at Puebla was to establish criteria for just societies that took into account the needs of the majority, while defending the rights of the individual within societies in which the church played an essential role. Permeating this was a desire to achieve change without promoting Marxist states and atheistic ideologies. Hence while the Latin American church has changed substantially, it has done so within limits. Nevertheless, because these changes occurred within a historically very conservative institution, its impact has been greater, not only within Latin America, but also without. Reinterpretation by the Latin American church of the societies in which it functions, and particularly the causes of poverty and authoritarianism, has increasingly been accepted by U.S. and other churches. The support of the U.S. bishops for the end of U.S. military aid to El Salvador and for negotiations between the ruling civilian-military junta and the opposing Frente Democrático Revolucionario (FDR) has been based on an analysis of the Salvadoran situation that has more progressive roots. Sharing with the Salvadoran church a belief that U.S. policymakers misunderstand the nature of the present conflict in El Salvador, Archbishop James A. Hickey in testimony for the U.S. Catholic Conference before the House of Representatives Inter-American Affairs Subcommittee stated in March of 1981 that he wanted:

> to stress the value of an historical perspective for the debate regarding the present conflict in El Salvador. Couched largely in terms of "superpower politics" the current discussion seems to forget that for a long time the people of El Salvador have been struggling for social justice and for participation in the life of their society. The conflict which now captures our attention has been going on, admittedly in less visible and less noteworthy terms, for decades. We need perhaps to reflect on the infamous massacre of the campesinos in 1932. The nature of the conflict in El Salvador is a perduring one. My point is that long before there were charges of outside intervention there was a struggle on behalf of large numbers in El Salvador for social, political and economic change. The conflict has been over land, wages, the right to organize and the issue of political participation. To ignore this long struggle of a people for justice, dignity and freedom is to misunderstand the nature of the conflict today in El Salvador.[6]

The structural, theological, and pastoral transformation of the Latin American church, which has probably been greater than in any other geographic area, has thus clearly had impact outside Latin America. The documents flowing from Medellín and Puebla, as well as other official statements, would not have had as much influence, however, if there had not been growing awareness within the church worldwide of the prevalence of social injustice in Latin America. This was facilitated by the increasing frequency of exchanges between Latin American churchpeople and their counterparts elsewhere, the presence of foreign missionaries, and greater attention by both the ecclesiastical and secular media. It was further advanced by the church breaking out of its traditional urban strongholds and pursuits at a time when the contradictions within Latin American society were being accentuated by post-World War II socioeconomic developments. It was also stimulated by increasing government violation of human rights.

Vatican II, as well as Medellín and Puebla, characterized the denunciation of such violations as a prime responsibility of the church. Hence the Catholic church became more vocal in denouncing those responsible for such abuses, including government officials. As a result, it too, became the object of state terrorism. This has had a catalyzing effect not only on the Central American church, but also on the international church. Both increasingly share a sense of obligation to take such stances even at the risk of jeopardizing churchpeople or institutions. As the Episcopal Conference of El Salvador (CEDES) phrased it in 1977:

> The Church and all Christians are going through a painful and real process of conversion. Since Vatican II and especially after Medellín, there is an awareness that God says "No" to our sin of omission; and in a greater or lesser measure we are collaborating for a more human society which we know is the approximation of the Kingdom of God. Not only in our country but in many others in Latin America, whenever Christians and the official Church are faithful to the prophetic mission of denouncing sin and working towards a more just society which cares for its dispossessed and marginated, whether they are peasants, laborers, Indians, or slum dwellers, the reaction is always the same: the power structures bear down upon these Christians and there have been deaths, disappearances, expulsions and threats.[7]

Such a position has brought the Catholic church into the front lines of political combat in Central America and prompted it to take a leading role in crisis situations such as those in Nicaragua in 1979 and subsequently in El Salvador. While the church's role in Guatemala, Honduras, and Costa Rica has not yet evolved to the same extent as in El Salvador and Nicaragua, there are indications that it may well do so.

El Salvador

The first time in recent years that the weight of the international Catholic church was brought heavily to bear in Central America was in 1977 in El Salvador. Relations between the church and rightist elements, including some within the government, had deteriorated to such a degree that between February and May of that year two priests were assassinated, five tortured, eight expelled from the country, and ten exiled.[8] While fliers were circulated in San Salvador urging Salvadorans to "Be a Patriot! Kill a Priest!" a rightist paramilitary group threatened to kill all Jesuits in the country if they did not leave. The Jesuits, especially Father Rutilio Grande, helped create some of the first comunidades eclesiales de base. These CEBs provided a base political demand-making for some of the poorest communities in Salvadoran society and spread quickly as a result of the efforts of some clerics and lay leaders, particularly catechists and Delegates of the Word. The latter frequently penetrated rural areas that had remained relatively unevangelized despite the presence of the Catholic church since the sixteenth century. The rapid expansion of the CEBs and the Delegates of the Word is affirmed by the fact that, from September 1973 to June 1974, some 37 such groups were organized while 326 Delegates were trained.[9] Jesuit activities, in line with the Society of Jesus' historical emphasis on education, also included the expansion of the Universidad Centroamericana José Simeon Canas (UCA). By 1970, organs of this institution had begun to criticize the government for failure to deal in an effective way with widespread socioeconomic injustice. By the mid-1970s the university and the Jesuits were widely identified with the leftist opposition to the government.[10]

Also active were Maryknoll priests and nuns from the United States. This order emphasized seeing to the needs of the poor worldwide. In the 1960s it increased its activities in areas such as Central America, opening health clinics, soup kitchens, and other facilities, as well as promoting community self-help programs. Other religious groups that expanded their social welfare activities in the area included the Capuchins, Italian Franciscans, Christian Brothers, and Sisters of Notre Dame. Some U.S. dioceses, such as Cleveland and Seattle, also sent personnel. The Jesuits and Maryknollers were most notable, not only because of their overall progressivism, but also because of the extent of their international networks, which could be counted on to respond in crisis situations.

Even prior to the establishment of the UCA and the CEBs, some Catholic clerics had been involved in organizing peasants to defend their rights principally through the Federación Christiana de Campesinos Salvadorenos (FECCAS). This group, which was begun in 1964, was involved in protests over rural working conditions, as well as the rights of peasants to land. By the mid-1970s FECCAS had spread throughout the country and had become a focal point of pressure on the government for agrarian reform. This issue dominated political discourse in El Salvador throughout the 1970s, with the church strongly supporting reform as early as 1970 at the abortive national Agrarian Reform Congress.[11]

By 1977 such factors convinced right-wing elements in El Salvador that one of their principal enemies was the Catholic church which, they alleged, had been penetrated by Marxists. Because of their activities and openness to liberation theology, Jesuits and Maryknollers were particularly suspect. The resultant repression tended for a time to diminish divisions within the church, and in March of 1977 the Salvadoran bishops, who were rather conservative, condemned the government and right-wing elements for repression of peasants and those working to conscientize them. They also denounced the increasing use of torture as a means of intimidation or to extract extrajudicial confessions, as well as the abduction and assassination of both lay and religious leaders. The expulsion and exiling of priests was denounced, and the bishops called upon Christians everywhere to bring pressure to bear on the government to cease human rights violations.[12]

Meanwhile the Jesuits depended on their colleagues in other countries voluntarily to mount campaigns to publicize the situation in El Salvador, a process that was facilitated by the bishops' pastoral letters. The network of Catholic and Protestant church groups that became active remained in existence even after the threat to the Jesuits and other clerics subsided. In 1978 and 1979 it was brought into play to support those working for the overthrow of the government of Anastasio Somoza in Nicaragua.

More recently it has served to help convince the United States Catholic Conference (USCC) to oppose U.S. military aid to El Salvador on the grounds that its government is a major violator of human rights. While also condemning the alleged supply of arms to the left by the Soviet Union and its allies, the bishops fear that U.S. military aid will reduce the possibility of a political solution to the civil strife. This position has been presented in a series of public statements and private representations by USCC officials that are unparalleled in the history of the church in the United States.

Catholic officials have justified this action on the grounds of the church's responsibility to speak out when U.S. policy threatens the well-being of "large numbers of the poor and oppressed."[13] They have also criticized giving support to governments (such as El Salvador's) that justify gross violations of human rights on the basis of a Communist threat. They argue that "the United States should not place itself on the side of those who say 'security' requires postponement of justice and suppression of human rights."[14] Implicit in this stance is acceptance of the position enunciated by the Apostolic Administrator of

San Salvador, Arturo Rivera Damas—that the church even in the face of Communist gains must "be true to herself and defend human rights. She can't pull back from that."[15] As will be seen in the examination of church-state relations in post-Somoza Nicaragua, anti-Marxist sentiment continues to prevail within some sectors of the church even if it is sometimes moderated when faced with gross violations of human rights.

Instead of military aid to El Salvador, the USCC urged that the United States bring pressure to bear on the present civilian-military junta to enact extensive socioeconomic reforms. These would require long-term U.S. economic aid, as well as immediate emergency aid. Priority, according to the bishops, should be given to development assistance that would benefit the working man and woman. This reflects the influence of the priorities established by Vatican II and the preferential option for the poor promoted by the Latin American church. On the diplomatic front the USCC has repeatedly urged the United States, in conjunction with other nations, to encourage dialogue between the Salvadoran government and the opposition, principally the Frente Democrático Revolucionario (FDR). The purpose is to lay the basis for a negotiated settlement that would ultimately result in reconciliation and national reconstruction. This is the same strategy that has been recommended by the Salvadoran episcopal conference.[16]

The bishops of El Salvador, and in particular Bishop Rivera Damas, have been one of the chief supports of international mediation to resolve the civil strife. Such mediation has been urged by the Socialist International, as well as a number of Latin American countries, including Mexico. A frequently mentioned possibility is a body including representatives of the Socialist International, Christian Democrats, the Mexican government, a member of the U.S. Congress, and a church official. Rivera Damas has been the most mentioned for the latter slot, and much of his energy of late has been dedicated to generating international support for the proposal.

This has included seeking Vatican cooperation. Rivera Damas' success in this respect has allegedly been somewhat limited because of lack of confidence in him by some clerical officials, as well as the head of CELAM, Bishop López Trujillo. Representing the more conservative elements in Rome and Latin America, they fear that negotiations might lead to increased Marxist influence in El Salvador. Moderates at the Vatican, including Secretary of State Agostino Casaroli, appear disposed to explore the possibility of mediation and reportedly have had their fears of the motives of the FDR reduced somewhat after a meeting with its representatives in early 1981.

The role of Rivera Damas is further limited by his isolation within the conservative Salvadoran episcopacy, as well as by the fact that a number of his principal liberal advisors have had to leave the country. The bishop has been criticized by both the right and left among the Salvadoran clergy and religious for not having fully supported their respective interpretations of the conflict in El Salvador. There is at present little apparent inclination on the part of the Salvadoran government to engage in negotiations.[17] Mediation by the Vatican is even more unlikely, while the possibility of the U.S. bishops exercising any role other than to pressure the U.S. government to favor negotiations is slight.

Support for the position of the U.S. bishops from the clergy, religious, and laity within the United States has been strong. It was reinforced by outrage over the assassination of Archbishop Oscar Arnulfo Romero in March 1980 while he was saying Mass. A strong opponent of U.S. military aid to El Salvador, Romero exemplified the tendency within liberation theology that emphasized defense of the poor through denunciation of their oppressors. Romero did not, however, use Marxist socioeconomic analysis in arriving at his conclusions. Rather he was moved by empathetic identification with those who suffered. The murders of three U.S. nuns and one lay worker near San Salvador in December 1980 further galvanized the Catholic church, as well as U.S. Protestants and nonbelievers. Church-based solidarity groups experienced an upsurge of support, while the USCC received increased indications of grass-roots approval of its criticism of U.S. policy toward El Salvador. Suggestions by Secretary of State Alexander M. Haig and U.S. Ambassador to the United Nations Jeane Kirkpatrick that the four women had exceeded the proper limits of their missionary work brought a sharp rejection by the USCC of any attempt to call into question the evangelical objectives of the four women. This prompted the State Department to disclaim any such intent and appears to have ended such public statements by Reagan administration officials.[18]

A good number of Protestant leaders in the United States have been supportive of the position of the USCC on El Salvador, joining them in opposing U.S. military aid. Their motives are similar to those of the Catholic leadership and flow from a preferential option for the well-being of the Salvadoran poor. As one group of Protestant leaders expressed it:

> Mainline American Protestants see the Gospel as both a call to justice and an invitation to grace. The suffering of the people in El Salvador demands that Christians in the United States, in response to their commitments, act by calling our government to work for "a negotiated

peace grounded in justice." [Furthermore, they asserted that:] Neither ideological triumph over communism nor political advantage over the Soviet Union, nor renewed national self-confidence, nor any other cause can justify our government's support of the systematic slaughter of the Salvadorean people.[19]

There is, in addition, widespread Protestant support for a negotiated solution.

The Canadian Catholic bishops have also been outspoken in their support of the Salvadoran church and of opposition to U.S. military aid to the junta. This is in spite of reports of Vatican pressure on them not to make public statements on El Salvador that could be construed as supportive of the FDR. Rome's argument is reportedly that the situation is too confused to make competent judgments.

Some Irish, British, and Dutch bishops have been even more outspoken in publicly condemning the junta as illegitimate and genocidal. Support has flowed from these countries to Socorro Jurídico, the major human rights agency of the Catholic church in El Salvador, even after allegations were made that it was too closely linked to the FDR. The German and French churches have been less active, with divisions within the German church reflecting the split between Social Democrats and Christian Democrats in secular politics. The French bishops have deplored the violence in El Salvador and provided some humanitarian aid.

Nicaragua

The critical nature of the crisis in contemporary El Salvador and the repression of the church there have called forth a strong response from the international church that has been unmatched elsewhere in Central America. Even in Nicaragua when the Somoza government attempted to repress certain elements within the church, there was not such widespread international involvement. In part, this was the result of ambiguities in the position of the Nicaraguan church and, in particular, that of the episcopacy. While some bishops opposed Somoza for years prior to his 1979 fall, it was only in June of that year that the episcopacy came out publicly in support of his overthrow. Throughout the 1970s, however, some churchpeople, both clerical and lay, had incorporated themselves in the Frente Sandinista de Liberación Nacional (FSLN) and were actively seeking the downfall of the government. This was partially the result of the radicalizing effect of some grass-roots church activities developed in the context of worsening conditions for the poor, particularly after the 1972 earthquake. Structural, theological, and doctrinal change all had a leavening effect on the Nicaraguan church, creating within it an active progressive sector that virtually did not exist prior to 1960.

The Catholic church in Nicaragua in the 1960s and 1970s became increasingly politicized especially at the grass roots, largely because of the introduction of base communities, catechists, Delegates of the Word, liberation theology, and increased involvement in social action programs. By the mid-1970s Somoza's National Guard was harassing the CEBs, as well as individual churchpeople. The church defended its institutions and members against such attacks, while the bishops remained somewhat uneasy about grass-roots progressivism and autonomy. The bishops were largely conservative, although some like the archbishop of Managua, Miguel Obando y Bravo, took no pains to hide their public distaste for Somoza and his government. In fact, in August 1978 the prelate publicly called upon Somoza to resign. By 1979 it is estimated that 85 percent of the approximately 120 priests in the country, plus the majority of nuns, were strongly opposed to Somoza.[20] The Jesuits, Maryknollers, and Capuchins were in the forefront of clerical opposition to the regime, but it was not until the late 1970s that a good number began cooperating with the FSLN. During the final stages of the struggle in 1978–1979, church groups not only provided humanitarian and other assistance but served to publicize the issues involved in the struggle outside Nicaragua and to mobilize international support for the opposition.

One month before the final toppling of Somoza, the Nicaraguan bishops came out in favor of insurrection on the grounds that they could not support a system and structures that resulted in grave inequalities between classes and citizens. Failure of the government to guarantee civil and political rights, as well as to promote the fulfillment of basic needs undercut, in the bishops' minds, the legitimacy of the government. The existence of prolonged denial of the fundamental rights of the individual justified the insurrection, as witnessed by its broad-based popular support. The bishops cautioned, however, that care must be taken in any process of reconstruction to overcome political partisanship, ideological differences, and special interests. Furthermore, the bishops warned that the maintenance of political pluralism was indispensable and that socioeconomic improvements must be linked to popular participation.[21]

Shortly after Somoza's fall, the bishops issued another pastoral letter urging that Nicaraguans beware of all "imperialisms" and freely mold their own political and social structures. These should incorporate those human values that implied authentic liberation and were free from the domination of state idolatries. The government, in raising the political consciousness of the people, should be careful not to encourage massification. Furthermore, belief in God must not be excluded from the task of national reconstruction for this "would newly enslave the people, not liberate them."[22]

At the same time that the bishops were expressing their preoccupations with the possible direction of the new government, several priests were incorporating themselves into it. Maryknoller Miguel D'Escoto was named foreign minister, while a Trappist-trained diocesan priest, Ernesto Cardenal, became minister of culture. The Jesuit, Xavier Gorostiaga, became head of national planning and Cardenal's Jesuit brother Fernando was made director of the national literacy campaign. A number of other priests also accepted official positions. Their actions pointed up the fact that among the clergy there was less caution in supporting the Sandinista government.[23]

Episcopal disquiet over possible Marxist inroads was expressed in a November 17, 1979, pastoral letter that also affirmed support for the government of national reconstruction. The bishops are clearly worried that the creation and expansion of Sandinista organizations and other mechanisms such as the literacy campaign will be used to inculcate atheism and lead to the ultimate abandonment of the church by the people. This fear places a premium on maintaining unity within the church that encourages the maintenance of somewhat ambiguous positions in order to incorporate a fairly wide spectrum of opinions. In November 1979 the Episcopal Conference urged recognition of the "risks, the dangers, the errors of this revolutionary process while being conscious of the fact that in history there are no absolutely pure human processes. Therefore we must give importance to a freedom of expression and criticism as the only way of indicating and correcting errors in order to perfect the achievements of the revolutionary process."[24] The bishops further asserted that their commitment to the revolutionary process should not be interpreted as signifying "naivete or blind enthusiasm." Moreover, "dignity, respect, and Christian liberty are irrenounceable rights within an active participation in the revolutionary process."[25]

Coming as they did at a time of increasing criticism by Nicaraguan conservatives, the cautionary words of the bishops were interpreted by some as support for those elements. It appears that the episcopacy wanted to establish the legitimacy of the church as a critic of the revolutionary process and as a nonpartisan actor whose actions stemmed from concern for individuals of all political persuasions. The bishops did compliment the revolutionary government on its accomplishments and urged it to continue in its attempts to satisfy basic needs and reduce injustice. This, the prelates asserted, could only be accomplished through the transfer of power to the common people, thereby encouraging them to assume responsibility and realize the Christian duty to perfect the world.[26]

Motivated in part by the November pastoral letter, the Sandinistas prepared a position paper on religion that was intended to reassure the Catholic leadership that the Sandinistas would respect religious liberty and recognize the role of the church within Nicaraguan society. The bishops reacted by preparing a detailed criticism of the Sandinista statement. It reflected fear of the emergence of a single-party state that propounded an atheistic ideology and what the bishops called massification of society. It also denied the government the authority, which the Sandinistas had asserted, to decide if political parties or individuals were trying to convert religious activities into political events.[27] Reflecting the distance between episcopal opinions and that of many of the clergy and laity, the bishops' statement was criticized as harmful to the process of national reconstruction by a number of CEBs, youth and student organizations, the Jesuits, the National Conference of the Religions (CONFER), and some social action and study groups.[28]

A good number of the latter have promoted efforts to increase Marxist-Christian dialogue and Christian participation in the Revolution. In September 1979, a seminar was held at the Universidad Centroamericana in Managua to explore ways the church could contribute to the Revolution. Participants included junta members, priests, Protestant ministers, and CEB leaders. It resulted in the mobilization of the University's Instituto Histórico under the direction of the Jesuit Alvaro Argüello to assist in the analysis of the role of the church in national reconstruction. The institute represents some of the most progressive elements in the church and, as the result of criticism from within the university, has tended to seek a somewhat independent identity. In August 1979, the Centro Antonio Valdivieso was created to help promote support for the Revolution among Christians and to assist ecclesiastical leaders to understand the process. It had the further objective of countering rightist influences on the churches. Headed by an ecumenical team of a Franciscan and a Baptist minister, it aimed to work with church leaders, as well as the CEBs. There is some evidence that the strength of the latter has been somewhat reduced in areas where Sandinista organizations have expanded.[29] This has confirmed the fears of some Nicaraguan Catholics.

The ambiguities of the position of the Nicaraguan church have been communicated to the international church, and hence there has not been as much activity with respect to Nicaragua as to El Salvador. The USCC did, however, beginning in late 1978, repeatedly condemn human rights violations by the Somoza government. It also strongly supported U.S. economic aid to the new government. There has also been less communication from Nicaraguan than from Salvadoran church officials, and hence there is less knowledge and understanding of the local situation. Reflecting the attitudes of the Nicaraguan bishops, as well as their own inclinations, there is some preoccupation with Marxist inroads, although most U.S. bishops do not accept the Reagan administration's view that the country is being transformed into a Communist outpost.

Conservatives at the Vatican are uneasy with the course of the Nicaraguan Revolution, although others, including Secretary of State Cardinal Casaroli, apparently have flexible attitudes. There is no apparent official policy in Rome other than maintaining openness and waiting to see how the situation develops. CELAM, under the direction of López Trujillo, provided funds for Cursos de Formación (basic religious instruction) in every diocese immediately after the fall of Somoza. Using catechists from Mexico and materials that emphasized traditional Catholic concerns, rather than social action and liberation theology, the program has been criticized by some Nicaraguans as a return to the past and an effort to undercut the Revolution. The bishops have, nevertheless, expressed considerable gratitude to CELAM for its efforts.[30] Humanitarian aid and economic development projects have also been provided by Protestant and Catholic agencies in Canada and Europe.

Guatemala, Honduras, and Costa Rica

In Guatemala, Honduras, and Costa Rica there have been fewer structural innovations and less experimentation with new theological and pastoral formulations than in El Salvador and Nicaragua. Nevertheless, there has been a growing involvement of the Catholic church with the rural and urban poor, greater politicization of clergy and laity, and increased attacks on churchpeople and institutions. This process has proceeded furthest in Guatemala, where an incipient state of civil war has increased pressures on the church from all sides.

Government repression has resulted in the departure of priests, and other religious from some parts of Guatemala, and assassinations and disappearances of clerics have escalated. The head of the episcopal conference, Bishop Juan Gerardi, a Guatemalan by birth and a liberal, was refused readmission into the country by government officials in December 1980. Most of the seventeen bishops in Guatemala are relatively conservative, including Cardinal Mario Casariego, who has cooperated with the government in expelling liberal or progressive priests. Government threats have caused some clerics, as well as some Protestant leaders, to go underground. A few have joined guerrilla groups.

In spite of their overall conservatism, in June 1980 the Guatemalan bishops issued a pastoral letter condemning the persecution of the church by the kidnapping, torture, and assassination of catechists, Delegates of the Word, and other churchpeople. Accusations that the church was increasingly serving as a vehicle of atheistic communism were rejected with the assertion that the Catholic message was above all ideologies and did not favor any particular socioeconomic system. The prelates urged dialogue among the contending forces within the country and ascribed violence to the loss of spiritual values and the assertion of man's basest instincts. The solution the bishops proposed was acceptance of the Christian message and a revitalization of the faith. Critical to the accomplishment of this was the strengthening of unity within an increasingly divided church.[31]

To date the U.S. Catholic Conference has not taken a formal position on Guatemala, although there are indications that they are unhappy with U.S. military aid to the country. The heads of a number of religious congregations with missionaries in Guatemala, including the Maryknollers, Christian Brothers, and Capuchins, have expressed their deep concern over the situation in Guatemala to U.S. bishops. They have also published materials and increased their efforts to inform the U.S. public and members of Congress. Individual bishops, such as Lawrence H. Welsh of Spokane, whose diocese has missionaries in Guatemala, have spoken out strongly against government repression and the persecution of church workers.[32] He has also urged the people in his diocese to write their congressional representatives about the situation.

While the violence and repression in Honduras have not reached the levels in El Salvador and Guatemala, endemic poverty and the growing number of Salvadoran refugees have increased societal tension and conflict. The massacre of an estimated six hundred refugees at Río Sumpul in 1980 prompted denunciations by the Honduran Episcopal Conference and the bishop of Santa Rosa de Copán, José Carranza Chávez. Both justified their actions on the grounds that it was the church's responsibility to defend the poor and oppressed. The bishops hastened to add that their action should not be interpreted as acting in contradiction of the state.[33] The Honduran episcopacy clearly accepts the role of the church as protector of human rights without going so far as to denounce the causes of the violations.

Bishop Carranza and others have, however. In a June 19, 1980 pastoral letter, Carranza and other clerics denounced "institutionalized evil" in Central America and laid the blame for the Sumpul massacre at the feet of the oligarchy and the Salvadoran army; OAS officials were condemned for ignoring the facts of the massacre, while the Honduran government was described as an accomplice. Political parties and other institutions that "remained silent in the face of the tragedy" were criticized. Carranza recommended that the CEBs in Honduras use the massacre as the basis for theological reflection and action to pressure for better treatment of the refugees.[34]

The reaction to the Río Sumpul massacre occurred against a background of substantial divisions within the Honduran church. The conservative archbishop of Tegucigalpa, for example, has cooperated with the government in expelling progressive clerics. In the absence of a high degree of government repression of the church, unity has not been forged.

In Costa Rica, where a democratically elected civilian government is in power, relations between the church and state are relatively good, although some churchpeople have become increasingly critical of corruption in government and the deteriorating economic situation. There is a certain amount of pressure by conservative prelates on progressive priests, but no specific government repression of the church. Even the Jesuits in Costa Rica are less socially active than in other parts of Central America. However, such attitudes and behavior are not unlike those ten years earlier in Nicaragua where, in calling for a halt to government repression, the freeing of political prisoners, and a more just economic order, clerics took pains to disclaim that they were being political.[35] This continues to be a common theme. Recently, for example, the Salvadoran episcopal conference defended the legitimacy and apolitical nature of its criticism of the government on the grounds that "To struggle for justice, peace, human development and defense of the basic rights of man is not politics, rather it is working for the common good."[36] This is a position that is not widely shared by government officials throughout Latin America and hence increases the likelihood of future church-state conflicts.

Conclusion

The assertion of the Catholic church's commitment to the poor and oppressed since the Second Vatican Council forced the church in Central America into increasing confrontations with political authorities. In order to withstand the consequent repression, local churches turned to the international church for both material and moral support.

The provision of humanitarian aid by both the Catholic and Protestant churches worldwide has been substantial. Catholic Relief Services, as well as other church groups, provided critical assistance, particularly for refugees, during the Nicaraguan insurrection and more recently in El Salvador and Honduras. This has resulted in a raising of consciousness about conditions in Third World areas within the Catholic church, particularly in North America and Europe. Repression of local churches and churchpeople has also contributed to greater international solidarity within the Catholic church, an institution where regional differences had traditionally been strong. The result has been an increase in the church's effectiveness as an international actor.

Structural, theological, and pastoral changes within Catholicism worldwide have contributed substantially to the increasingly progressive positions the church has taken in Central America. The preferential option for the poor and the commitment to social justice and human rights enunciated at the Second Vatican Council, Medellín, and Puebla have caused the church increasingly to oppose the status quo. Growing social activism in the 1960s and 1970s led to the substantial expansion of grass-roots organizations among the poor, whose greater incorporation into the church increased knowledge and outrage over their exploitation. The opening up of the decisionmaking process within the church to greater participation by local bishops' conferences, the clergy, and the laity increased the voices speaking for the church, as well as the variety of opinions expressed. It also resulted in more pressure on the church as an institution to take public stands on social issues in crisis situations. The tradition of the hierarchical exercise of authority within the church was modified somewhat as horizontal links were built among national bishops' conferences, members of religious orders, and progressives in different countries, as well as Catholics and non-Catholics united on specific issues. The development of liberation theology in Latin America, while it is held by only a minority, provided legitimation for the more progressive Catholic sectors and opened the way for cooperation with secular groups with similar concerns for justice issues.

Perhaps the most notable development has been the increasing number of Catholics who conceive of the church as a community of believers rather than as an institution. This has been a prime result of structural and pastoral innovations such as the CEBs. They have also increased substantially the autonomy of some groups and individuals within the church, especially at the base and diminished somewhat the authority of the hierarchy and Rome. In order to reduce the threat of grass-roots independence and guarantee institutional survival, the hierarchy has had to broaden its traditional positions in order to maintain such groups and individuals within the church. The fact that progressives can and do invoke the preferential option for the poor asserted by Vatican II and the encyclicals of Pope John XXIII, Paul VI, and John Paul II limits the capacity of even very conservative prelates to resist.

It has become clear that the vision of the grass-roots church in Central America as a community of believers strongly committed to the creation of more just societies has led to the building of strategies and alliances not always acceptable to the hierarchy. In particular, the promotion of socialist options perturbs, not only most bishops, but also some of the clergy and lay leaders. As a consequence, there has been increasing tension between the titular leadership and the base, with the real possibility of ruptures. The flexibility of the hierarchy, as well as Rome, in the face of the radical behavior of some sectors of the church has been, in part, dictated by a desire to avoid such splits. There is, nevertheless, likelihood that they will occur.

Pressures from secular authorities and outright attacks on the church have also augmented the hierarchy's desire to limit internal divisions. They have also increased the value of maintaining and cultivating relations with the Catholic church in countries that can provide material and moral support. While the official church continues to insist that it is above politics, there is no doubt that it has become politicized, particularly in contexts such as Central America. The church's repeated assertion of its preferential option for the poor in countries such as El Salvador and Guatemala can only be interpreted as taking a political position. While the official church has not supported any specific political and economic options, the polarization in some Central American societies leads to its identification with the left. Once leftist groups succeed, as in Nicaragua, however, the tendency of the institutional church has been to attempt to reassert its universalistic appeal and to carve out a role for itself as a neutral critic of the government. This is resisted by those, both within and without the church, who feel that, because of its historical identification with the status quo, the church must first legitimate itself by insertion into the process of building a new society. There are strong doubts among churchpeople that Socialism and Communism will necessarily ensure a more just society in which religious and other individual liberties are guaranteed. Overall, the church in Central America is attempting to reconcile its tradition of not excluding any class or individual from evangelization while at the same time exercising its preferential option for the poor. The difficulties inherent in this are reflected in the varying reactions of the international church to the current situation in Central America.

Strongly supportive of local churches and churchpeople under attack, foreign bishops and Vatican officials tend to close ranks even if they disagree with the positions propounded by the former. Widespread violations of civil and political rights, particularly violations of the physical integrity of clergy and laity, have prompted considerable moral outrage and expressions of solidarity. Neither the Vatican nor the churches in North America and Europe have as progressive bases as the Central American churches and hence are not very supportive of armed struggles for liberation or the construction of socialism. They, like the Nicaraguan bishops, limit themselves to denunciations of state terror and partial insertion into change-oriented processes in a desire to influence their direction. For an institution that in the midtwentieth century was overwhelmingly supportive of the status quo, this is a considerable advance. Its future direction both on a national and international basis will be largely determined by developments within and around the church, particularly those originating from the base and the nature of processes such as that currently under way in Nicaragua. If the Catholic church in that country can carve a secure place for itself, it will probably continue to be supportive of change. If it cannot, both the Nicaraguan church and the church internationally may very well experience a resurgence of conservatism.

NOTES

1. This chapter will focus on the Catholic church in Central America, since it has been the principal religious actor in the area for close to five hundred years and continues to dominate. While the number of Protestants in Central America has increased substantially in recent years, and they play a role in recent developments, their impact has not been as great internationally or locally as that of the Catholic church.

2. On Medellín, see Conferencia del Episcopado Latinoamericano (CELAM), *The Church in the Present Day Transformation of Latin America in the Light of the Council* (Bogotá: CELAM, 1970). On Puebla, see CELAM, *III Conferencia General del Episcopado Latinoamericano, Puebla: La Evangelización en el Presente y en el Fúturo de América Latina* (Bogotà: CELAM, 1979).

3. The theology of liberation focuses on the realization of the Kingdom of God on earth as a prime means of salvation rather than strictly on individual rectitude. More attention is paid to promoting societal change than has traditionally been the case in the Catholic church. Some liberation theologians use Marxist socioeconomic analysis in their evaluations of contemporary issues and support a species of humanistic socialism. However, many who subscribe to liberation theology do not, focusing instead on pastoral activities that promote popular self-determination. Liberation theology has had considerable impact on the comunidades eclesiales de base, as well as other progressive Catholic groups that proliferated in the 1960s and 1970s. Emphasizing communal reflection and action, these groups tend to encourage increased political

activism on the part of both lay and clerical participants. In societies rife with inequality and repression, such organizations tend to become identified with opposition to the existing political, economic and social order.

4. For the conclusions of this meeting, see W. Abbott, *The Documents of Vatican II* (New York: America Press, 1966).

5. Illustrative of this were the Cursillos de Capacitación Social (study groups focusing on contemporary socioeconomic problems) developed in Central America from 1962 to 1967. Drawing their inspiration from the condemnations of political and economic structures that resulted in unremitting poverty contained in Pope John XXIII's 1961 encyclicals *Mater et Magistra* and *Pacem in Terris,* participants examined contemporary social problems in the light of the gospels and recent Catholic social doctrine. Critical analyses of Central American conditions led to a growing belief in the necessity of radical change to be achieved by nonviolent means if possible. If this was not the case, then violence was regarded as justified, as well in response to institutionalized violence. The radicalization of the participants disturbed, not only ecclesiastical authorities, but also secular authorities and in 1967 the cursillos were forced to dissolve. Some of their clerical and lay leaders went into exile while others incorporated themselves into secular revolutionary movements. Shortly after their demise, other progressive church-based organizations began to emerge, including youth and student groups, peasant unions, and most notably the comunidades ecclesiales de base. For a description of the Cursillos de Capacitación Social, see Blase Bonpane, "The Church and Revolutionary Struggle in Central America," *Latin American Perspectives* 7, nos. 2–3 (Spring–Summer 1980), pp. 182–186.

6. James A. Hickey, "Testimony of Most Reverend James A. Hickey for the United States Catholic Conference before the Inter-American Affairs Subcommittee of the House Foreign Affairs Committee on U.S. Policy toward El Salvador," Mar. 5, 1981, Washington, D.C., p. 2.

7. Conferencia Episcopal de El Salvador (CEDES), "Pastoral Letter, San Salvador, Mar. 5, 1977," *El Salvador I: Voices of the Church* (Washington, D.C.: LADOC, 1980), pp. 3–4.

8. Tommie Sue Montgomery, "The Church in El Salvador," Mss. (1980), p. 20. To be published as chapter IV of Tommie Sue Montgomery, *Revolution in El Salvador: Origins and Evolution* (Boulder, Colorado: Westview Press, forthcoming).

9. Ibid., p. 13.

10. In spite of the chaos in El Salvador, as well as pressure on the Jesuits, the provincial of the Society of Jesus reported in February 1981 that its university had never had more students. César Jérez, S.J., briefing, Feb. 20, 1981, Washington, D.C. The closure by the government of the national university undoubtably was a contributing factor.

11. The strong statements of Father José Inocencio Alas in support of agrarian reform at that meeting resulted in his abduction by the government, the first such incident in El Salvador. The auxiliary bishop of San Salvador, Monsignor Arturo Rivera Damas (currently apostolic administrator), promptly went to the office of the minister of defense and threatened not to leave until

Alas was located and released. The strategy worked, but the incident was the first of an increasing number of church-state confrontations. A mid-1981 news report indicated that many peasants originally organized by FECCAS were then fighting with the armed opposition to the government. Alma Guillermoprieto, "Salvadoran Villagers Abandon Town to Cast Their Lot with Guerrillas," *Washington Post,* July 14, 1981, p. A6.

12. CEDES, p. 27.

13. Hickey, p. 1.

14. J. Bryan Hehir, "Testimony of Rev. J. Bryan Hehir for the United States Catholic Conference before the Foreign Operations Subcommittee of the House Appropriations Committee on U.S. Policy toward El Salvador, Feb. 25, 1981, Washington, D.C., p. 8.

15. Speech by Bishop Arturo Rivera Damas, Apr. 6, 1981, Washington, D.C.

16. E.g., Statement of Monsignor Freddy Delgado, general secretary of the Episcopal Conference of El Salvador, Apr. 2, 1981, Washington, D.C., p. 1. See also Hehir, pp. 7–10; Hickey, pp. 7–8 and United States Catholic Conference (USCC), "Resolution on El Salvador of the Bishops' Administrative Board," Apr. 13, 1981, Washington, D.C., p. 4.

17. An offer of mediation by the Socialist International was specifically rejected by the president of El Salvador, José Napoleón Duarte, in late May 1981. *New York Times,* May 29, 1981, p. 3.

18. Letter of Archbishop John R. Roach of Saint Paul and Minneapolis, President of the National Conference of Catholic Bishops, NCCB, to the Honorable Alexander M. Haig, Secretary of State, March 26, 1981, Washington, D.C.; letter of the Honorable Walter J. Stroessel, Acting Secretary of State to the Most Reverend John R. Roach, Archbishop of Saint Paul and Minneapolis, President, National Conference of Catholic Bishops, NCCB, Apr. 11, 1981, Washington, D.C.

19. "Statement by Church Leaders Concerned about Human Rights in El Salvador," Apr. 17, 1981, Washington, D.C., p. 1. See also "Council of Churches Raps Reagan on Rights Policies," *Washington Post,* May 16, 1981, p. A8.

20. Sergio Mendez Arceo, bishop of Cuernavaca, Mexico, "Introduction to Pastoral Letter of the Episcopal Conference of Nicaragua," Nov. 17, 1979, Managua, p. 2.

21. Conferencia Episcopal de Nicaragua, *Presencia Cristiana en la Revolución: Dos Mensajes—Momento Insurreccional 2 de junio 1979; Iniciando la Reconstrucción, 30 de julio 1979* (Managua: Cristianos en el Mundo, Comisión, Justicia y Paz, Documentos, 1979), pp. 4–8.

22. Ibid., 30 de julio de 1979, p. 14.

23. The 1980 Vatican directive that priests should not hold political office was not insisted upon by the Nicaraguan bishops until June of 1981. In resisting the pressure from the local episcopacy, as well as from Rome, a number of priests holding high office claimed that their obligation to the Nicaraguan people overrode their responsibility to accept episcopal authority. At a two-day meeting in mid-July 1981 a compromise was reached between the Nicaraguan

Episcopal Conference and the priests. The latter would retain their political offices, but would not in any way use their clerical status to support the government. The priests also committed themselves to remain obedient to and in close communication with the hierarchy. Acceptance on the part of the episcopacy of the continuance in office of the priests reflected the bishops desire to avoid a breach, not only with the lower clergy, but also with the government. Further, not every bishop felt the priests should be forced to abandon their secular posts. Christopher Dickey, "Nicaraguan Priests to Stay in Office under Compromise," *Washington Post,* July 17, 1981, p. A24.

24. Pastoral Letter, Nov. 17, 1979, Managua, p. 2.

25. Ibid., p. 3.

26. Ibid., p. 4.

27. "La Iglesia en Nicaragua," *CELAM,* vol. 19, no. 158 (enero de 1981), pp. 11–21.

28. National Catholic News Service, Nov. 7, 1980, p. 1.

29. Michael Dodson and Tommie Sue Montgomery, "The Churches in the Nicaraguan Revolution," paper presented at the Latin American Studies Association National Meeting, Bloomington, Ind., Oct. 16–19, 1980, pp. 29–32, forthcoming in Thomas Walker, ed., *Nicaragua in Revolution* (New York, Praeger).

30. "Letter of Conferencia Episcopal de Nicaragua to CELAM," in *CELAM,* vol. 19, no. 158 (enero de 1981), p. 21.

31. Episcopal Conference of Guatemala, "Catholic Church of Guatemala Addresses Guatemalan People," *LADOC,* vol. 11, no. 3 (January-February 1981), pp. 45–48.

32. Bishop Lawrence H. Welsh, "Pastoral Letter," October 1980, Spokane, Washington, pp. 1–2.

33. Episcopal Conference of Honduras, "Declaration of Honduran Episcopal Conference Regarding Río Sumpul Movement," *LADOC,* vol. 11, no. 3 (January-February 1981), pp. 22–23.

34. José Carranza Chávez (bishop of Santa Rosa de Copán), et al., "Honduran Diocese Denounces Peasant Massacre at Río Sumpul," ibid., p. 29.

35. See, for example, "Declaración de Sacerdotes Nicaraguenses," *Cuadernos de Marcha,* 17 (septiembre de 1968), pp. 31–32.

36. CEDES, p.5.

PART FOUR

The Central American Response

11. National (and Factional) Adaptation in Central America: Options for the 1980s

James N. Rosenau

To assess Central America today is, inescapably, to engage in a theoretical enterprise.* Conclusions about what is likely to occur in the region and recommendations about what ought to be done in any or all of its countries are bound to be an admixture of several general theories to which one, knowingly or otherwise, subscribes. This is not because a dearth of information necessitates speculation, but rather because so much is changing and so little is remaining constant that only resort to theory can enable us to trace the course of events from one point in time to the next.

Stated differently, the pace, scope, and scale of change within and among the states of Central America highlight their discontinuities and obscure their trend lines, thus requiring the observer to impose order on what seems like sheer chaos. An archbishop is assassinated, a harvest is poor, a junta is formed, a party is fragmented, a decree is issued, a secret document is captured, a commodity price collapses, a public rally fizzles—endless events such as these compel politicians and analysts alike to fall back on their underlying conceptions of the dynamics of conflict, the reversibility of polarization, the vulnerability of revolutionary situations to self-fulfilling prophecies, the limits of moderation and the role of brute force, the fragility of coalitions, the fluidity of popular support, the flexibility of left-wing organizations, the consequences of land

*I am grateful to Craig Etcheson and Elizabeth Nelson for their help in preparing this chapter. The support of the Institute for Transnational Studies at the University of Southern California is also happily acknowledged.

reform, and the susceptibility of underlying social, economic, and political institutions and processes to manipulation by leaders at home and interested parties abroad. Indeed, if they were not so pervaded with tragedy and suffering as well as so potentially capable of escalating into a global crisis, the present circumstances of Central America could be viewed as an extraordinary opportunity for reexamining our fundamental theories as to what holds societies together and what tears them apart.

To recognize that one is juggling several theories as one assesses the Central American scene is not, however, to simplify greatly the task of comprehending its dynamics. For each of the countries of the isthmus has its own history and traditions, and these are sufficiently differentiated to render regionwide generalizations hazardous.[1] Furthermore, notwithstanding the fact that all five of the countries are small, even miniscule, in comparison to most of the world's states, their present upheavals are no less complex for their lack of size. Small scale does not mean simplicity. Nor does it signify the presence of fewer variables or a narrower range across which they vary. If anything, in fact, smallness may add to the complexity of change processes because the repercussions of each variable may be greater by virtue of the smaller scale within which the changes in its value occur.[2]

Yet, to repeat, we have no choice but to resort to our theoretical impulses as we seek to evaluate the likely and desirable course of events in Central America. Despite the differences and complexity that mark the region, the breakdown of its established continuities means that our evaluations can only be as sound as the theoretical underpinnings on which they rest, theoretical underpinnings that are informed by knowledge of particular individuals, groups, and traditions in Costa Rica, El Salvador, Guatemala, Honduras, and Nicaragua but that derive mainly from our general understanding of political dynamics.

But what kind of theory is most relevant to present-day circumstances in Central America? There is no single answer to this question. Much depends on how the problems we seek to clarify are posed. If the dilemma concerns the prospects for democratic institutions evolving in the region, then models of the origin and breakdown of authoritarian regimes can usefully be employed.[3] If the problem involves the prospects for stability and continuity in the region, irrespective of whether it is founded on democratic institutions, we might turn to two types of models—on the one hand, to foreign policy models that allow for the roles the United States, the Soviet Union, Cuba, and other interested nations might play in Central America;[4] and, on the other hand, to political economy models that allow for the way in which the countries of Central America are locked into patterns of production and trade.[5] If our concern is with the possibility of reversing the processes of polarization, it might prove helpful to examine and adapt Coser's model of the dynamics of conflict.[6]

A Theoretical Perspective

Valuable as such models are, they all suffer from at least one of two defects: either they are static and fail to allow for the dynamics of change, or they focus on internal or external phenomena and fail to allow for how the world's mounting interdependence is intensifying the interaction between domestic and foreign affairs. Models of political development and the decline of authoritarian regimes do build in propositions that anticipate change, but they also hold the international environment constant and thus can only account for changes induced and sustained internally. Much the same can be said of conflict models. Foreign policy and political economy frameworks, on the other hand, do focus on the interaction of internal and external variables, but (leaving aside Marxist models) they tend to posit a cross-national design and ignore the transformations that occur through time. Furthermore, all the foregoing approaches concentrate on the nation-state and largely dismiss as peripheral the many different types of transnational actors that have emerged as the world becomes increasingly interdependent.

These deficiencies in the available theory are especially consequential when one focuses on the countries of Central America, several of which have extensive histories as client states and all of which have long been influenced by major transnational actors as well as the omnipresent superpower to the north. Consider, for example, this excerpt from a 1927 State Department memorandum by Under Secretary of State Robert Olds:

> Our ministers accredited to the five little republics, stretching from the Mexican border to Panama. . . . have been advisers whose advice has been accepted virtually as law in the capitals where they respectively reside . . . We do control the destinies of Central America and we do so for the simple reason that the national interest absolutely dictates such a course. . . . Until now Central America has always understood that governments which we recognize and support stay in power, while those we do not recognize and support fail.[7]

Plainly, any theory of political development in Central America is bound to be conspicuously wanting if it does not allow for the operation of such an important external variable as that so vividly depicted by Olds. Nor is the necessity of building in the U.S. factor any less because American influence in the region has diminished since 1977. The potential for diverse American responses has not lessened and (given geography and the relative power balance) probably never will. Hence "it is no exaggeration to say [in 1981] that not a single political movement or initiative is launched in these republics that does not take into account the likely reaction of the United States."[8] If actors in the region cannot ignore external variables, certainly those of us who theorize about it can do no differently.

Nor can the need to include private actors as well as governments in the analysis of external variables be understated: "It is no longer possible to understand inter-American relations without reference to the activities of a broad variety of interest groups."[9] The recent kidnapping of an American working in Colombia for the Wycliffe Bible Translators, an organization viewed by the kidnappers as "an affront to . . . our national sovereignty" and "a means by which the plunder of our national resources is institutionalized,"[10] is a poignant symbol of the importance of private actors to the course of inter-American affairs. And two stories adjacent to each other on the same page of the *Los Angeles Times* perhaps make the operational implications of this point even more incisively: in one the United States Secretary of State spoke of the possible need to ship arms to El Salvador while, in the other story, Los Angeles local leaders of the Longshoremen's and Warehousemen's Union spoke of not loading arms for shipment to El Salvador.[11]

What is needed, in short, is a theoretical perspective that somehow combines variables derived from national, international, and transnational models. More accurately, if the problem is defined as one of comprehending the alternative routes the countries of Central America may traverse as they respond to and cope with the dynamics presently besetting them from within and without, a theory combining the several levels of analysis would surely yield more incisive results.

It would be presumptuous to suggest that what follows meets the requirements of a theory that can adequately account for constancy and change in the maelstrom of Central American politics. Time and space limitations, not to mention the limits of imagination and training, do not permit an effort to develop here a theory that encompasses all the relevant variables at the several levels of analysis. But the ensuing formulation does offer a point of departure, since it takes into account the interaction of internal and external variables and also allows for profound transformations in political structures and processes. It is a formulation that I call *a theory of national adaptation.*[12] The theory has proven helpful in exploring the dilemmas of relatively autonomous and internally coherent small states[13] and may, with modifications, thus lend itself to the analysis of the less autonomous, strife-ridden states of Central America. At the very least it is a formulation that enables us to probe how the various factions and parties contending for power in the region may assess and address the options open to them.

Let me first summarize the theory. In its original and most general formulation, the adaptation perspective focuses on any state, irrespective of whether it is large or small, developed or underdeveloped, united or divided, authoritatian or democratic (to mention only a few of the salient dimensions of states). As long as its sovereignty as an international actor is accepted, every state is conceived to be faced with the problem of adapting to changing circumstances if it is to persist through time and space as a cohesive social unit. The survival of the national state is not theoretically assumed, but is treated as an empirical question. Although few states are likely to be conquered militarily today, collapse from within is an ever-present possibility. Hence, while most states persist, some go under, and those that do point up the delicacy of the mechanisms through which national adaptation occurs. In identifying four types of national adaptation, in other words, I do not mean to imply that the continued existence of any historic nation-state is assured. The theory allows for a fifth alternative: maladaptation that is so severe as to amount to extinction.

National adaptation is defined as a process through which fluctuations in the essential structures of states are kept within limits acceptable to their members. The essential structures are those basic interactions patterns (e.g., the economy, polity, society) that sustain the life of national actors and that undergo fluctuation in response to changing circumstances at home and abroad. These changes are posited as demands with which a nation must cope. Because the demands are both internal and external, the nation is seen as achieving (or failing to achieve) adaptation through the basic orientations whereby the interplay between the demands from at home and abroad is handled.

Built into the theory, in other words, is an internal-external balance that is always present but that can undergo enormous shifts, depending on the relative potency of the internal and external demands and the orientations of the nation's leaders and publics toward these relative potencies. The degree of adaptation and maladaptation at any point in time is conceived to be a function of the discrepancy between the relative strength of the key internal and external variables and the orientations toward the balance between them. If the discrepancy is great, maladaptation will ensue, with either extinction or transformation to a more appropriate set of orientations occurring thereafter. If the discrepancy is slight or nonexistent, then neither extinction nor adaptive transformation will follow.

The theory postulates the nation, like any human entity, as always pursuing one of four basic and mutually exclusive adaptive orientations if it is to maintain its essential structures and survive. It can seek to adjust its present self to its present environment; it can try to shape its present environment to its present self; it can attempt to create a new equilibrium between its present self and its present environment; or it can accept the existing equilibrium between its present self and its present environment. In order to simplify discussion, these four alternative sets of self-environment orientations have been designated as giving rise to, respectively, the politics of acquiescent adaptation, the politics of intransigent adaptation, the politics of promotive adaptation, and the politics of preservative adaptation. Present-day Afghanistan, South Africa, Libya, and Great Britain might be cited, respectively, as illustrative of the four types.[14] Table 11.1 delineates the four types in terms of the decisionmaking orientations inherent in each.

It is important to stress that each of the self-environment orientations is conceived to constitute a basic posture from which all policy decisions spring. All four are viewed as stable and enduring as long as the relative strength of the demands emanating from within the national actor and of those from its present environment do not change or are not perceived to have changed. If changes occur and/or are perceived as such, then the national actor is seen as either undergoing a transformation to one of the other three adaptive orientations or failing to survive. This means that the theory allows for twelve possible transformations. It must be reemphasized, however, that the four types of adaptive orientations are conceived as deep-seated and not transitory in nature, as undergoing transformation only in response to profound social and technological change, either internally or in the international system. The theory posits an electoral or violent ouster of political leaderships as normally necessary to the initiation of any of the twelve possible transformations, and for some of them (especially the transformation from either intransigent or acquiescent to preservative adaptation), a major societal upheaval would appear to be a prerequisite.[15]

The Adaptation of Small States: Modifying the Theory

The original formulation of the adaptation model was pervaded with the implicit assumption that the external environment of small states is

Table 11.1 THE NATURE OF DECISIONMAKING IN DIFFERENT PATTERNS OF ADAPTATION

Patterns of Adaptation	Demands and changes Emanating from a society's External environment	Demands and changes Emanating from the essential structures of a society
Acquiescent	+	−
Intransigent	−	+
Promotive	−	−
Preservative	+	+

SOURCE: James N. Rosenau, *The Study of Political Adaptation* (New York: Nichols Publishing Co., 1981), p. 61.

+ Officials responsive to changes and demands, either because the changes and demands are intense or because their intensity is perceived to be increasing

− Officials unresponsive to changes and demands, either because the changes and demands are not sufficiently intense or because their intensity is perceived to be decreasing

predominant, locking them into situations from which transformation is unlikely and thus giving rise either to the politics of acquiescent adaptation if their internal demands are perceived as relatively minimal or to the politics of preservative adaptation if the internal demands are viewed as sufficiently great to offset those from abroad. This assumption now appears untenable. The changing structure of world politics has facilitated, perhaps even encouraged, the emergence of some small states that have managed to lessen substantially their orientations toward their external environments or to raise substantially their orientations toward the needs of their essential structures. That is, some small states have successfully moved their politics from acquiescent to preservative adaptation (e.g., Panama), from acquiescent to promotive adaptation (Cuba), from preservative to promotive adaptation (Libya), or from preservative to intransigent adaptation (Cambodia in the mid-1970s). In effect, the original formulation was founded on the faulty reasoning that equates smallness with weakness and that treats objective circumstances as determinative of external behavior. Consequently, dependency was presumed to mark small-state survival, whereas now it is clear that defiance and different degrees of autonomy are also forms of survival available to them.

A number of factors can be cited as sources of the various adaptive transformations experienced by some small states. The breakdown of the bipolar world and the resulting greater tolerance of great powers for the autonomy of small states, the advent of ever greater numbers of small states, and the cohesive consequences of the intense nationalism through which many of them came into existence, the relatively lessened importance of military-security issues, and the relatively greater importance of socioeconomic and scientific issues, the growing number of transnational actors from which small states can procure assistance, and the dynamism of modern technology and the greater interdependence it has fostered are among the more obvious reasons why the adaptive options open to small states have multiplied.

Although it is the totality of such factors that comprises the world to which all nations must adapt, one of these changes seems especially salient as a source of the dynamics whereby small states have been able to evolve new adaptive orientations. The shift from a world in which military issues and strategy are predominant to one in which economic conflicts and tactics are paramount—what might be viewed as a shift from foul- to fair-weather politics—has appeared to have had profound consequences for the way in which small states define their self-environment relationships. When the context of world politics is cast predominantly in terms of military security, with the threat of armed intervention ever present and the demand for adherence to alliance commitments serving as a constant pressure, the officials of small states are likely to perceive their external environments as a series of forces to be deflected, dodged, or otherwise warded off. With the greater prevalence of economic concerns, however, the external environment emerges not as a wellspring of threats, but as a vast reservoir of desired possessions. Instead of being viewed as an ominous source of challenges to be thwarted, the environment comes to be seen as an endless resource from which to procure. To begin to redefine the external environment as a site from which demands emanate to one in which resources are available is, in terms of adaptive orientations, to begin to undergo a transformation from acquiescent to the other three types of adaptation or from preservative to promotive or intransigent adaptation. Such a redefinition of the external environment would appear to be under way among many small states, mainly those in the Third World but also on the part of some in the industrial world. For them the superpowers and other large states are decreasingly seen as armed camps and are increasingly viewed as marketplaces where goods and expertise can be acquired. And, equipped for the first time with this conception of the outside world as offering procurement opportunities, small states are in the position of considering alternative strategies for coping with their external environments.

There is a curious paradox here. While large states and superpowers, still needing to be attentive to problems of military strategy and for the first time experiencing a substantial degree of dependence on foreign resources, are moving in the direction of preservative adaptation in which a balance is sought between external and internal demands, small states are increasingly able to tip the balance in favor of their internal needs. More accurately, in the case of those small states whose internal structures are basically coherent and not racked by dissension, the external environment is emerging as a place where it is possible to strive for the formation of new arrangements and processes that can yield previously unobtainable benefits. In effect, small states may be the only ones capable of evolving and sustaining the orientations that underlie promotive adaptation.

Such an interpretation seems especially logical for those small states that are richly endowed with a resource needed in the industrial world. The oil-rich states of the Arab world, once so dependent on the West and so acquiescent in their adaptive orientations, have clearly benefited from the shift from foul- to fair-weather politics and been able to evolve perceptions of the world as a vast marketplace in which their oil products can serve as an effective currency with which to promote new arrangements abroad and new dimensions of their essential structures at home. It would be a mistake, however, to conclude that only those small states possessing resources in short supply in the West are capable of redefining their relationship to their external environments. The sight of superpowers becoming increasingly vulnerable and linked to changes abroad, supplemented by the example of small states such as Cuba defying their larger neighbors, would seem to have encouraged other less richly endowed small states to reconsider their self-environment relationships. In some instances (such as Panama) the reconsideration has been hastened by vigorous demands for greater national autonomy on the part of domestic groups, while in other instances (such as Bahrain) the effort to initiate adaptive transformations has its root in the calculations of top-level elites. But, whatever the source, a process of emulation would appear to be sweeping the world of small states, encouraging all of them to be much more ready to reexamine whether their dependency form of survival is necessary and to explore strategies for moving toward greater autonomy.

It is here, of course, that the theory has relevance for the states of Central America. All of them are being swept by change, and three of them have clearly entered a period of adaptive transformation. After a long history of acquiescent adaptation in which successive leaderships were oriented to give greater priority to the policies of the United States than to internal demands, El Salvador, Guatemala, and Nicaragua are now undergoing the domestic upheaval that precedes the emergence of new self-environment orientations. Which set of orientations will actually emerge as predominant in these three countries is, obviously, the paramount policy question presently confronting all the actors, domestic and foreign, caught up in the Central American maelstrom.

The Adaptation of Central American States: Further Modifications

As it has been developed thus far, however, the theory of national adaptation provides only a point of departure for examining the current Central American scene. Its application to small states yielded a number of useful hypotheses founded on the assumption of coherent and strife-free internal structures,[16] but such a condition certainly does not obtain today in El Salvador, Guatemala, and Nicaragua. All three are presently racked by factional conflict among groups and parties scattered across the left, center, and right ranges of the political spectrum. And, unfortunately, the theory has not yet been elaborated in such a way as to allow for the derivation of hypotheses about likely internal strategies and external policies while states are undergoing adaptive transformations. For such transformations arise when the self-environment orientations of different factions have moved from peaceful competition to mortal combat, with the result that the internal strategies and external policies pursued during such periods may be more in the nature of short-term accommodations to the immediate requirements and crises of combat than they are derivatives of deep-seated, long-term adaptive orientations. Thus some theorists argue, for example, that in Nicaragua the tolerance of moderate political parties on the part of the Sandinista government is a tactical retreat from their underlying self-environment orientation, a window-dressing designed to sustain the flow of outside aid from the United States and Venezuela until such time as an effective switch over to Cuban, Soviet, and other Communist sources can be pulled off.

Through a five-step process of analysis, however, it is possible to redesign the adaptation model as a conceptual tool that can be fruitfully applied to the current circumstances of Central America: first, the model's focus on nation-states is scaled down in such a way that the faction, be it an opposition group or a fragile government, is treated as the adapting entity; second, those aspects of the current scene in Central America that we, as detached observers, consider central to the course of events in the region are identified and the extent to which each variable can be manipulated by a faction or a regime is assessed; third, the interaction among the variables is analyzed; fourth, the degree of manipulability of each varible is then reassessed from the perspective of the four adaptive orientations; and, finally, the fundamental adaptive orientations of the various factions presently struggling for predominance in the several countries are determined through a careful review of their activities and pronouncements. As a newcomer to the study of Central America, I can contribute only to the first four of these steps, but I hope what follows in this regard will enable specialists on the region to implement the fifth step and thereby develop insights into the options and maneuvers that the competing factions might pursue as the dynamics of change unfold throughout the isthmus.

To look within the nation-state and treat the various factions in the several countries as adaptive entities present some analytic problems, but none of these are insurmountable. From this scaled-down perspective, any faction's self-environment orientations are examined in such a way that its constituent elements and resources constitute the "self" (i.e., the source of internal demands) while the rest of the society and the world beyond the state's formal boundaries comprise the "environment" (the source of external demands). The faction's preferred balance between these demands may undergo short-term accommodations in response to the exigencies of the ongoing struggle for control, but their conceptions of which demands need to be accommodated and which can be resisted, thwarted, manipulated, or otherwise managed are likely to stem from their underlying orientations toward themselves in relation to their environment. Thus can an analysis of the competing factions facilitate estimates of how each faction is likely to assess the options open to it during the period of transformation.

Furthermore, the device of scaling down the adaptation model to the subnational level enables us to frame expectations as to the policies and strategies the various factions are likely to follow in the event they emerge as winners of their country's power struggle. Of course, to compete for power is not the same as wielding power. As the faction becomes the government and its responsibilities become societywide in scope, its definition of the self may be enlarged enough to alter the adaptive orientations with which it came to power. Promotive or intransigent orientations, for example, may give way to the preservative kind as new internal and external "realities" are encountered for the first time. On the other hand, it seems highly improbable that the self-environment orientations of a victorious faction would undergo immediate change. At the very least the adaptive orientations it articulated during the struggle for power are likely to be a forerunner of how the faction's leaders initially define the "realities"—what can and cannot be manipulated at home and abroad—when they become the government. Surely, for instance, the early months of a new regime previously committed to promotive self-environment orientations will be marked by different responses to the United States than will a regime that brought preservative orientations into office. In short, scaling the adaptation model down to the factional level allows us to look beyond the present chaos and polarization in the region if we assume that eventually stable (if not consensual) regimes will emerge in each of the troubled countries, thereby enabling them to pass out of the transformation phase into a new era·of predominant self-environment orientations fashioned by the faction that takes over the reins of government.[17]

Another advantage of analyzing Central American factions and parties as adaptive entities is that doing so frees us from the conceptual blinders inherent in the tendency to classify factions on the left-right political spectrum. The distinctions between left, center, and right do describe important ideological and policy differences, and they also identify crucial socioeconomic and class differences in the support bases of factions. But such differences do not enable us to anticipate the readiness of a faction to contest or accommodate new developments at home and fresh challenges from abroad. By examining factions in the context of the relative significance they attach to internal and external demands, however, we are in a position to estimate the range within which they are likely to tailor their ideological commitments to the economic, political, and military "realities" with which they have to contend. To classify the Sandinistas as a left-wing regime, for example, is to provide clues as to its policies toward land reform, banks, and other burning issues; but such a classification does not facilitate an answer to the question of what the Sandinistas will do when faced with the possibility of a cut-off of U.S. aid to Nicaragua. Yet such questions can be meaningfully handled by interpreting the empirical indicators of the Sandinistas' adaptive orientations. Whatever the dictates of their ideology and whatever their location on the left side of the political spectrum, they will respond differently to U.S. challenges if they are intransigently, promotively, or preservatively oriented.

There is, to be sure, an overlap between the left-center-right political model and the adaptation scheme. Other things being equal, in the nature of their ideological commitments and socioeconomic support bases, left-wing factions are likely to maintain promotive orientations and those on the right are likely to be intransigently oriented, while those located in the democratic center will probably adhere to preservative orientations. But other things are not equal in Central America. Local economies are too impoverished and the need for external assistance is too great to allow us simply to overlay the left-right spectrum onto the adaptation types. The two models should be seen, rather, as supplementary, with a faction's political ideology perhaps underlying its initial predispositions in any situation, but with these then being filtered through its self-environment orientations.

Controls over and Interactions among the Relevant Variables

Let us turn now to the next steps in applying the adaptation model to Central America—those of enumerating the relevant variables and assessing their manipulability. On the basis of a careful survey of journalistic accounts of events in the region since 1977 (a year when the isthmus was characterized as quiescent, even "simple and controlled"[18]), sixty-one recurrent features of its several situations emerge as relevant to future outcomes and thus as variables that may or may not be subject to manipulation by the factions and regimes that wield power in the various countries. These are listed in the left-hand column of table 11.2. Although far from exhaustive, this listing makes clear the extraordinary complexity and delicacy of the transformations now under way in Central America. Each of the sixty-one variables can reasonably be said to be interactive with most or all of the others, so that a change in the value of any of them seems bound to result in the alteration of some of the others. Such, of course, is the nature of adaptive transformations. They render constants into variables and slow-changing variables into short-term fluctuations. And their rippling

Table 11.2 SOME MAJOR VARIABLES CURRENTLY OPERATIVE IN CENTRAL AMERICA (1981)

Variables	Estimated Degree of Manipulability (Other Things Being Equal)							
	Leaders of the adapting entity if their self-environment orientations allow them to attempt alteration of the variable				External actors if their adaptive orientations allow them to attempt alteration of the variable			
	Readily manipulable	Possibly manipulable in the short term	Possibly manipulable over the long term	Probably not manipulable	Readily manipulable	Possibly manipulable in the short term	Possibly manipulable over the long term	Probably not manipulable
1. The political skills, education of a country's population	...	x	...	...	...	...	...	x
2. The literacy of a country's population	...	...	x	...	...	...	...	x
3. The military skills of a country's population	...	x	...	...	...	...	x	...
4. The technical skills of a country's population	...	...	x	...	...	...	x	...
5. A country's trading patterns	...	...	...	x	...	...	x	...
6. Coffee prices and other foreign markets	...	...	...	x	...	...	...	x
7. Harvests, food supplies	...	...	x	...	...	...	x	...
8. Balance of payments and dependence on foreign aid	...	...	...	x	...	...	...	x
9. State of the economy	...	...	x	...	...	...	x	...
10. State and pace of land reform	...	x	...	...	...	...	x	...
11. Population size and structure	...	...	x	...	...	...	...	x
12. Class structure and consciousness	...	...	x	...	...	...	...	x
13. Strength of the business sector	...	...	x	...	...	...	...	x
14. Degree of state control	...	...	x	...	...	...	...	x
15. Degree of press freedom	...	x	...	...	...	...	...	x
16. Degree of independence of the judiciary	...	x	...	...	...	...	...	x
17. Degree of private investment guaranteed against a takeover by the state	...	x	...	...	...	...	...	x
18. Size of foreign debt	...	...	x	...	...	...	...	x
19. The level and solidarity of popular support	...	x	...	...	...	...	x	...
20. Readiness of population to be mobilized	...	x	...	...	...	...	...	x
21. Potential for and growth of opposition	...	...	x	...	...	...	...	x
22. Appearance of momentum toward greater or lesser support	x	...	...	...	...	x	...	...

Table 11.2—*Continued*

	Estimated Degree of Manipulability (Other Things Being Equal)							
	Leaders of the adapting entity if their self-environment orientations allow them to attempt alteration of the variable				External actors if their adaptive orientations allow them to attempt alteration of the variable			
	Readily manipulable	Possibly manipulable in the short term	Possibly manipulable over the long term	Probably not manipulable	Readily manipulable	Possibly manipulable in the short term	Possibly manipulable over the long term	Probably not manipulable
23. Ability of a faction to create publicity calling attention to its claims.	x	...	...	...	...	x	...	...
24. The extent and pace of polarization among a country's factions.	x	...	...	...	...	...	...	x
25. Degree of consensus among a country's factions.	...	...	x	...	...	...	...	x
26. The extent of support for and coherence within and among right-wing factions.	...	x	...	...	...	...	...	x
27. The extent of support for and coherence within and among center factions.	...	x	...	...	...	...	...	x
28. The extent of support for and coherence within and among left-wing factions.	...	x	...	...	...	...	...	x
29. The extent of support for and coherence within and among military elites.	...	x	...	...	...	...	...	x
30. The extent to which the political regime controls the military.	...	x	...	...	...	...	...	x
31. The extent of support for and coherence within and among religious elites.	...	x	...	...	...	...	...	x
32. The degree of activity on the part of religious elites.	...	x	...	...	...	...	...	x
33. The extent of support for and coherence within and among business elites.	...	x	...	...	...	...	...	x
34. The readiness of business elites to increase productivity.	...	x	...	...	...	...	x	...
35. The readiness of a faction or regime to resort to violence (assassinations, kidnappings, death squads, harassment).	...	...	x	...	...	...	...	x
36. The readiness of a faction or regime to prevent or curb increasing violence.	...	x	...	...	...	...	x	...

Table 11.2—*Continued*

| | Estimated Degree of Manipulability (Other Things Being Equal) | | | | | | | |
| | Leaders of the adapting entity if their self-environment orientations allow them to attempt alteration of the variable | | | | External actors if their adaptive orientations allow them to attempt alteration of the variable | | | |
	Readily manipulable	Possibly manipulable in the short term	Possibly manipulable over the long term	Probably not manipulable	Readily manipulable	Possibly manipulable in the short term	Possibly manipulable over the long term	Probably not manipulable
37. The readiness of a faction or regime to resort to censorship.	X						X	
38. The readiness of a faction or regime to correct corruption.	X						X	
39. The readiness of a faction or regime to curb or facilitate shipment of arms to neighboring countries.	X						X	
40. The readiness of a faction or regime to press land reforms, institute press reforms, nationalize banks, etc.		X					X	
41. A faction's ties to west European countries.			X				X	
42. A faction's ties to the U.S. State Department, members and committees of Congress, the Defense Department, etc.			X				X	
43. A faction's ties to private groups in the United States (church, media, etc.).			X				X	
44. A faction's ties to the Soviet Union, Cuba, and/or other Communist actors.			X				X	
45. A faction's ties to Venezuela, Mexico, and other non-Communist actors.			X				X	
46. A faction's readiness to cut all ties to the United States or to make compromises in order to obtain assistance.			X				X	
47. Availability of an international black market in arms.		X					X	
48. Availability of international private credit.		X					X	
49. Readiness of the United States to insist on human rights, land reform, free elections, etc.		X				X		

Table 11.2—*Continued*

| | Estimated Degree of Manipulability (Other Things Being Equal) | | | | | | | |
| | Leaders of the adapting entity if their self-environment orientations allow them to attempt alteration of the variable | | | | External actors if their adaptive orientations allow them to attempt alteration of the variable | | | |
	Readily manipulable	Possibly manipulable in the short term	Possibly manipulable over the long term	Probably not manipulable	Readily manipulable	Possibly manipulable in the short term	Possibly manipulable over the long term	Probably not manipulable
50. Readiness of the United States to provide economic, military, and/or diplomatic aid....................	...	...	x	...	...	...	x	...
51. Readiness of the United States to make military commitments in Central America......................	...	...	x	...	...	...	x	...
52. Readiness of the United States to send military advisers.............	...	...	x	...	...	...	x	...
53. Readiness of the United States to reverse its policies................	...	...	x	...	...	...	x	...
54. Readiness of the United States to bring pressures on others to support its policies in the region...........	...	...	x	...	...	...	x	...
55. Readiness and ability of factions and other regimes in Central America to provide assistance, channel arms, etc........................	...	x	...	...	...	...	...	x
56. Readiness and ability of Cuba and other Communist countries to provide arms, economic assistance, etc.	...	x	...	...	...	...	...	x
57. Readiness of Communist countries to back off under U.S. pressure....	...	...	...	x	...	...	...	x
58. Readiness of Socialist International to support counterparts in Central America.......................	...	x	...	...	...	...	...	x
59. Readiness of Christian Democratic parties outside Central America to support their Central American counterparts.....................	...	x	...	...	...	...	...	x
60. Readiness of a faction or regime to tamper with evidence relative to controversial developments........	x	...	...	...	...	...	...	x
61. Availability and accuracy of evidence in regard to arms supplies from abroad.	x	...	...	...	...	...	...	x

effects make it easier for actors to precipitate change but harder to control its outcome.

Since many of the listed variables involve actions, policies, and resources external to Central America, table 11.2 also makes clear the high degree to which the interdependence of domestic and foreign affairs marks the politics of the region. That is, many of the interactions among the variables span national boundaries, with the result that decisions ِaken abroad can have repercussions within a faction, regime, or country, and vice versa. As will be seen, it is with respect to these internal-external interactions that the adaptation model is especially clarifying.

The right-hand columns of table 11.2 employ a simple coding scheme to assess the extent to which the listed variables appear (to a detached observer) subject to control by the leaders of a faction or regime seeking to advance their goals and by external actors pursuing foreign policies toward the region. A book-length manuscript would be needed to explain each of the assessments, but certain patterns they form are worthy of comment here. First, it seems clear that the factions and regimes in Central America are, other things being equal, much more capable of manipulating developments within their countries than are any external actors who might seek to exercise control in the region. Second, other things being equal, there remain severe limits on the extent to which the factions or regimes can effect desired changes within their countries, particularly in the short run. The values of many of the variables do change in the short term, but this is because of dynamics at work in the polity, economy, and society, and not because leaderships are able to get the compliance on which control is founded. Third, to the extent that any of the variables are manipulable, and again assuming that other things are equal, the external actors are no better able to manipulate the intraregional variables than are faction or regime actors able to impact on the extraregional variables.

Some of the limits of control from abroad and at home are amplified in the ensuing more specific analysis, but these three general patterns highlight an important overall reminder for those who ponder appropriate policies to be pursued by the United States and/or its favored factions or regimes in the region—namely, that in periods of profound and rapid transformation the limits to policy effectiveness are much less than they might otherwise appear, that the options open to either external or internal actors are not very great and involve incremental and marginal impacts, and that the few viable options are more likely to involve controlling the pace of change than they are the fact of it.[19]

In order to facilitate the next steps in the analysis, the sixty-one variables listed in table 11.2 have been reduced to nine broad clusters.

Table 11.3 ESTIMATED INTERACTION AMONG MAJOR VARIABL
(1981)

Variable Clusters

I. SOCIOECONOMIC STRUCTURES (1–18*)
(rigid ↔ flexible)

II. POPULAR SUPPORT (19–22*)
(decline ↔ growth)

III. POLARIZATION PROCESSES among a
country's factions (24–25*)
(lessens ↔ heightens)

IV. ELITE COHERENCE within factions (26–34*)
(fragmented ↔ unified)

V. readiness to resort to DOMESTIC
VIOLENCE (35–36, 39*)
(low ↔ high)

VI. readiness to resort to new,
REDISTRIBUTIVE DOMESTIC POLICIES (38, 40*)
(reluctant ↔ eager)

VII. readiness to resort to new
FOREIGN POLICIES (41–46*)
(maintain old relationships ↔ establish
new contacts)

VIII. capacity to PROCURE economic, financial,
and/or military AID abroad (47–59*)
(limited ↔ considerable)

IX. readiness to provide accurate EVIDENCE in
regard to the course of events (23, 37, 60–61*)
(minimum ↔ maximum)

+   As the value of the row variable moves from left to right across its indicated (in par
−   As the value of the row variable increases or decreases across its indicated range, c
+ , − The interaction between the row and column variables can go in either direction, de
?   Unclear as to how the row and column variables may be linked or, indeed, whether
*   These are the variables (as numbered in table 2) encompassed by the clusters.

I	II	III	IV	V	VI	VII	VIII	IX
/////////	1 +	2 −	3 −	4 +,−	5 +	6 ?	7 ?	8 +,−
9 +	/////////	10 −	11 −	12 +,−	13 +	14 ?	15 +	16 +,−
17 −	18 −	/////////	19 +	20 +	21 +,−	22 +	23 −	24 +,−
25 −	26 +,−	27 +	/////////	28 +	29 +,−	30 +	31 +	32 +,−
33 −	34 −	35 +	36 +,−	/////////	37 ?	38 +	39 +,−	40 ?
41 +	42 +	43 +	44 +	45 ?	/////////	46 +	47 +,−	48 ?
49 ?	50 ?	51 +	52 +,−	53 ?	54 +	/////////	55 +	56 +,−
57 ?	58 +	59 ?	60 +	61 +,−	62 +,−	63 +	/////////	64 +,−
65 ?	66 +,−	67 +,−	68 +,−	69 ?	70 ?	71 +,−	72 +,−	/////////

) range, similar movement is likely with respect to the column variable.
movement is likely with respect to the column variable.
on the identity of the adapting faction.
meaningful and systematic connection between them.

Although the variables are highly interactive, each has been assigned only to one cluster so as to highlight some of the more important interactions among them through an examination of how the mutually exclusive clusters impact on each other. The nine clusters and a crucial range across which each can vary are set forth in the rows of table 11.3, while their listing in the columns permit a crude assessment in the cells as to whether, other things being equal, each cluster is directly or inversely linked to the other eight.

Perhaps the most interesting, or at least the most currently salient, relationship depicted in table 11.3 is to be found in cells 39, 47, 61, and 62, These involve the interaction between a faction's or regime's capacity to generate support abroad and its inclination to hold firm or alter the domestic policies it pursues. Other things being equal, the foreign supplier seeks to impact on the faction's domestic policies by offering or withholding economic, military, or political support, but the faction, being deeply committed to its own political and philosophical foundations, is reluctant to accede fully to the external demands if they are viewed as too risky or noxious. Thus, other things being equal, a delicate balance evolves as the internal and external actors assess each other and juggle their assessments with the other demands made upon them. This is what is occurring to the junta in Nicaragua as it faces the prospect of losing U.S. aid if it supplies or permits the supplying of arms to El Salvador's rebel factions. And it is also the current experience of the Salvadoran junta as it seeks to balance the need for U.S. support with U.S. demands that land reform and other liberal policies be aggressively advanced by the junta.

Another set of crucial dynamics that will determine the outcome of the transformations unfolding in Central America are those represented by cells 15 and 58 in table 11.3. Involved here are the complex ways in which the amount of tangible and intangible support a faction can procure abroad is linked to the extent of the support it has, or appears to have, at home. "Popular support"—as journalists summarily describe the strikes that paralyze, the rallies that fizzle, the funeral processions that lengthen, the kidnapings that persist, and the many other types of events that may reflect the shifting tides of public sentiment—appears to be endlessly volatile, as if waiting to coalesce around a victor who can bring both progress and stability. Under these conditions a faction needs to demonstrate underlying viability if potential friends abroad are to maximize their moral and material support. Ideological affinity is not enough to ensure unqualified backing. Counterparts abroad cannot long afford to endorse a loser and will quickly back away from concrete commitments if the momentum seems to shift and popular support seems to slip. Thus, other things being equal, factions have to be careful that their claims of public support are essentially accurate, lest they be embarrassed by discrepancies between their claimed support and the realities of the way it is expressed. This happened recently in El Salvador when spokespersons for the left-wing insurgents announced a forthcoming military drive to oust the Duarte regime. The drive failed as the anticipated public support did not materialize, an outcome that led the insurgents' friends abroad to modify their previously unqualified support by calling for a negotiated settlement of the conflict.

The distinction between assertions about the political climate and the realities of that climate call attention to still another important set of interactions identified in table 11.3. These are represented by the cells comprising both the ninth row and the ninth column, and they testify to the large (but subtle) role played by information and evidence—be it scarce or plentiful, accurate or distorted—in Central America today. Any fluid and volatile situation, where each increment of domestic or foreign support seems capable of tipping the balance in a new direction, is bound to highlight the importance of images, of indicators of growing strength, for those who are party to the situation and hope to turn it to their advantage. The extent to which images and evidence are presently being contested in El Salvador and Nicaragua is thus a measure of the uncertainty and explosiveness of those situations. In trying to maximize public support, for example, all parties to the conflict in El Salvador are seeking to create an image of momentum that reflects growing unity among their previously divided factions, that is bringing in outside aid that will further ensure success, that is daily adding to the ranks of supporters, and that, all told, is sweeping them unerringly toward their goals.

Whether it involves the pace of land reform or the flow of goods from abroad, in other words, often the image can be as important as the reality in the current Central American scene. And, under these circumstances, the nature and solidity of the evidence for claims and counterclaims can, other things being equal, be as much an issue as the conflicts to which the evidence pertains. Thus, to cite but a few recent examples from the conflict in El Salvador, did major controversies with widespread repercussions arise over such questions as the authenticity of captured rebel documents depicting the flow of aid from the Communist world, the validity of an ID card indicating the presence of American combat soldiers, the identity of those who fired first at Archbishop Romero's funeral, the origins of the wood in the hull of a boat used to smuggle arms into the country, and the affiliations of the killers of four Catholic missionaries.

Or consider the large degree to which information and evidence bears on the underlying political values to which a faction may or may not be committed. Consider, for example the important consequences that flow from where the Duarte regime is located on the political spectrum in El Salvador. The U.S. government contends that it is backing a centrist regime, whereas a former U.S. ambassador to that country, Murat W. Williams, argues that the regime is "neither centrist, nor Christian, nor democratic, nor reform-minded."[20] Which characterization does one accept, and what evidence on the matter does one find credible? The elusiveness of the answers to these questions serves to demonstrate the considerable extent to which the faction that creates the most effective images and offers the most persuasive evidence—and which can sustain the reputation for these qualities—has a distinct advantage in the struggle for power in the region. The capacity to provide "proof" has, in effect, become a crucial ingredient of national and factional power in Central America.

The *ceteris paribus* phrase that peppers the previous paragraphs points up the analytic limits of the relationships identified in table 3. Other things, of course, are never equal. The table depicts variables and not constants. The outcomes of the interactions among the variables are thus bound to differ as their values differ from one country to the next or change within a country from one situation to the next.

One obvious way in which other things are never equal concerns the policies of foreign countries toward specific factions and the isthmus in general. These may have been essentially constant in earlier eras but, as change sweeps Central America and brings its affairs high onto the agendas of foreign powers, the constancy of its external environment has come apart. The United States has vacillated between pressing human rights and supporting authoritarian regimes.[21] Cuba, Mexico, and Venezuela have been actively concerned about the course of events throughout the isthmus.[22] The Soviet Union and several of its allies have been cited as suppliers of military and economic aid to the region.[23] The support of Social Democratic parties in Europe and elsewhere has been sought by the left in El Salvador while President Duarte, the head of its junta, has directed similar efforts toward fellow Christian Democrats abroad.[24] In short, the relevant external environment of Central America has enlarged in recent years and, accordingly, so have the options open to its factions and regimes increased in number. Stated differently (and in the terms that the external variables have been clustered together in table 11.3), the capacity of each faction or regime to procure aid abroad has been altered and is now subject to much more variability than ever before.

This is not to imply that generating external support has become easier for any of the factions and regimes in Central America. To be more salient on the global agenda and thereby have more options is no guarantee of an increased capacity to bargain for or otherwise procure more aid abroad. The countries remain small and poor, and their ability to drive hard bargains continues to be constrained by the "realities" of their geographic location and their historic patterns of production and trade. Furthermore, even if they were somehow prepared to set aside their growing reluctance to use internal structures and policies as bargaining chips to attract foreign powers, their capacity to procure aid abroad is limited by the obvious fact that the readiness of each of the foreign countries to respond to requests for aid is affected by a host of other considerations, from its own domestic pressures to its other external commitments, that have no relevance to Central America and that have a higher priority than providing support to factions in the region. Many current examples could be cited. Mexico's close ties to Cuba precede (and condition) its links to El Salvador. Several governments in Western Europe, especially those where Socialists hold or share power, put plans for deploying nuclear missiles in Europe ahead of temptations to side with counterparts in Central America.[25] In the United States the Reagan administration does not want the situation in El Salvador to divert attention from or otherwise undermine its efforts to mobilize support for its new economic program.[26]

The capacity to procure support abroad, in other words, can never be treated as given by any faction or regime in Central America. It varies, not only in terms of the faction's or regime's success in managing its internal affairs and otherwise remaining attractive to would-be outside supporters (i.e., in terms of the interactive phenomena represented by all the cells in the next to last row and column of table 3), but it is also a capacity that is as variable as the foreign policies of the countries with which the faction has or might establish links (phenomena not depicted in table 11.3).

Thus it is difficult to estimate the viability of the greater number of options abroad open to Central American factions. On the one hand, much depends on the importance the United States attaches to the region. While America's geopolitical credibility has been eroded with the erosion of its superpower status, it still commands sufficient clout to dominate the region if it chooses to do so. More accurately, although the United States may no longer be able to preserve or promote desired structures within the countries of the region, it still appears competent to prevent those countries from freely (and successfully?) pursuing the new external options that have emerged with the decline of its credibility. That is, the United States' proximity to the region, its history of sending in the Marines, its long-standing availability as a prime market for Central American produce, and its capacity to proffer or withhold economic and financial assistance to friendly factions are all considerations that no faction or regime can ignore as it assesses the possibility of alternative sources of foreign support. If the United States chooses, for example, it can probably prevent Nicaragua from remaining within the Western financial and trading system while developing close security ties with Cuba.

On the other hand, the United States is not without limits in the region. Its freedom to maneuver in Central America is generally constrained by the lessons it learned in Vietnam[27] and, more particularly, by the need to maintain productive relations with oil-rich Mexico and Venezuela, not to mention the rest of Latin America; and the need to do so serves as an important constraint on its freedom to maneuver in Central America. The diplomatic costs of a military operation or an unqualified backing of a right-wing faction, for example, would be so high that the United States is unlikely, other things being equal, to wield all the clout available to it in the region. And such constraints, reinforced as they are periodically by warnings from Mexico and other interested nations, enhance the viability of the options open to factions toward the center and left of the political spectrum. The latter have to move carefully to explore new contacts and sources of aid abroad, but there would appear to be some room for them to act independently of, even contrary to, the demands emanating from Washington.

But even if the viability of all the emerging external options open to Central American factions and regimes were somehow to remain constant, there is another important way in which *ceteris paribus* obscures the dynamics of the relationships set forth in table 11.3. For factions to consider pursuing a new option—by identifying the leverage it offers vis-à-vis the United States and by determining whether the necessary domestic concessions can be made in exchange for foreign support—they have to assess the importance of the self in relation to the environment. Options do not loom as options unless an actor is oriented to perceive them as such. It follows that the viability of any option is bound to be different depending on how the phenomena it encompasses are seen as a link between the self and the environment.

This line of reasoning leads us to the next step in applying the adaptation model to the current Central American scene. To reduce the extent to which other things have to be equal for us to grasp the dynamics of the nine variable clusters, each of these can usefully be assessed in the context of the four adaptive orientations. The outlines of such an assessment are presented in table 11.4. Here is it clear that the world abroad is seen in a very different light when approached from different adaptive perspectives. As the seventh and eighth rows of table 11.4 indicate, many more policy options are open to promotively oriented factions than to those with any of the other three self-environment orientations. A comparison across the other rows, moreover, reveals that promotive adaptation leads to a wider array of options, not only because it allows for a greater readiness to strike bargains with external actors, but also because it imposes fewer domestic constraints on efforts to be innovative abroad than do any of the other adaptive orientations.

Policy Implications

A more immediate utility of the formulation summarized in table 11.4 concerns the urgent policy questions of how the various factions will respond to diverse and conflicting pressures for change presently converging upon them. Will the Sandinistas in Nicaragua and the Democratic Revolutionary Front in El Salvador seek to widen their support bases through negotiating with business and other center groups and accommodating the United States? Or will they avoid compromise and seek to impose authoritarian solutions on their divided countries with the help of new supporters in the Communist world? Will the regime in El Salvador continue to press for land reform and free elections? Or will it be overwhelmed by the processes of polarization, abandon its centrist policies, and succumb to pressures from groups on the right? And should a coup d'état bring the right to power in El Salvador, will its leaders resist American pressures for reform and seek to impose an authoritarian solution? How will comparable groups in Guatemala make comparable choices in the event the processes of revolutionary change follow a comparable course in that country?

The answers to these questions become clearer when the history, structure, and internal tensions of each of the factions are assessed in the context of table 11.4. If the left-wing groups interpret the realities of their circumstances through the filter of promotive orientations, their conduct through this period of transformation will be quite different than if their circumstances loom as increasingly constraining and encourage them to evolve preservative orientations. Likewise, the question of how right-wing groups will conduct themselves can be considerably clarified by determining whether their circumstances induce them to evolve intransigent or preservative forms of adaptation.

There remains the problem of how to assess the probable evolution of each faction's adaptive orientations as the period of transformation unfolds. This is not, admittedly, an easy analytic task. Unforeseen events lie ahead, and any of these might influence which adaptive path a faction traverses. On the other hand, the problem is not as difficult as it may seem. If those who specialize in Central American affairs and have intimate knowledge of the predispositions and thinking of the various factional leaders can identify hard empirical indicators that

Table 11.4 THE NINE VARIABLE CLUSTERS AS THEY MIGH
IN TERMS OF THE FOUR TYPES O

	Acquiescent Adaptation	*Intransigent Adaptation*
I. SOCIO-ECONOMIC STRUCTURES	assumed to be beyond manipula- tion unless of concern to the ex- ternal sources of support	a consequence of nature and/or history and thus not subject to alteration
II. POPULAR SUPPORT	of concern only to the extent that external sources of support are concerned	not of concern, except as a threat to existing socio-economic struc- tures; repressive measures taken if support for the structures wanes and opposition builds
III. POLARIZATION PROCESSES among factions	resisted, accepted, or furthered, depending on the posture of the external sources of support	seen as a price for maintaining existing socio-economic structures and thus accepted
IV. ELITE COHERENCE within factions	inclusion or exclusion of individu- als or groups viewed as dependent on the wishes of external sources of support	viewed as crucial to maintaining existing socio-economic structures; hence defections not acceptable and force used to prevent or offset them
V. readiness to resort to DOMESTIC VIOLENCE	only as encouraged by external sources of support	high, if existing socio-economic structures perceived as challenged
VI. readiness to resort to new REDISTRIBUTIVE DOMESTIC POLICIES	only if external sources of support insist	adamantly against any policies that would undermine existing socio- economic structures
VII. readiness to resort to NEW FOREIGN POLICIES	only as required by external sources of support	willing to abandon old ties abroad and establish new ones if con- tinuance of existing socio-eco- nomic structures thereby served
VIII. capacity to procure FOREIGN AID	ready to pursue domestic policies dictated by external sources of foreign aid	unwilling to bargain alterations in existing structures for external aid
IX. readiness to provide accurate EVIDENCE	release and distortion of informa- tion guided by external sources of support	only information supportive of existing socio-economic structure seen as credible and worthy of distribution; damaging evidence withheld

Promotive Adaptation	Preservative Adaptation
subject to extensive alteration through long-range training programs and consistent redistributive policies	subject to some modifications necessary to maintain popular support and flow of external aid
of great concern, as popular support necessary to the development of new and desired socio-economic structures	of concern to the extent that support for existing socio-economic structures wanes, in which case a readiness to adopt domestic measures necessary to the maintenance of support
seen as possibly necessary to the development of new socio-economic structures and, if so, welcomed	seen as a threat to existing socio-economic structures and thus contested
viewed as crucial to developing new socio-economic structures; hence ideological purity stressed and defections acceptable	viewed pragmatically, with compromises made in order to enlarge support for socio-economic structures deemed essential
high, if seen as necessary to overcome opposition to the development of new socio-economic structures	low, only as a last resort to protect existing socio-economic policies or structures
anxious to initiate new policies that will lead to desired socio-economic structures	appreciate that some new policies may be necessary to meet changing conditions
prepared to establish any new ties abroad that will facilitate the development of the denied internal structures	appreciate that some new ties abroad may help protect essential structures at home, especially if these can be developed without jeapordizing existing relationships
willing to make concessions, or give the appearance of so doing, in order to get the foreign aid necessary to promote new domestic structures	ready to bargain with any foreign sources over domestic structures in exchange for aid that will preserve essential structures
willing to tamper with evidence if will enhance the development of new socio-economic structures	credibility deemed important and thus some effort to provide reliable information

locate the leaders in, say, two or three of the cells of the same column of table 11.4, it should be possible to anticipate how any faction is likely to conduct itself in response to any challenge that the coming months may bring. This may seem like a grandiose conclusion, but it is the kind that a theoretical perspective allows. Whether or not its implications should form the basis for policy decisions is, of course, another question. The answer depends on whether policymakers are prepared to posit self-environment orientations as the core impulse in politics to the same extent as the adaptation model does.

At the same time it might be argued that table 11.4 highlights another overall conclusion, one that is no less grandiose but surely much less satisfying: namely, the possibility that the period of transformation will not culminate in clear-cut outcomes. Such a conclusion would stress how very differently the four types of adaptation dispose their adherents toward the dynamics presently at work in Central America. These differences suggest the large extent to which the various factions and regimes may be locked into a highly structured set of perspectives toward their country, its groups, and their conflicts, once they evolve their values as to the relative importance of internal and external demands. If this is so, and if the major factions of the several countries persist in clinging to various types of adaptation, it is reasonable to expect that the processes of polarization will continue apace and that the period of transformation racking the isthmus will continue to lengthen its trail of chaos and suffering across time and space. Indeed, as long as the major factions are so differentially adaptive, it seems conceivable that none of the emergent options available to them abroad will be sufficient to inhibit the steady movement of the states of Central America toward maladaptation and eventual extinction as viable sociopolitical units.

NOTES

1. Cf. Federico G. Gil, Enrique A. Baloyra, and Lars Schoultz, "The Deterioration and Breakdown of Reactionary Despotism in Central America," a paper prepared for the U.S. Department of State (Washington, D.C., xerox, January 1981), pp. 3–4.

2. Thus it is not surprising, for example, that even a seemingly obvious, bivariate hypothesis anticipating a link between fluctuating coffee prices and regime stability in El Salvador and Guatemala was not readily affirmed when subjected to data for a ninety-five-year period ending in 1975. The analysts managed to tease out "the existence of a relationship" between these two

National (and Factional) Adaptation: Options for the 1980s **267**

variables, but their qualifications of this finding make it clear that too many other factors intervene between a shift in coffee prices and an alteration in the degree of domestic conflict to expect the former to impact directly and simultaneously on the latter. Cf., ibid., pp. 17–22.

3. For a valuable inquiry founded on such a model, see Federico G. Gil, Enrique A. Baloyra, and Lars Schoultz, "Democracy in Latin America: Prospects and Implications," a paper prepared for the U.S. Department of State (Washington, D.C.: xerox December 1980). For a more general model, see Barrington Moore, *Social Origins of Dictatorship and Democracy* (Boston: Beacon Press, 1966).

4. General frameworks that might provide guidance here are Maurice A. East, Stephen A. Salmore, Charles F. Hermann, *Why Nations Act: Theoretical Perspectives for Comparative Foreign Policy Studies* (Beverly Hills: Sage Publications, 1978), and Jonathan Wilkenfeld, Gerald W. Hopple, Paul J. Rossa, Stephen J. Andriole, *Foreign Policy Behavior: The Interstate Behavior Analysis Model* (Beverly Hills: Sage Publications, 1980).

5. In this connection, see Fernando Henrique and Enso Faletto, *Dependency and Development in Latin America* (Berkeley: Univ. of California Press, 1979), and Albert O. Hirschman, "The Turn to Authoritarianism in Latin America and the Search for Its Economic Determinants," in David Collier, ed. *The New Authoritarianism in Latin America* (Princeton: Princeton Univ. Press, 1979), pp. 61–98.

6. Lewis Coser, *The Functions of Social Conflict* (New York: Free Press, 1956), and Lewis Coser, *Continuities in the Study of Social Conflict* (New York: Free Press, 1967).

7. Cited in Richard Millett, "Central American Paralysis," *Foreign Policy,* no. 39 (Summer 1980), p. 101.

8. Gil, Baloyra, and Schoultz, "The Deterioration and Breakdown of Reactionary Despotism in Central America," p. 5.

9. Ibid., p. 9.

10. *Los Angeles Times,* Feb. 8, 1981, p. 1.

11. Ibid., Feb. 18, 1981.

12. The theory is spelled out in James N. Rosenau, *The Study of Political Adaptation* (New York: Nichols Publishing Co., 1981).

13. See James N. Rosenau, "The Adaptation of Small States," a paper presented at the Conference on Contemporary Trends and Issues in Caribbean International Affairs, Institute of International Relations, Univ. of the West Indies (May 1977), and reproduced in ibid., chapter 6. Several paragraphs that follow have been taken from that essay. For a critical reaction to the essay, see Herb Adoo, "A Letter to Rosenau on the Three Basic Fallacies Attaching to His Theory of Adaptation of Small States," (Saint Augustine, Trinidad: Institute of International Relations, xerox, August 1979).

14. For a full analysis of each type, see Rosenau, *The Study of Political Adaptation,* pp. 63–79.

15. A discussion of the twelve adaptive transformations can be found in ibid., pp. 80–87.

16. Ibid., pp. 113–123.

17. It is possible, of course, that the polarization of any of these societies will persist for so long as to render the transformation phase a permanent condition. The theory treats such an outcome as a continual process of maladaptation leading to extinction of the national system in its present structure and form. A plaintive recognition of this possibility was recently recorded by Nicaragua's interior minister, Tomas Borge Martinez, in relation to a failed guerrilla offensive in El Salvador: "The guerrillas could not defeat the army and the army could not defeat the guerrillas. Things cannot continue like this. It is convenient neither for the government nor for the guerrillas, neither for the United States nor for us. No defeat and no victory seems possible." *New York Times,* Feb. 16, 1981, p. 7.

18. Millett, "Central American Paralysis," p. 100.

19. For a lengthy theoretical discussion on the limits of control, see my essays entitled "Calculated Control as a Unifying Concept in the Study of International Politics and Foreign Policy," in J. N. Rosenau, *The Scientific Study of Foreign Policy,* (New York: Nichols Publishing Co., rev. ed., 1980), chap. 10; and "Capabilities and Control in an Interdependent World," reproduced in J. N. Rosenau, *The Study of Global Interdependence* (New York: Nichols Publishing Co., 1980), chap. 3.

20. *Los Angeles Times,* Mar. 11, 1981, p. 2.

21. For cogent discussions of the complex roles played by the United States in Central America, see chapter 2 by James Kurth and chapter 4 by Margaret Daly Hayes in this book.

22. The involvement of these three countries in Central America derives from diverse sources, including a long-standing rivalry between Cuba and Venezuela and a long-standing friendship between Cuba and Mexico. Perhaps no less relevant is Cuba's aspiration to extend its influence and ideology into the isthmus, Venezuela's desire to prevent the expansion of left-wing revolutionary movements into Central America, and Mexico's eagerness to use the conflicts of the region as a means of demonstrating its independence of the United States. In addition, both Mexico and Venezuela have expressed alarm that United States policy toward the Nicaraguan and El Salvadoran conflicts could transform the Caribbean basin into the site of a prolonged East-West power struggle. For an elaboration of these considerations, see chapter 8 by Robert Bond in this book.

23. For an analysis of the Communist world's involvement in Central American affairs, see chapter 6 by Jiri Valenta.

24. Chapter 9 in this book by Wolf Grabendorff elaborates on how both sides have involved the political parties of Western Europe in the affairs of Central America.

25. *New York Times,* Feb. 22, 1981.

26. *Los Angeles Times,* Feb. 28, 1981.

27. For empirical materials highlighting the impact of Vietnam on the foreign policy orientations of a broad segment of the American leadership community, see the following inquiries by Ole R. Holsti and myself: "Vietnam, Consensus, and the Belief Systems of American Leaders," *World Politics* 32 (October 1979), pp. 1–56; "America's Foreign Policy Agenda: The Post-Vietnam Beliefs of American Leaders," in C. W. Kegley and P. J. McGowan, eds.,

Challenges to America: United States Foreign Policy in the 1980's (Beverly Hills: Sage Publications, 1979), pp. 231–268; and "Cold War Axioms in the Post-Vietnam Era," in A. George, O. R. Holsti, and R. M. Siverson, eds., *Change in the International System* (Boulder: Westview Press, 1980), pp. 263–301.

Index